The .NET Languages:
A Quick Translation Guide

BRIAN BISCHOF

The .NET Languages: A Quick Translation Guide

Copyright ©2002 by Brian Bischof

ISBN (pbk): 1-893115-48-8

Printed and bound in the United States of America 12345678910

Technical Reviewer: Dan Appleman

Editorial Directors: Dan Appleman, Gary Cornell, Jason Gilmore, Karen Watterson

Marketing Manager: Stephanie Rodriguez

Project Manager: Grace Wong

Copy Editor: Nicole LeClerc

Production Editor: Kari Brooks

Compositor: Susan Glinert

Indexer: Rebecca Plunkett

Cover Designer: Tom Debolski

Distributed to the book trade in the United States by Springer-Verlag New York, Inc.,175 Fifth Avenue, New York, NY, 10010

and outside the United States by Springer-Verlag GmbH & Co. KG, Tiergartenstr. 17, 69112 Heidelberg, Germany

In the United States, phone 1-800-SPRINGER, email orders@springer-ny.com, or visit http://www.springer-ny.com.

Outside the United States, fax +49 6221 345229, email orders@springer.de, or visit http://www.springer.de.

For information on translations, please contact Apress directly at 901 Grayson Street, Suite 204, Berkeley, CA 94710.

Phone 510-549-5938, fax: 510-549-5939, email info@apress.com, or visit http://www.apress.com.

Dedicated to Mom and Dad. You've always been there to offer advice, and you have supported.my decisions, no matter how crazy they seemed. There is no one else I would dedicate this book to but you. I love you both.

Contents at a Glance

Acknowledgments .... *xiii*

About the Author.. *xv*

Chapter 1   Introduction.. *1*

Chapter 2   Program Fundamentals *3*

Chapter 3   Data Types and Operators *25*

Chapter 4   Program Flow.. *61*

Chapter 5   Exception Handling... *79*

Chapter 6   Classes.. *99*

Chapter 7   Class Interfaces... *125*

Chapter 8   Class Inheritance... *139*

Chapter 9   Events.. *151*

Chapter 10   String Management.. *165*

Chapter 11   Windows Form Applications *193*

Chapter 12   File Access.. *217*

Chapter 13   ADO.NET *243*

Chapter 14   Date and Time Functions *277*

Chapter 15   Math and Financial Functions... *287*

Chapter 16   Collections.. *299*

Chapter 17   Program Interaction *313*

Chapter 18   The App Object.. *335*

Chapter 19   Drawing with Forms and Printers.................................... *345*

Index *359*

Contents

Acknowledgments xiii

About the Author xv

Chapter 1   Introduction   1

Chapter 2   Program Fundamentals   3

Overview   4
Starting with the Code Template   4
Case Sensitivity   5
Writing Code across Multiple Lines   6
Comments   6
Declaring Variables   9
Modifying a Variable's Scope   11
Declaring Procedures   12
Passing Arguments to Procedures   13
Calling Procedures   17
Example 2-1. Calculate Test Score Functions   19

Chapter 3   Data Types and Operators   25

Overview   27
Simple Data Types   27
Converting between Data Types   38
Using Arithmetic Operators   42
Using Relational Operators   44
Using Logical Operators   44
Turning Option Strict On   45
Example 3-1. Declaring and Using Variables   46
Example 3-2. Using Enumerators to Print
     Employee Information   51
Example 3-3. Comparing Boolean Operators   54

Chapter 4   Program Flow *61*

Overview *62*
Testing Conditions with the If Statement *62*
Select Case/switch *63*
For Loops *66*
While Loops *68*
Do Loops *69*
For Each Loops *70*
Example 4-1. Logging In a User and Looping
*   Through a Collection* *71*

Chapter 5   Exception Handling *79*

Overview *79*
Using the Exception Class *80*
Handling Errors *80*
Throwing Exceptions *86*
Creating Custom Exception Classes *89*
Example 5-1. Copying a File *89*

Chapter 6   Classes *99*

Overview *99*
Declaring Classes and Objects *100*
Declaring the Class *101*
Using Shared/static Members *102*
Initializing the Class with Constructors *104*
Shared/static Constructors *106*
Declaring Methods *106*
Declaring Properties *107*
Shadowing Variables *110*
Destroying the Class with Finalizers *111*
Overloading Class Methods *113*
Instantiating Objects *115*
Using With Statements *117*
Using Structs *117*
Example 6-1. Writing to a Log File *119*

Chapter 7   Class Interfaces *125*

Overview *125*
Defining an Interface *126*

Implementing an Interface *127*
Implementing Multiple Interfaces *128*
Applying Interfaces *130*
Example 7-1. Managing a Checking Account *132*

Chapter 8   Class Inheritance *139*

Overview *139*
Inheriting a Class *139*
Extending the Base Class with New Methods *141*
Overriding Existing Methods *142*
Inheriting Constructors *144*
Forcing Inheritance *145*
Preventing Inheritance *145*
Example 8-1. Calculating the Price of Items for Sale *145*

Chapter 9   Events *151*

Overview *151*
Declaring an Event *152*
Raising the Event *153*
Handling the Event *154*
Linking the Event to the Event Handler *155*
Example 9-1. Managing a Checking Account *157*

Chapter 10 String Management *165*

Overview *169*
Using the StringBuilder Class *169*
Working with Characters *173*
Using String Functions *175*
Formatting Output *185*
Example 10-1. Manipulating an Input String *186*

Chapter 11 Windows Form Applications *193*

Overview *197*
Default Windows Form Source Code *197*
Using the Visual Studio IDE *198*
Using Common Controls *200*

Chapter 12 File Access *217*

Overview *218*
Managing Files *218*
Reading and Writing Text Files *226*
Example 12-1. Managing Files and Directories *230*
Example 12-2. Reading and Writing Text Files *237*

Chapter 13 ADO.NET *243*

Overview *244*
Introduction to ADO.NET *245*
Opening a Connection *250*
Calling Stored Procedures and Using SQL Statements *251*
Using a Table for Forward-Only Access *254*
Reading and Modifying Individual Records *256*
Viewing Data with the DataGrid Control *265*
Example 13-1. Viewing and Updating the
* Northwind Database* *267*

Chapter 14 Date and Time Functions *277*

Overview *278*
Storing Date and Time Values *278*
Getting the Current Date and Time *278*
Inputting Dates *279*
Using the TimeSpan Class *283*
Example 14-1. Working with Your Birthday *284*

Chapter 15 Math and Financial Functions *287*

Overview *288*
Math Functions *288*
Financial Functions *291*
Example 15-1. Minimum and Maximum Numbers *292*
Example 15-2. Common Financial Functions *294*

Chapter 16 Collections *299*

Overview *299*
Declaring a Collection *300*
Adding Elements *301*
Accessing and Modifying Elements *302*

Examining the Elements 304
Other Collections in .NET 304
Example 16-1. Managing a Collection 304

Chapter 17 Program Interaction 313

Overview 313
Working with COM Objects 313
Early Binding to COM Objects 313
Late Binding to COM Objects 316
Working with the System Registry 319
Example 17-1. Getting a Program's Version Number
    Using Early Binding 324
Example 17-2. Getting a Program's Version Number
    Using Late Binding 325
Example 17-3. A Generic COM Interface Class 327
Example 17-4. A RegEditor Class 330

Chapter 18 The App Object 335

Overview 336
Getting Application-Specific Details 336
Writing to the Event Log 338
Example 18-1. Displaying Application Information 339
Example 18-2. Logging Errors Using the Event Log 342

Chapter 19 Drawing with Forms and Printers 345

Overview 345
Efficient Memory Management for Graphics Objects 346
Drawing on a Form 347
Printing Documents 349
Drawing Graphics 352

Index 359

Acknowledgments

CESAR SERNA HELPED MAKE this book possible. He gave me insight, helped me brainstorm, and provided just enough harassment to get me off my butt and do it.

Many people contributed to this book with their ideas and criticisms. They didn't hesitate to volunteer their time when I asked them to read and comment on different chapters. They are Anthony Burton, Christina Che, Jason Colbert, Mike Kalousek, Mike Khorrami, Tom Kiefer, Humberto Morales, Ramraj Ramamurthy, Mark Ristich, Jeff Ross, and Judith Sopher. All of their comments have really helped the development of this book.

Thanks to Mike Smith and Kurt Schroder, my best friends from high school, for letting me cancel our long overdue reunion so that I could finish the book on time. Thanks to Traci Simonsen for giving me my daily affirmations that kept me focused. Thanks to Mike Curtis for taking on a lot of my workload so that I had time to write this book.

I also want to thank everyone at Apress for making this possible. Thanks to Dan Appleman for taking a chance on an unknown author. Thanks to the rest of the Apress team, Kari Brooks, Susan Glinert, Nicole LeClerc, Grace Wong, and Rebecca Plunkett, for agreeing to work on a crazy schedule so we could print the book quickly. This was an intense experience, and everyone really went into overdrive to make it happen.

About the Author

BRIAN BISCHOF, CPA, MCSD, AND MCT, discovered a marketing niche early in his career. Many software consultants were adequate working with software applications but did not understand or know the language to discover a company's true needs. Contrarily, business managers knew what they wanted to improve their business processes but did not know how to communicate this information to a computer "tech." So began the inception of Bischof Systems, Inc., a software development and training firm that provides a unique merger of business expertise and technical knowledge.

Bischof Systems, Inc., a 12-year-old firm, is a catalyst in assisting small businesses and Fortune 500 companies remain technologically competitive by providing expert advice, custom solutions, and training in a continually fluctuating technological market. Bischof understands the end product is not the software or the staff training Bischof Systems provides, but rather it is a level of commitment to its customers to support the ongoing technical changes a company experiences as it grows and develops.

You can learn more about the author and Bischof Systems, Inc., by visiting the company's Web site at http://www.BischofSystems.com.

CHAPTER 1

Introduction

THIS BOOK IS A QUICK reference guide to help you navigate through the .NET languages. It is designed to be used by two types of programmers. The first type is a VB 6.0 programmer deciding to program in either VB .NET or C#. Deciding which language to use can be a daunting task. Being able to see each one side by side can help with this decision. Once you decide upon a particular language, learning it is easier when you can do a side-by-side comparison with VB 6.0. The second type is a programmer working in one of the .NET languages and still having to use/review code in the other language. This programmer may work in a corporate environment where programmers are writing objects written in one language that are being integrated with objects written in the other language. This book quickly translates one language into the other language without requiring you to become proficient in it.

If you are the first type of programmer, you are migrating your skills from VB 6.0 to VB .NET. This means unlearning a syntax that you have become accustomed to and learning a new syntax that is much more robust. Alternatively, you may have decided to do away with the VB language altogether and migrate your skills to C#. You are learning a totally new language with a syntax that may not be at all familiar to you. Although either task may appear to be quite an undertaking, neither is beyond the realm of your abilities. This is because both languages require the same logic skills that you already have. You can build upon them regardless of the particular syntax used.

If you are the second type of programmer, many times you will need to understand code written in a language different from what you are using. For example, your company may have a VB .NET team writing front-end Web pages and they are calling objects written by the C# team. Given the fact that documentation is usually written well after the time that the program is finished, both teams will frequently have to read the other team's code to find out about an object's interface. There may also be a time when you are told that a book on a certain topic (e.g., ADO.NET) is really well written and is a must-have for your library. Unfortunately, you are a C# programmer and it was written for the VB .NET language. Just because it was written for a different language doesn't mean you shouldn't be able to get just as much out of it as a VB .NET programmer.

Working with the two different languages simultaneously does pose some challenges, but not as many as you might think. Microsoft decided to make the two languages compatible with the Common Language Specification (CLS), and as a result they created two languages that are very similar, although their syntax is different. Thus, what can be done in C# can also be done in VB .NET. There are some exceptions to this rule (and this book will point them out), but on the whole it is true. This now puts the VB programmers on equal footing with the C# programmers and has given them a new level of respect.

This reference guide is here to help you migrate from VB 6.0 to either VB .NET or C#, and it also aims to help you read code written in another language and quickly understand it. A word of warning: If you are moving from VB 6.0 to the .NET platform, it is essential that you learn more than just syntax changes. The .NET platform totally changes programming for Windows development. Although it is possible to go from VB 6.0 to .NET based primarily on syntax changes, unless you understand the internal workings of the .NET platform your productivity and effectiveness as a programmer will be severely limited. There are other books written for that, one of which I recommend is *Moving to VB .NET: Strategies, Concepts, and Code,* by Dan Appleman (Apress). However, if you are simply trying to declare a string array and you can only remember how to do it in VB 6.0, there is no reason to search through a 500+-page book to find a good example of a simple `Dim` statement.

This book is organized so that you can quickly convert the syntax among the three languages. At the beginning of each chapter is a table showing a one-to-one quick conversion between languages. Below that is an Overview section that gives a summary of language differences. After the Overview section, numerous examples are duplicated for each language. These examples provide you with a real-world perspective of how the languages are used. You won't find small code snippets that explain a concept, but leave you hanging when you want to see how it works within the scope of a full project. Each example shows the complete code and its output.

This book offers you the ability to quickly look up the syntax for any language as well as convert code between languages.

CHAPTER 2
Program Fundamentals

Table 2-1. Program Fundamentals Equivalent Chart

VB 6.0	VB .NET	C#
' Comment	' Comment	//Comment

		/*Start of comments
		
		  ...
		  End of comments */

		///XML comments
Dim var As type	Dim var As type	type var;
Dim var As type var = num	Dim var As type = num	type var=num;
Dim var1 As type, var2 As type	Dim var1, var2 As type	type var1, var2;
	Dim var1 As type = num,_ var2 As type = num	type var1=num, var2=num;

Table 2-2. Procedure Declaration Equivalent Chart

VB 6.0	VB .NET	C#

Public Sub procedure()
End Sub
	Public Sub procedure()
	End Sub
		public void procedure()
		{
		}

Public Function procedure() As _
type
   procedure = value
End Function
	Public Function procedure() As
	type
	   return value
	End Function
		public type procedure()
		{
		   return value;
		}

Public Sub procedure(ByRef _ param As type)	Public Sub procedure(ByRef param As type)	public void procedure(ref type param)
ByVal	ByVal	
ByRef	ByRef	ref
		out
Public Sub procedure(Optional _ param As type)	Public Sub procedure(Optional _ param As type)	

Table 2-2. Procedure Declaration Equivalent Chart (Continued)

VB 6.0	VB .NET	C#
Public Sub procedure (ParamArray _ param() As type)	Public Sub procedure (ParamArray _ param() As type)	public void procedure(type params[])
procedure param1, param2	procedure(param1, param2)	procedure(param1, param2);
var = function(param1, param2)	var = function(param1, param2)	var = function(param1, param2);

Overview

Program fundamentals consist of all the little things that are required of almost every program, including writing code across multiple lines, writing comments, declaring variables, and declaring procedures. Although each of these tasks can seem almost trivial when compared to the other aspects of programming, it's essential to have a thorough understanding of how they work.

Starting with the Code Template

When you open a project using Visual Studio .NET, it prompts you to select a Project Template to start with. There are many options to choose from. A couple of the more common choices are VB .NET Web Service and C# Windows Application. With the exception of the chapter on Windows controls, all the examples in this book create console applications in either VB .NET or C#. This is because the book's focus is on the programming language. The best way to show the details of the language is to use examples that don't have the extra code needed when writing a Windows application.

The examples at the end of each chapter always show you the entire code template that is generated by Visual Studio. Nothing has been removed. This section will make it easier to read the examples in each chapter. This section offers a quick introduction to what the different lines of code do. The programming statements are described in more detail in various places throughout the book.

The C# template is much more involved than the VB .NET template. By comparison, a VB .NET console application is simple. It consists of a module declaration and within the module block is the Main() procedure. It is your job to fill in the starting code within the Main() procedure and add any additional procedures and classes after that.

The C# template gives you a lot more to work with. First of all, there is the using System statement. It tells the compiler that you want to use classes from the System namespace without typing System in front of each class. VB .NET doesn't need this line because the System namespace is built in to the IDE. The VB .NET equivalent for the using statement is Imports.

C# uses the Namespace keyword to define the application's namespace. It defaults to the name of your application, but you can type in a different name. A namespace declares the scope for objects within it and helps you organize your code. VB .NET doesn't use the Namespace keyword by default (though it is supported in the language). Instead, the namespace is set via the IDE menu. Select Project ➤ Properties and you can enter the VB .NET application's namespace in the dialog box.

Next in the C# template are the XML comments. This is simply an example of how XML comments look and it gives you some starter comments. VB .NET doesn't have these comments in its template because it doesn't have the capability to do XML comments.

C# defines a default class for you. VB .NET uses a module instead. VB .NET modules are similar to a class, but they are shared and accessible anywhere (i.e., global scope) within their namespace.

C# defines the Main() procedure inside the default class. It uses the static modifier because the Main() procedure isn't associated with an instance of the class. VB .NET puts the Main() procedure within the module. The Main() procedure is where an application starts. There can only be one per application.

Case Sensitivity

If a compiler is case sensitive, it treats as unique procedures and variables with the same name if the case of the letters do not match.

VB 6.0 and VB .NET are not case sensitive. A variable called FirstName is the same as the variable called firstName. Because of this, the IDE for both languages automatically converts the case of your procedure and variable names to match how they were declared. This ensures that you don't mistakenly think that two variables are different.

C# is case sensitive. If you are coming from a VB 6.0 background, you might have the habit of only worrying about entering the proper case when declaring a variable. You know that after you declare a variable properly you can just enter it as lowercase and the IDE will fix it for you. This doesn't work with C#.

A common way of declaring variables in C# is to use camelCasing for private members of a class and use PascalCasing for anything exposed externally. camelCasing uses uppercase for the first letter of every word except the first word. For example, firstName and socialSecurityNumber use camelCasing. PascalCasing uses uppercase for the first letter of every word. For example, FirstName and SocialSecurityNumber is PascalCasing. Although VB .NET isn't case sensitive, I find this naming convention useful in VB .NET because I can immediately recognize which variables are arguments in the procedure declaration.

Writing Code across Multiple Lines

Writing your code so that it crosses multiple lines can make it more readable. Given the width constraints of monitors, it can be helpful to have a programming statement use two or more lines. In VB this is done using the underscore character (_). In C# this isn't an issue because the compiler uses a semicolon (;) to mark the end of a line.

VB 6.0/VB .NET

Use the underscore character to mark that a statement will continue to the next line. It is important to remember, and easy to miss, that the underscore must be preceded with a space. A common error is to type the underscore immediately after typing the last character on a line.

```
'Demonstrate concatenating two strings together with the "&". The strings are
'on different lines. The "_" is used to tell the compiler to use the
'second line.
var = "This is a very, very, very long string " & _
      "that takes two lines to write."
```

C#

Because each statement ends with a semicolon, no line continuation character is needed to mark that a statement continues to the next line. The exception to this is the // comment tag that only applies to the line it is on. This is discussed in the next section.

```
//Demonstrate concatenating two strings together with the "+". The strings are
//on different lines.
var = "This is a very, very, very long string " +
      "that takes two lines to write.";
```

Comments

Comments play an essential part in documenting your code. This ensures that your program is understandable and maintainable by other programmers (as well as yourself). Although many programs have separately written programmer's documentation, nothing can take the place of a bunch of short, in-line comments placed at critical points in your program code.

What can be even more important than comments is writing self-documenting code. There isn't anything language specific about self-documenting code. It's a self-imposed discipline that every good programmer uses. It simply consists of taking an extra second or two to use variable names and procedure names that describe what their purpose is.

A problem for a lot of programmers entering the professional programming world is that many are accustomed to using variables and procedure names such as X and Test. This is fine if you are working on a simple program for a homework assignment or the program is out of a *Learn to Program in X Days* book. After you finish writing the program, you will probably never look at it again. But when you work on projects that will be used for months and years to come, many other programmers will be looking at your code. It's important to make it easy for them to immediately understand what your program does. Personally, I know that when I look at a program 6 months after I wrote it, the self-documenting code makes it so much easier to remember what I did and why.

Comments in both versions of VB are very simple. Use an apostrophe (') in front of the text that you want to comment out. This can either be at the beginning of a line or after a line of code. The compiler ignores everything after the apostrophe.

Comments in C# are much more robust. You have the option of using single-line comments, multiline comment blocks, and XML comments. Single-line comments are two forward slashes (//). They can be placed at the beginning of a line or at the end of a line of code. The compiler ignores everything after the two slashes.

C# also has multiline comment blocks that are used for making very detailed comments. They are represented by /* to start the block and */ to finish the block. They are useful for temporarily blocking out a large section of code for testing purposes.

XML comments in C# are a new concept to make it easier to document your code. They are designed so that you can have "intelligent" comments that use tags to describe the different parts of your program. You can view these comments using an XML reader (e.g., Internet Explorer). Because this is a totally new concept, it remains to be seen how C# programmers will take to it. This chapter does not teach you the concepts of writing XML comments, but Table 2-3 provides an easy lookup chart for the standard tags that Microsoft recommends.

VB 6.0/VB .NET

Comments use a single apostrophe and the compiler ignores everything that comes after it.

```
'This is a comment on a line by itself
Dim Month As String    'This is a comment after a line of code
```

C#

Single-line comments use two forward slashes (//).

```
//This is a comment on a line by itself
string month;    //This is a comment after a line of code
```

Multiline comment blocks use /* and */ to begin and end a block of comments.

```
/* This is the start of some comments.
    This is the end of the comments. */
/* Comment out a block code for testing purposes
string month;
month = "July";
*/
```

XML comments are defined using three forward slashes (///) and they must follow the standards for well-defined XML.

```
/// <summary>
/// This is a sample of XML code.
/// </summary>
///<code>
string month;
month = "September";
///</code>
```

You can create any tag you feel is necessary. However, there are some standard tags you should use to make your comments consistent with other programmers' work.[1]

Table 2-3. Standard Tags for Documenting Comments Using XML

XML TAG	DESCRIPTION
`<code>`	Mark a block of code
`<example>`	An example to demonstrate how to use the code
`<exception>`	Document a custom exception class
`<include>`	Refer to comments in another file that describe the types and members in your source code
`<list>`	A bulleted item list

1. From Microsoft's "C# Programmer's Reference," which you can find in the MSDN Help file. Use the index and type in **XML Documentation**.

Table 2-3. Standard Tags for Documenting Comments Using XML (Continued)

XML TAG	DESCRIPTION
`<para>`	A paragraph
`<param>`	Describe a parameter
`<paramref>`	Indicate that a word is a parameter
`<permission>`	Describe the access to a member
`<see>`	Specify a link to other text
`<seealso>`	Text that you want to appear in a See Also section
`<summary>`	Summarize an object
`<remarks>`	Specify overview information about a class or type
`<returns>`	A description of the return value
`<value>`	Describe a property

Declaring Variables

Declaring variables is a way of telling the compiler which data type a variable represents[2]. Each of the three languages does this differently. There are three major syntax differences to be aware of: declaring a single variable, declaring multiple variables on one line, and initializing a variable.

The syntax for declaring a variable in VB 6.0 and VB .NET uses the `Dim` and `As` keywords. C# uses a shorter notation by only stating the data type followed by the variable name. Thus, VB and C# are in the reverse order. This can make it a little confusing if you are VB programmer who is starting to learn C# programming. But you will probably adjust to it very quickly.

Declaring multiple variables on a single line in VB .NET has changed a lot from VB 6.0. Previously, every variable had to have its own data type assigned to it. Otherwise, it would be treated as a variant. In VB .NET this has been changed so that all variables listed between the `Dim` and the `As` keywords are of the same type. In C#, all variables listed between the data type and the semicolon are of the same type.

VB 6.0 does not allow you to initialize variables on the declaration line—this has to be done on another line of code. VB .NET now makes this possible by placing the equal sign (=) and a value after the data type. The C# syntax places the equal sign between the variable name and the semicolon.

---

2. Data types are described in Chapter 3.

VB 6.0

Declare a variable by listing the data type after the As keyword.

```
'Declare an integer variable
Dim var1 As Integer
'Declare and initialize an integer variable
Public var2 As Integer
var2 = 5
'Declare two variables: var3 is a Variant and var4 is a Single
Private var3, var4 As Single
'Declare two variables, all of which are of type Single
Dim var5 As Single, var6 As Single
```

VB .NET

Declare a variable by listing the data type after the As keyword. You can initialize the variable by assigning a value to it after the data type name. This won't work when you initialize more than one variable of the same type on one line.

```
'Declare an integer variable
Dim var1 As Integer
'Declare and initialize an integer variable
Public var2 As Integer = 5
'Declare two variables, both are of type Single
Private var3, var4 As Single
'Declare and initialize two variables
Private var5 As Integer = 5, var4 As Single = 6.5
```

C#

Declare a variable by putting the data type before the variable name. You can initialize the variable by assigning a value to it after the variable name. This will work when you initialize more than one variable of the same type on one line.

```
//Declare an integer variable
int var1;
//Declare and initialize an integer variable
public int var2 = 5;
//Declare and initialize two variables, both of which are of type float
private float var3=1.25, var4=5.6;
```

Modifying a Variable's Scope

The scope of a variable refers to who can access it and how long it exists in your program. This is useful for limiting the accessibility of a variable so that it can be used within a module or class, but not outside of it.

A variable exists as long as the context in which it was declared exists. For example, a variable declared within a procedure exists as long as the procedure is running. Once the procedure ends, all variables within the procedure are released. The same applies if a variable is declared within a class, or within a code block such as the For Next loop.

The Static keyword in VB 6.0 and VB .NET modifies a variable so that it lives for the entire life of the program. When the procedure ends, the static variable keeps its value in memory. When entering the procedure again, the variable will have the same value as when the procedure last ended. The scope is Private because it is only visible within the procedure it was declared in.

When declaring variables in a class, you can use the Shared modifier with variables in VB .NET. In a C# class, the static modifier is equivalent to both the Static and Shared modifiers in VB .NET. This is discussed in Chapter 6.

The standard access modifiers for setting the scope of a variable are Public, Private, Friend and internal, Dim, and Static.

- The Public modifier allows a variable to be accessed from anywhere in the program or from a program using the assembly. There are no restrictions.

- The Private modifier only allows a variable to be accessed from within its declaration context.

- The Friend (VB .NET) and internal (C#) modifiers allow a variable to be used from anywhere within its assembly. Programs using the assembly can't access it.

- The Dim (VB only) modifier has the same scope as Private. It cannot be used when declaring a procedure, class, or module.

- The Static modifier (VB only) exists for the entire life of the program. It has the same scope as Private.

VB 6.0

List the access modifier before the variable name.

```
Static var As type
```

VB .NET

List the access modifier before the variable name.

```
Friend var As type
```

C#

List the access modifier before the data type.

```
private type var;
```

Declaring Procedures

Declaring procedures is how you separate the different functionality within your code. The syntax for returning a value and passing parameters is different for each language.

In VB, procedures that don't return a value are *subroutines*. Procedures that do return a value are *functions*. C# doesn't differentiate between the two because every procedure must be declared as returning some data type. If you don't want the procedure to return a value, use the void data type. The void data type returns nothing.

The C# equivalent of a VB subroutine is a procedure with type void. The C# equivalent of a VB function is a procedure with any other data type.

Functions in VB 6.0 require that you assign the function name to the value that is to be returned. VB .NET still allows you to return values this way, and both VB .NET and C# now use the Return keyword to return a value. Simply list the value to return after the Return keyword and it will be passed back to the calling procedure.

VB 6.0

Procedures that don't return data are declared using the Sub keyword. Procedures that do return data use the Function keyword and after the procedure parameters you must list the data type that will be returned. Assign the return value to the function name.

```
Public Sub procedure()
End Sub

Public Function procedure() As type
    Dim var as type
    var = num
    procedure = var
End Function
```

VB .NET

Procedures that don't return data are declared using the Sub keyword. Procedures that do return data use the Function keyword and after the procedure parameters you must list the data type that will be returned. Either assign the return value to the function name or list the return value after the Return keyword.

```
Public Sub procedure()
End Sub

Public Function procedure() As type
    Dim var as type
    var = num
    procedure = var
End Function

'Demonstrate returning a value with the Return keyword
Public Function procedure() As type
    Dim var as type
    var = num
    Return var
End Function
```

C#

Every procedure has to have a return data type listed before the procedure name. If you don't want to return a value, use the void data type. List the return value after the return keyword.

```
public void procedure()
{
}

public type procedure()
{
    type var;
    var = num;
    return var;
}
```

Passing Arguments to Procedures

Passing data to procedures is done with parameter declarations. The data that is passed to the procedures are called *arguments*. The biggest change for VB programmers is that in VB 6.0, parameters are passed by reference as the default. This could cause problems because if you mistakenly change the value of a parameter without realizing it, you won't get an error. Instead, the data in the calling procedure would be changed and this would probably result in a hard-to-find bug. In .NET, both languages pass parameter data by value as the default. In fact, C# doesn't have a keyword for designating a parameter being passed by value. It only requires that you specify which parameters are passed by reference.

VB uses the ByVal keyword to specify a parameter as being passed by value. It uses the ByRef keyword to specify a parameter being passed by reference.

C# uses the ref keyword to specify a parameter as being passed by reference. It uses the out keyword to specify a parameter as only being used to pass data to the calling procedure. out differs from the ref keyword in that the calling procedure doesn't have to initialize the argument before passing it to the procedure. Normally, C# requires any argument passed to a procedure to be initialized first. The out keyword is useful when you want a procedure to return many values and you don't want to bother with initializing them.

A requirement in C# is that both the ref and out keywords must be used in the procedure declaration and in the procedure call. VB .NET doesn't have this requirement.

VB 6.0/VB .NET

Use the ByVal keyword to pass parameters by value. Use the ByRef keyword to pass parameters by reference. If not specified, the VB 6.0 default is ByRef. The VB .NET default is ByVal.

```
' VB .NET: param1 and param3 are both passed by value; param2 is passed by reference
' VB 6.0: param1 and param2 are both passed by reference; param3 is by value
Sub procedure(param1 As type, ByRef param2 As type, ByVal param3 As type)
```

C#

Passing parameters by value requires no extra coding. Use the ref keyword to pass parameters by reference. Use the out keyword to specify parameters whose only purpose is to return a value. The ref and out keywords must also be specified when calling the procedure.

```
//param1 is passed by value and param2 is passed by reference
void procedure(type param1, ref type param2, out type param3)

//Calling this procedure would look like this
procedure(val1, ref val2, out val3);
```

Optional Parameters

Optional parameters give you flexibility with how much data is required to be passed to a procedure. VB 6.0 and VB .NET use the Optional keyword to specify optional parameters. C# doesn't have optional parameters. As a substitute, you can use the parameter array that is described in the next section. You can also override methods as is discussed in Chapter 6.

Because a parameter is optional, you need a way to find out if the calling procedure passed an argument or not. In VB 6.0 this is done using the IsMissing() function. If IsMissing() returns True, no argument was passed and you can assign a default value to the parameter. The IsMissing() function isn't in VB .NET because it requires optional parameters to be given a default value in the procedure declaration.

A procedure can have as many optional parameters as needed, but they must be the last parameters listed. No standard parameters can be listed after them.

VB 6.0

Optional parameters use the Optional keyword.

```
Sub procedure(Optional param As type)
    If IsMissing(param) Then
        param = default
    End If
End Sub
```

VB .NET

Optional parameters use the Optional keyword. It is required that each optional parameter has a default value assigned to it.

```
Sub procedure(Optional param As type = default)

End Sub
```

C#

There are no optional parameters in C#.

Parameter Arrays

Parameter arrays give you the benefit of being able to pass from zero to an indefinite number of parameters to a procedure without having to declare each one individually.

Parameter arrays are declared in VB using the `ParamArray` keyword and in C# using the `params` keyword. There are two restrictions with parameter arrays: There can only be one parameter array declared per procedure, and it must be the last parameter listed.

A drawback to using a parameter array is that every element in the array is declared of the same type. To get around this obstacle, you can declare the array to be of type `Object`.

VB 6.0

Use the `ParamArray` keyword to declare a parameter array.

```
Sub procedure(ParamArray param() As type)
```

VB .NET

Use the `ParamArray` keyword to declare a parameter array.

```
Sub procedure(ParamArray param() As type)
```

C#

Use the `params` keyword to declare a parameter array.

```
void procedure(params type[] param)
```

Modifying a Procedure's Accessibility

You can determine which parts of a program can call a procedure by using an access modifier. The access modifier is placed at the beginning of the line, in front of the procedure declaration. The standard access modifiers for a procedure are `Public`, `Private`, and `Friend` and `internal`.[3]

- The `Public` modifier allows a procedure to be accessed from anywhere in the program or from a program using this assembly. There are no restrictions. This is the default for VB .NET procedures.

- The `Private` modifier allows a procedure to be accessed only from within its own declaration context. This includes being used within nested procedures. This is the default for C# procedures.

- The `Friend` (VB .NET) and `internal` (C#) modifiers allow a procedure to be accessed only from within the assembly.

---

3. There are other access modifiers available for classes. These are discussed in Chapter 6 and Chapter 8.

An interesting difference between VB .NET and C# is that they have different default modifiers. In VB .NET, procedures and functions declared in a module or class without an access modifier are treated as `Public`. In C#, methods declared in a class without an access modifier are `private` by default.

VB 6.0

List the access modifier before the procedure name.

```
Public Sub procedure()

Private Function procedure() As type
```

VB .NET

List the access modifier before the procedure name. A procedure without an access modifier will be declared as `Public`.

```
Sub procedure()      'This is Public

Public Sub procedure()

Private Function procedure() As type
```

C#

List the access modifier before the procedure data type. A procedure without an access modifier will be declared as `Private`.

```
void procedure()     //This is Private

public void procedure()

private type procedure()
```

Calling Procedures

Once you have declared a procedure, you need to call it so that its functionality can be used. Although this seems fairly simple, you need to be aware of the proper use of parentheses as well as how to properly pass arguments.

Before examining how to pass arguments, let's look at a change from VB 6.0 to VB .NET. It is now required in .NET to use parentheses when calling a procedure. This simplifies things because you will no longer get compiler errors stating that you need to have parentheses or that you are using them where they aren't required. Now parentheses are always required, so you don't have to think about it. C# also requires parentheses when calling a procedure.

When passing arguments to a procedure, VB has the advantage over C#. Normally, when you call a procedure you pass the arguments in the order that they are listed in the procedure declaration. This applies to both VB and C#. The advantage that VB has over C# is that in VB you can pass arguments by name. In other words, you do not have to pass arguments in the order that the procedure declaration says you should. This is very helpful when working with optional parameters because you can state which parameters you want to use and leave the others alone. You don't have to use an empty comma list and worry about inserting the correct number of commas. Simply list which parameters get which arguments. This makes your code look much cleaner. Because C# doesn't have optional parameters, it doesn't need the capability to pass arguments by name.

It should be noted that regardless of the language, when calling procedures that have a parameter array, you do not need to pass the procedure an actual array. You only need to pass it arguments separated by commas. The calling procedure will store these arguments in an array, but it is only expecting standard single-value arguments.

VB 6.0

Call subroutines without using parentheses. Call functions using parentheses. When passing arguments by name use := after the argument and give it a value.

```
procedure param1, param2
var = function(param1, param2)
procedure param2 := value
```

VB .NET

Call subroutines and functions using parentheses. When passing arguments by name use := after the argument and give it a value.

```
procedure (param1, param2)
var = function(param1, param2)
procedure (param2 := value)
```

C#

Call all procedures using parentheses.

```
procedure(param1, param2);
var = procedure(param1, param2);
```

Example 2-1. Calculate Test Score Functions

This example takes up to three test scores and displays the high score and the average score. Using reference parameters and an out parameter is demonstrated in the CalcHighScore() procedure. It returns the high score. The parameter array is demonstrated in the CalcAvgScore() function. It returns the average score via the function name.

VB 6.0

```
'Calculate Test Scores sample application using VB 6.0
'Copyright (c)2001 by Bischof Systems, Inc.

Sub Main()
    ProcessScores 80, 90, 75
End Sub

Public Sub ProcessScores(ByVal Score1 As Integer, ByVal Score2 As Integer, _
    ByVal Score3 As Integer)
    Dim HighScore As Integer
    Dim avgScore As Single
    'Write the scores we are working with
    DisplayScores Score1, Score2, Score3
    'Get the high score
    CalcHighScore Score1, Score2, Score3, HighScore
    Debug.Print "The high score is " & HighScore
    'Get the average score
    avgScore = CalcAvgScore(Score1, Score2, Score3)
    Debug.Print "The average score is " & Format(avgScore, "##.00")
End Sub

'Display all scores using a parameter array
Private Sub DisplayScores(ParamArray Scores())
    Dim CurrentScore As Integer
    Debug.Print "The scores being used are: "
    For CurrentScore = 0 To UBound(Scores)
        Debug.Print Scores(CurrentScore) & "  "
    Next
    Debug.Print
End Sub
```

```vbnet
'Use an out parameter to return the high score
Private Sub CalcHighScore(ByVal Score1 As Integer, ByVal Score2 As Integer, _
    ByVal Score3 As Integer, ByRef HighScore As Integer)
    'Assume score1 is the high score
    HighScore = Score1
    'Is Score2 higher?
    If (Score2 > Score1) Then
        HighScore = Score2
    End If
    'Does Score3 beat them all?
    If (Score3 > HighScore) Then
        HighScore = Score3
    End If
End Sub


'Use a function to calculate the average score
Private Function CalcAvgScore(ParamArray Scores()) As Single
    Dim TotalScore, CurrentScore As Integer
    For CurrentScore = 0 To UBound(Scores)
        TotalScore = TotalScore + Scores(CurrentScore)
    Next
    CalcAvgScore = TotalScore / (UBound(Scores) + 1)
End Function
```

VB .NET

```vbnet
'Calculate Test Scores sample application using VB .NET
'Copyright (c)2001 by Bischof Systems, Inc.

Module Module1

    Sub Main()
        ProcessScores(80, 90, 75)
        Console.ReadLine()
    End Sub

    Public Sub ProcessScores(ByVal Score1 As Integer, ByVal Score2 As Integer, _
        ByVal Score3 As Integer)
        Dim highScore As Integer
        Dim avgScore As Single
        'Write the scores we are working with
        DisplayScores(Score1, Score2, Score3)
        'Get the high score
        CalcHighScore(Score1, Score2, Score3, highScore)
```

```vbnet
        Console.WriteLine("The high score is {0}", highScore)
        'Get the average score
        avgScore = CalcAvgScore(Score1, Score2, Score3)
        Console.WriteLine("The average score is {0:N2}", avgScore)
    End Sub

    'Display all scores using a parameter array
    Private Sub DisplayScores(ByVal ParamArray Scores() As Integer)
        Dim currentScore As Integer
        Console.Write("The scores being used are: ")
        For currentScore = 0 To Scores.Length - 1
            Console.Write(Scores(currentScore).ToString & "  ")
        Next
        Console.WriteLine()
    End Sub

    'Use an out parameter to return the high score
    Private Sub CalcHighScore(ByVal Score1 As Integer, ByVal Score2 As Integer, _
        ByVal Score3 As Integer, ByRef HighScore As Integer)
        'Assume score1 is the high score
        HighScore = Score1
        'Is Score2 higher?
        If (Score2 > Score1) Then
            HighScore = Score2
        End If
        'Does Score3 beat them all?
        If (Score3 > HighScore) Then
            HighScore = Score3
        End If
    End Sub

    'Use a function to calculate the average score
    Private Function CalcAvgScore(ByVal ParamArray Scores() As Integer) As Single
        Dim TotalScore, CurrentScore As Integer
        For CurrentScore = 0 To Scores.Length - 1
            TotalScore += Scores(CurrentScore)
        Next
        Return CSng(TotalScore / Scores.Length)
    End Function
End Module
```

C#

```
//Calculate Test Scores sample application using C#
//Copyright (c)2001 by Bischof Systems, Inc.

using System;

namespace C_Fundamentals_TestScores
{
    class Class1
    {
        [STAThread]
        static void Main(string[] args)
        {
            ProcessScores(80, 90, 75);
            Console.ReadLine();
        }
        static public void ProcessScores(int Score1, int Score2, int Score3)
        {
            int highScore;
            float avgScore;
            //Write the scores we are working with
            DisplayScores(Score1, Score2, Score3);
            //Get the high score
            CalcHighScore(Score1, Score2, Score3, out highScore);
            Console.WriteLine("The high score is {0}", highScore);
            //Get the average score
            avgScore = CalcAvgScore(Score1, Score2, Score3);
            Console.WriteLine("The average score is {0:N2}", avgScore);
        }

        //Display all scores using a parameter array
        static internal void DisplayScores(params int[] Scores)
        {
            Console.Write("The scores being used are: ");
            for (int currentScore = 0; currentScore < Scores.Length;
                currentScore++)
            {
                Console.Write(Scores[currentScore] + "  ");
            }
            Console.WriteLine();
        }
```

```
        //Use an out parameter to return the high score
        static private void CalcHighScore(int Score1, int Score2, int Score3,
            out int highScore)
        {
            //Assume Score1 is the high score
            highScore=Score1;
            //Is Score2 higher?
            if (Score2 > Score1)
            {
                highScore = Score2;
            }
            //Does Score3 beat them all?
            if (Score3 > highScore)
            {
                highScore = Score3;
            }
        }


        //Use a function to calculate the average score
        static private float CalcAvgScore(params int[] Scores)
        {
            int totalScore=0;
            for (int currentScore = 0; currentScore < Scores.Length;
                currentScore++)
            {
                totalScore += Scores[currentScore];
            }
            return totalScore/(float)Scores.Length;
        }
    }
}
```

Example 2-1 Output

```
The scores being used are: 80  90  75
The high score is 90
The average score is 81.67
```

CHAPTER 3

Data Types and Operators

Table 3-1. Data Type Equivalent Chart

VB 6.0	VB .NET	C#
Byte	Byte	byte
Integer	Short	short
Long	Integer	int
	Long	long
Single	Single	float
Double	Double	double
Currency	Decimal	decimal
DateTime	Date	DateTime
Boolean	Boolean	bool
	Char	char
String	String	string
Variant	Object	object
Nothing	Nothing	null

Table 3-2. Arithmetic Operand Conversion Chart

VB 6.0	VB .NET	C#
x = x + y	x = x + y	x = x + y;
	x += y	x += y;
x = x - y	x = x - y	x = x - y;
	x -= y	x -= y;
x = x * y	x = x * y	x = x * y;
	x *= y	x *= y;

Table 3-2. Arithmetic Operand Conversion Chart (Continued)

VB 6.0	VB .NET	C#
x = x / y	x = x / y	x = x / y;
	x /= y	x /= y;
x = x \ y	x = x \ y	x = x \ y;
	x \= y	x \= y;
x = x + 1	x+=1	x++;
x = x - 1	x-=1	x--;
str = str & "string"	str = str & "string"	str = str + "string";
	str &= "string"	str += "string";
x = x Mod 10	x = x Mod 10	x = x % 10;
x = x ^ 2	x = x ^ 2	x = x ^ 2;

Table 3-3. Relational Operand Conversion Chart

VB 6.0	VB .NET	C#
If x = y Then ...	If x = y Then ...	if (x == y) {...}
If x <> y Then ...	If x <> y Then ...	if (x != y) {...}
If x < y Then ...	If x < y Then ...	if (x < y) {...}
If x <= y Then ...	If x <= y Then ...	if (x <= y) {...}
If x > y Then ...	If x > y Then ...	if (x > y) {...}
If x >= y Then ...	If x >= y Then ...	if (x >= y) {...}

Table 3-4. Boolean Operand Conversion Chart

VB 6.0	VB .NET	C#
And	And	&
	AndAlso	&&
Or	Or	|
	OrElse	||
Not	Not	! (logical) ~ bitwise

Overview

.NET introduces a variety of changes from VB 6.0 data types. A few of them are major, but most are just minor differences between the data types and there are some new operators.

Simple Data Types

The simple data types have primarily stayed the same. The biggest change is that Integer is now 32 bits and Long is 64 bits. In VB 6.0, Integer is 16 bits and Long is 32 bits. The purpose of this change is to make VB data types compatible with CLS-compliant data types. Because Windows computers are 32 bit, Integer is the most efficient data type.

Another change is that the Decimal data type has replaced the Currency data type. It provides high precision without rounding errors.

Dates in VB 6.0 are stored internally as a Double format and can be easily manipulated using common arithmetic functions. Dates in .NET are based off the System.DateTime class, manipulation of which requires you to access the class methods. To convert between DateTime and Double, use the ToDouble() and FromOADate() methods.

In VB 6.0 and VB .NET, simple data types are initialized to a default value. In general, numbers are defaulted to 0, Strings to an empty string, and Booleans to False. In C#, you must initialize every variable before using it. If you don't, the compiler will give you an error.

Variants and Objects

A major improvement from VB 6.0 to .NET is that the Variant data type has been removed from the language and the closest equivalent is now the Object data type.

Although the Variant data type allowed your code to be very flexible, your application incurred a large performance hit. Using Variant also encouraged poor programming practices, making your program harder to maintain and debug. The Object data type has been created to eliminate these problems. It is not an exact replacement for Variant, but it can be used in many places where Variant was previously required.

An Object variable is a pointer to a memory location storing a single piece of data. This variable can point to any data type because all data types in .NET inherit from the Object class. When you assign a different data type to an

Object variable, the original data type is unreferenced and the new data type is now pointed to. The garbage collector cleans up the original data.

An Object variable is based off the System.Object class. Each data type automatically inherits the following methods: ToString(), Equals(), ReferenceEquals(), GetType(), GetHashCode(), and Finalize(). Many data types override these methods to customize their functionality. You will probably find yourself frequently overriding the ToString() method in your own classes to give an accurate text representation of it.

In VB .NET, the Nothing keyword represents an uninitialized object or an object with no data. You can use the Is keyword to test an object variable for being equal to Nothing. C# uses the null keyword.

VB .NET

Test if an object variable references a valid object using the Is keyword followed by the Nothing keyword.

```
If var Is Nothing Then
    'No object is being referenced
    ...
End If
```

C#

Test if an object variable references a valid object using the null keyword.

```
if (var == null)
{
    //No object is being referenced
    ...
}
```

Booleans

A Boolean variable stores the value True or False. VB 6.0 allows your code to interchange Boolean and Integer variables. This is because False is represented as 0 and True is represented by any nonzero integer. Although this implicit conversion made it easier to write code, it can also make the code harder to understand and maintain. VB .NET requires Boolean variables to be assigned either True or False. C# is the same except that it uses all lowercase characters (e.g., true and false).

Characters

The character data type allows the storage of a single character using 16-bit Unicode format (for international characters). VB 6.0 doesn't have a character data type because it treats a string of length 1 as a character. In .NET, using a string with only one character in it is very expensive because of the way strings are managed. It's a lot more efficient in .NET to work with single characters using the character data type. Define a literal in VB .NET as a single character string followed by c. Define a literal in C# as a character enclosed in single quotes.

Converting between a character and its ASCII equivalent is covered in Chapter 10.

VB 6.0

A character is a String of length 1.

```
Dim var as String*1
var = "x"
```

VB .NET

A character is declared using the Char data type. A character can be typed in directly by using a single character String followed by c.

```
Dim var as Char
var = "x"c
```

C#

A character is declared using the char data type. A character can be typed in directly by enclosing it in a pair of single quotes.

```
char var = 'x';
```

Strings

.NET changes the String data type from VB 6.0 in two ways: It is now a class and it is also immutable.

Because the String data type is now a class, it has a variety of methods that can perform operations on the string. Thus, rather than using built-in string functions, you now use the methods that are part of the String class.

Saying that a string is immutable means that a string can never change its value. Instead, when you make a change to a string variable, a new string is created using the string's original value and that original string is unreferenced. The garbage collector cleans it up.

The downfall of making strings immutable is that making a lot of changes to a string incurs extra overhead. This is because every time a string changes, its modified contents must be copied to a new memory location and the old string is unreferenced. This requires a lot of processing when compared to just changing one character. An alternative to modifying a string variable is to use the StringBuilder class. This class is used to perform basic string modifications in a very efficient manner. It works by allocating more memory than necessary for a string, and any changes made to the string are done within the original memory location. Any characters appended to the string are done so within the extra memory space that was originally allocated. If more memory is needed, a new string is created and the contents are copied to it. If you have to make a lot of modifications to a string, the StringBuilder class can really improve your program's performance.

C# strings can be written using escape sequences. For example, creating a string to represent a line feed is written as "\n". The backslash character (\) tells the compiler that this is an escape sequence. If you wish to use a backslash character that isn't an escape sequence, put the at sign (@) in front of the string to tell the compiler to ignore escape sequences in the string, or remember to use \\ (which is the escape sequence for a single backslash character). This is especially important when you are writing filenames and you are using the backslash as a directory separator. The VB .NET compiler doesn't have this syntax because it can't use escape sequences in strings.

Chapter 10 covers all the functions that manage string data and also discusses the StringBuilder class in detail.

VB 6.0/VB .NET

Strings are declared using the String keyword.

```
Dim var1 As String
var1 = "New String"
```

C#

Strings are declared using the string keyword.

```
string var1;
var1 = "New String";
//Demonstrate assigning a filename to a string
fileName = @"C:\Directory\Filename.txt"
```

Arrays

An array is a group of elements referenced by an index. There is one major difference between arrays in VB 6.0 and .NET. Arrays in VB 6.0 can use the Option Base keyword to specify the default lower bounds of an array. Alternatively, a lower bound could be specified when declaring the array. This is not possible in .NET. Arrays in .NET are always zero-based.

The syntax for declaring a static sized array is the same for both VB 6.0 and VB .NET. When you declare the array, pass it a size initializer. The size initializer is placed between a pair of parentheses and listed after the array name. C# requires the size initializer to be placed between a pair of square brackets and listed after the data type.

VB 6.0/VB .NET

Declare a static sized array by passing the size between a pair of parentheses.

```
Dim var(n) As datatype

'Demonstrate creating an array of integers
Dim var(2) As Integer
'Initialize its elements
var(0) = 23
var(1) = 41
var(2) = 50
```

C#

Declare a static sized array by passing the size between a pair of square brackets. Assign the variable to a new instance of the data type and pass the size initializer between a pair of square brackets. This can be done on one or two lines.

```
datatype[] var = new datatype[size];

//Demonstrate creating an array of strings using two lines
string[] myArray;
myArray = new string[2];
myArray[0] = "St. Xavier";
myArray[1] = "Louisville, Kentucky";
```

The syntax for creating a dynamic array is the same for VB 6.0 and VB .NET. Declare a dynamic array using a pair of empty parentheses (i.e., no size initializer) after the variable name. Use the ReDim statement to give it an appropriate size. The ReDim statement will reinitialize the array's values when resizing it. If you want to resize an array after you've been using it, and you don't want to lose its data, use the Preserve keyword. Both VB .NET and C# support element initialization when declaring the array. This is described at the end of this section.

C# doesn't have arrays that can by dynamically changed as the program executes. You should use the ArrayList class if you need to use arrays that must be resized.[1]

VB 6.0/VB .NET

Declare a dynamic array using a pair of empty parentheses. Use the ReDim statement to modify its size. If you want to keep the values of the array intact, use the Preserve keyword after the ReDim statement.

```
Dim var() As Integer
Redim var(size)
ReDim Preserve var(size)
```

Depending on whether you are working in VB .NET or C#, specifying the size initializer has a different effect on the number of elements in an array.

In VB 6.0 and VB .NET, the size initializer is used to determine the upper bounds of the array. Declaring an array with a size initializer of 20 creates an array with 21 elements. The first element has an index of 0 and the last element has an index of 20.

In C# the size initializer specifies the number of elements in the array. Declaring an array with a size initializer of 20 creates an array with 20 elements. The first element has an index of 0 and the last element has an index of 19.

Because there can be a lot of confusion about the size of an array and its upper bound element, .NET arrays have multiple methods for getting this information. VB 6.0 uses the UBound() function to find the upper-bound element number. VB .NET and C# can take advantage of many new methods in the .NET Framework. The GetUpperBound() method is the .NET equivalent of the VB 6.0 UBound() function. The GetLength() method indicates how many elements are in the array for a particular dimension. The Length() property indicates the total number of elements in the array. For a multidimension array, this is equivalent to calling the GetLength() method for each dimension and adding the results together.

VB 6.0

The UBound() function takes the array name as the first parameter. An optional second parameter is the dimension. The dimension is base 1 and 1 is also the default dimension.

---

1. If you want to research this in MSDN, use the index and type in **ArrayList class**.

```
Dim myArray(5, 10) As Integer
Debug.Print UBound(myArray)     'Prints 5
Debug.Print UBound(myArray, 2)  'Prints 10
```

VB .NET

The methods GetUpperBound() and GetLength() both take the array dimension as their parameter. Unlike VB 6.0, the dimension is base 0. The Length property doesn't take any parameters.

```
Dim myArray(5, 10) As Integer
Console.WriteLine(myArray.GetUpperBound(1)) 'Prints 10
Console.WriteLine(myArray.GetLength(1))     'Prints 11
Console.WriteLine(myArray.Length)           'Prints 66
```

C#

The methods GetUpperBound() and GetLength() both take the array dimension as their parameter. The dimension is base 0. The Length property doesn't take any parameters.

```
int[,] myArray = new int[5,10];
Console.WriteLine(myArray.GetUpperBound(0)); //Prints 4
Console.WriteLine(myArray.GetLength(0));     //Prints 5
Console.WriteLine(myArray.Length);           //Prints 50
```

A very nice feature in both VB .NET and C# that has always been part of C++ but not VB (although I do remember using it in BASIC for MS-DOS) is element initializers. When declaring the array, a data list can be passed within a set of curly brackets and this is used to populate the array.

VB .NET

Initialize the array's elements by assigning a data list enclosed in curly brackets to the array variable. If you are declaring the array and initializing it on the same line, using the New keyword is optional.

```
'Create an array on one line and initialize its elements
Dim var() as Integer = {22, 99, 18}
 'Create an array on one line and initialize its elements using the New keyword
Dim var() as Integer = New Integer() {22, 99, 18}
'Create an array and initialize its elements using two lines
Dim var() as Integer
var = New Integer() {22, 99, 18}
```

C#

Initialize the array's elements by assigning a data list enclosed in curly brackets to the array variable. If you are declaring the array and initializing it on the same line, using the new keyword is optional.

```
//Create an array on one line and initialize its elements
int[] var = {22, 99, 18};
//Create a two dimension array on one line and initialize its elements
int[,] var = new int[,] {{22, 99, 18},{5, 14, 23}};
//Create an array and initialize its elements using two lines
int[] var;
var = new int[] {22, 99, 18};
```

Grouping Constants with Enumerators

Enumerators provide a means of storing a set of related constants into a single group. There are times when identifying items in a group with numeric constants is not very obvious. Enumerators let you assign a value to a variable using a name rather than a cryptic number. They provide an easy way to make your code self-documenting and easier to maintain.

Enumerated data types must be declared as a module-level variable or as a class variable. They can't be defined within a procedure because once that procedure is finished, the enumerated type will be destroyed. This would eliminate its usefulness in the program.

Because an enumerated data type is a member of a class, it can be used with any of the typical member accessors: Public, Private, Protected, Friend or internal, and Shadows (VB .NET only). This only applies to the .NET languages.

The syntax for listing the entries is the same for both versions of VB, but different for C#. The VB compiler expects each entry to be on a separate line. Thus, you can't put more than one entry on the same line. C# is different because it uses the semicolon to designate the end of the line. Rather than putting semicolons after each entry, it uses a comma-separated list. You can put entries on separate lines or all on the same line, but they must always be separated by commas.

VB 6.0/VB .NET

Put each entry on a separate line.

```
Enum Months
    Jan
    Feb
    Mar
```

```
        Apr
        May
        Jun
        Jul
        Aug
        Sep
        Oct
        Nov
        Dec
End Enum
```

C#

Put each entry on a separate line and separate each entry with a comma.

```
enum Months
{   Jan,
    Feb,
    Mar,
    Apr,
    May,
    Jun,
    Jul,
    Aug,
    Sep,
    Oct,
    Nov,
    Dec
}
//Demonstrate putting all entries on the same line
enum Months {Jan, Feb, Mar, Apr, May, Jun, Jul, Aug, Sep, Oct, Nov, Dec}
```

When creating an enumerated type, you can let the computer assign values to each entry or you can assign them yourself. If you let the computer do it, it will assign 0 to the first entry and each entry after that will be incremented by one.

It is possible to assign values to some entries and not to others. If you leave an entry unassigned, the compiler will assign it the next sequential number based on the entry before it. As an example, if an entry is assigned 5 and the next entry is unassigned, it will get the value 6. Each time an entry is assigned a value, the compiler resets the internal counter. You can also assign an entry a value based on another entry. It's perfectly acceptable to do arithmetic between entries and assign the result to another entry.

All three languages work the same way. Let's look at an example using a VB .NET module.

VB .NET

```
Module EnumExample
    Enum myEnum
        A
        B
        C = 9
        D
        E = C * D
        F = E + 5
    End Enum

    Sub Main()
        Console.WriteLine(myEnum.A)
        Console.WriteLine(myEnum.B)
        Console.WriteLine(myEnum.C)
        Console.WriteLine(myEnum.D)
        Console.WriteLine(myEnum.E)
        Console.WriteLine(myEnum.F)
        Console.ReadLine()
    End Sub
End Module
```

Output

```
0
1
9
10
90
95
```

Entry A is 0 because it was the first entry in the list and you didn't assign it a number. You also didn't assign a value to entry B, and as a result it is 1. The compiler assigned it the next sequential number after A. C is 9 because you assigned it that. D is 10 because that is the next sequential number after 9. E is the result of multiplying C and D. F is the result of adding 5 to E.

A new feature for enumerated types in .NET is the ability to use the Flags attribute. This enables you to perform Boolean operations among multiple entries. Using a Boolean variable to store a value is a way to save multiple pieces of data without having to create multiple variables. You can test if a variable has a bit set by doing Boolean operations on it.

VB .NET

Use the `<Flags()>` attribute to signify an enumerated type that stores Boolean values.

```
<Flags()> Enum Bits
        Entry1 = &H1
        Entry2 = &H2
        Entry3 = &H4
End Enum
```

C#

Use the `<Flags()>` attribute to signify an enumerated type that stores Boolean values.

```
[Flags] enum Bits
{
    Entry1 = 0x1,
    Entry2 = 0x2,
    Entry3 = 0x4
}
```

Assigning a value to a variable is stricter in .NET than it is in VB 6.0. In VB 6.0 you can assign an enumerated constant to a variable by using only the enumerated entry's name. This is not so in .NET. You must use the fully qualified name to assign it to a variable. Thus, you must use the enumerated type name as well as the entry name.

VB 6.0

Assign a value to a variable using either the fully qualified name or the name of the entry.

```
Dim var As myEnum
var = myEnum.myEntry1
```

Or

```
var = myEntry2
```

VB .NET

Assign a value to a variable using the fully qualified name.

```
Dim var As myEnum
var = myEnum.myEntry1
```

C#

Assign a value to a variable using the fully qualified name.

```
myEnum var;
var = myEnum.myEntry1;
```

You can examine a variable declared as an enumerated type by printing either its value as an integer or its name as a string. To get its value in VB .NET, reference its fully qualified name. In C# you have to cast the variable as an int. To print the name as a string, both languages use the ToString() method.

VB .NET

```
Dim var As myEnum
var = myEnum.myEntry
'Print the value of the variable as an integer
Console.WriteLine(var)
'Print the name of the enumerated type as a string
Console.WriteLin(var.ToString())
```

C#

```
myEnum var;
//Print the value of the variable as an int
Console.WriteLine((int)var);
//Print the name of the enumerated type as a string
Console.WriteLine(var.ToString());
```

Converting between Data Types

When you use a lot of different data types in a program, it is often necessary to convert a variable into a different data type. This can happen when you are calling a procedure and it expects a certain data type or when you are converting strings into their numerical equivalent. The .NET Framework provides three different ways of converting between data types. You can use the System.Convert class, use explicit casting, or use the Parse() method of a base data type.

Using the System.Convert Class

VB 6.0 has a variety of conversion functions built into the language. Some of these are CInt(), CDouble(), and CDate(). These functions are also available in VB .NET, but the .NET Framework uses the System.Convert class to perform data type conversions.

The System.Convert class consists of many methods to convert between data types. Each method is overloaded so that it can be passed different data types and it returns a value of the specified data type. Sometimes conversions from a larger size data type to a smaller size data type can result in a loss of precision. If the target variable is too small to hold the value, an overflow exception is thrown. Table 3-5 lists the different methods of the System.Convert class.

VB 6.0

Pass a variable to the Cxxx() function and it returns a value of the appropriate data type.

```
varTo = Cxxx(varFrom)
'Demonstrate converting data types
var = CInt(1234)
var = CDate("8/27/33")
```

VB .NET

Pass a variable to the Cxxx() function and it returns a value of the appropriate data type.

```
varTo = Cxxx(varFrom)
'Demonstrate converting data types
var = CInt(12345678)
var = CDate("5/29/1973")
```

Each method of the System.Convert class is passed a variable or constant and it returns a value of the specified data type.

```
varTo = Convert.ToInt32(varFrom)
'Demonstrate converting a 0 to Boolean False
Dim var As Boolean
var = Convert.ToBoolean(0)
```

C#

Each method of the System.Convert class is passed a variable or constant and it returns a value of the specified data type.

```
varTo = Convert.ToInt32(varFrom)
//Demonstrate converting a 0 to Boolean false
int varTo;
varTo = Convert.ToInt32(12345678);
```

Table 3-5. Methods of the System.Convert Class

CONVERT METHOD	DESCRIPTION
ToByte(), ToUInt16(), ToUInt32(), ToUInt64()	Convert to an unsigned integer of the specified number of bytes
ToSByte(), ToInt16(), ToInt32(), ToInt64()	Convert to a signed integer of the specified number of bytes
ToDecimal()	Convert to a Decimal
ToDouble()	Convert to a Double
ToSingle()	Convert to a Single
ToDateTime()	Convert to a DateTime
ToBoolean()	Convert to a Boolean
ToChar()	Convert to a Unicode character
ToString()	Convert to a String

Explicit Variable Casting

Explicit casting consists of taking a variable of one type and telling the compiler to treat it as a variable of another type. This is done differently in VB .NET and C#. VB .NET uses the CType() built-in function. C# has you prefix the variable with the data type to convert it into.

VB .NET

Use the CType() built-in function to explicitly cast a variable. The first parameter is the variable to convert. The second parameter is the data type to convert it into.

```
varTo = CType(varFrom, datatype)
'Demonstrate converting a string to a Boolean
Dim var As Boolean
var = CType("True", Boolean)
```

C#

C# uses a syntax of prefixing the variable you want to convert with the data type to convert it into. The data type is enclosed in parentheses.

```
varTo = (datatype) varFrom;
//Demonstrate converting a double to an int
double myVar = 12345678;
int varTo;
varTo = (int)myVar;
```

Using the Parse() Method

Each of the base numeric data types has a `Parse()` method that converts a string into the base type. Pass the `Parse()` method a string, and it returns the numeric equivalent in the data type specified by the class name used.

```
var = int.Parse("23");
```

If the string contains non-numeric characters, such as a comma or parentheses, you need to pass the `Parse()` method an enumerator telling it what characters are in the string. If you don't do this, it will fail. This enumerator is part of the `Globalization.NumberStyles` class, and it is passed as the second parameter. Table 3-6 lists the enumerators of the `Globalization.NumberStyles` class.

For example, if you have a string that uses commas to designate the thousands position, you need to use the enumerator `AllowThousands`. If you have a string that uses a decimal, you need to use the enumerator `AllowDecimal`. If you have more than one type of character to allow for, add the enumerators together.

VB .NET

Use the `Parse()` method of the data type class to convert a string to the data type. Pass the string as the first parameter. If the string has non-numeric characters, tell the `Parse()` method to allow them by passing a `NumberStyles` enumerator as the second parameter.

```
datatype.Parse(myString, Globalization.NumberStyles.enumerator)

Imports Globalization
...
'Demonstrate converting strings
var = Integer.Parse("1234")
var = Integer.Parse("1,234", NumberStyles.AllowThousands)
```

C#

Use the `Parse()` method of the data type class to convert a string to the data type. Pass the string as the first parameter. If the string has non-numeric characters, tell the `Parse()` method to allow them by passing a `NumberStyles` enumerator as the second parameter.

```
datatype.Parse(myString, Globalization.NumberStyles.enumerator);

using Globalization;
...
//Demonstrate converting strings
var = Single.Parse("$1,234.56", NumberStyles.AllowCurrencySymbol +
        NumberStyles.AllowThousands + NumberStyles.AllowDecimal);
var = Integer.Parse("3e2", NumberStyles.AllowExponent);
```

Table 3-6. The Enumerators of the NumberStyles Class

NUMBERSTYLES ENUMERATOR	DESCRIPTION
AllowCurrencySymbol	The string has the currency symbol.
AllowDecimalPoint	The string has the decimal symbol.
AllowExponent	The string is an exponential number.
AllowHexSpecifier	The string is a hexadecimal number.
AllowLeadingSign	The string has a positive or negative sign before the number.
AllowLeadingWhite	The string has white spaces in front of it.
AllowParentheses	There are parentheses around the number.
AllowThousands	The string has the thousands symbol.
AllowTrailingSign	The string has a positive or negative sign following the number.
AllowTrailingWhite	The string has white spaces following it.

Using Arithmetic Operators

Arithmetic operators enable you to perform a variety of calculations. With the exception of concatenation operators, arithmetic operators are pretty much the same in .NET as they are in VB 6.0.

In VB 6.0, performing calculations is done by putting a variable on the left side of the equal statement and also putting it on the right side of the equal statement, along with the calculation to perform.

```
Price = Price + SalesTax
```

Repeating the variable twice is eliminated when using concatenation operators. These operators let you perform an operation on a variable and assign the result back to the variable. This is done by putting the variable on the left side of the concatenation operator and putting the numeric modifier on the right side. The syntax of a concatenation operator is the standard arithmetic operator followed the equal sign.

```
Price += SalesTax
```

As you can see from the previous example, this is a quick and concise way of performing calculations. C# also has concatenation operators.

C# has a cool set of operators to quickly add or subtract 1 from a variable. It uses ++ to add 1 to a variable and -- to subtract 1 from a variable.

VB 6.0
Standard arithmetic operators are surrounded by a single operand. The result is usually assigned to a variable. Concatenation operators are not available in VB 6.0.

```
var1 = var2 / 2
var3 = var3 + var4
```

VB .NET
Standard arithmetic operators are surrounded by a single operand. The result is usually assigned to a variable.

```
var1 = var2 + 2
var3 = var3 + var4
```

Concatenation operators are used with a variable on the left side and an operand on the right side.

```
var5 += 10
var6 -= 27
```

C#
Standard arithmetic operators are surrounded by a single operand. The result is usually assigned to a variable.

```
var1 = var2 * 3;
var3 = var3 / var4;
```

Concatenation operators are used with a variable on the left side and an operand on the right side.

```
var5 *= 10;
var6 += 27;
```

Add or subtract 1 from a variable using ++ or --.

```
var++;    //Equivalent to var = var + 1
var--;    //Equivalent to var = var - 1
```

Using Relational Operators

Relational operators are very similar between VB and C#. VB 6.0 and VB .NET share the same operators and they basically consist of less-than, less-than or equal to, greater-than, and so on. With one exception, C# is the same. C# has a different operator to represent equal and not equal. Equal is represented in VB with = and in C# with ==. Not equal is represented in VB with <> and in C# with !=.

To get the opposite of a Boolean variable, use logical negation. In VB this is Not and in C# this is !.

Using Logical Operators

Logical operators are used to join multiple conditions together to determine a single Boolean result. VB .NET has made an improvement over VB 6.0 in that there are now two keywords that are short-circuiting logical operators. This means that once the final Boolean result has been determined, no more testing is done. If the result can be determined after doing only one test, that is enough. The VB .NET short-circuited operators are AndAlso and OrElse. For example, in VB .NET the AndAlso operator does not evaluate the second expression if the first expression is False. The OrElse operator does not evaluate the second expression if the first expression is True. Hence, the statement has been short-circuited because in some circumstances not all the tests are done. In C#, the AndAlso and OrElse equivalent operators are both short-circuited and they are represented by && and ||, respectively.

In both VB 6.0 and VB .NET, the And and Or operators always evaluate both expressions regardless of the value of the first expression. In C#, the equivalent operators are & and | respectively.

You can use short-circuiting logic to improve the performance of your application. When you call multiple expressions that are separated by short-circuited logical operators, put the one that runs fastest first. If it results in not needing to call the second expression, which takes longer, your application will increase in performance.

VB 6.0

The format for using a logical operator is as follows: Condition1 operator Condition2.

```
'Use the If statement to demonstrate logical operators
If Condition1 And Condition2 Then ...
If Condition1 Or Condition2 Then ...
```

VB .NET

The format for using a logical operator is as follows: Condition1 operator Condition2.

```
'Use the If statement to demonstrate logical operators
If Condition1 And Condition2 Then ...
If Condition1 AndAlso Condition2 Then ...
If Condition1 Or Condition2 Then ...
If Condition1 OrElse Condition2 Then ...
```

C#

The format for using a logical operator is as follows: Condition1 operator Condition2.

```
'Use the if statement to demonstrate logical operators
if (condition1 & condition2) then{...}
if (condition1 && condition2) then{...}
if (condition1 | condition2) then{...}
if (condition1 || condition2) then{...}
```

Turning Option Strict On

The Option Strict option in VB .NET allows you to decide whether the compiler should do implicit data type conversions in your program. This means you can assign a variable of one type to a variable of a different type, and the compiler will attempt to convert it for you.

On the surface, this probably seems like a good idea because you don't have to write as much code. Unfortunately, what can seem like a blessing can actually be a curse. When the compiler does an implicit conversion, it tries to figure out what you are attempting to do. Sometimes it will get it right, but sometimes it won't. If it does get it wrong, you will have a bug that's very difficult to track down and can waste a lot of your time. I recommend that you always turn Option Strict on right when you open a new project. To turn Option Strict on, right click on the project name in the Solution Explorer and select the Build tab. It is the second dropdown box.

Although turning Option Strict on is optional, I personally don't want the reliabilty of my code dependent upon the compiler guessing correctly. All the code samples in this book have Option Strict turned on.

C# enforces Option Strict to be turned on as part of the language. It is not an option you can set.

Example 3-1. Declaring and Using Variables

This example shows how to declare and use variables by taking a script and processing commands from it. The script consists of multiple commands separated by commas. The first letter of the command is a code and the rest of the string is raw text. The code tells the computer how to process the text. The codes are as follows:

- B: Convert the text to Boolean and print it.

- D: Convert the text to a month and print the first and last day of the month.

- I: Convert the text to Integer and print it.

This example shows variables declared as Integer, Boolean, DateTime, String, and Char. Initializing an array is demonstrated by creating an integer array of the days of the month. Notice how characters are handled differently among the languages.

VB 6.0

```
'Declaring and Using Variables in VB6.0
'Copyright (c)2001 by Bischof Systems, Inc.

Public Sub Main()
    ProcessScript ("D1,Btrue,bfalse,I4453")
End Sub
```

```
Private Sub ProcessScript(ByVal Script As String)
    'Declare an array and automatically populate its values
    Dim DaysOfMonth(11) As Integer
    'Both date variables are declared as a Date
    Dim FirstDate As Date, LastDate As Date
    Dim IntegerData As Integer, StringData As String, BooleanData As Boolean
    Dim Command As String * 1
    Dim Scripts() As String
    Dim ScriptCount As Integer
    'Initialize the DaysOfMonth array
    DaysOfMonth(0) = 31: DaysOfMonth(1) = 28: DaysOfMonth(2) = 31
    DaysOfMonth(3) = 30: DaysOfMonth(4) = 31: DaysOfMonth(5) = 30
    DaysOfMonth(6) = 31: DaysOfMonth(7) = 31: DaysOfMonth(8) = 30
    DaysOfMonth(9) = 31: DaysOfMonth(10) = 30: DaysOfMonth(11) = 31
    If Not Script = "" Then
        Debug.Print "The script is: " & Script
        Debug.Print
        'Split the string into a string array based upon the comma seperator
        Scripts = Split(Script, ",")
        For ScriptCount = 0 To UBound(Scripts)
            Command = UCase(Left(Scripts(ScriptCount), 1))
            StringData = Mid(Scripts(ScriptCount), 2)
            Select Case Command
                Case "B"        'Boolean
                    If UCase(StringData) = "TRUE" Then
                        BooleanData = True
                    Else
                        BooleanData = False
                    End If
                    Debug.Print BooleanData
                Case "D"        'Date
                    FirstDate = CDate(StringData & "/1/" & Year(Now))
                    LastDate = CDate(StringData & "/" & _
                        DaysOfMonth(CInt(StringData) - 1) & "/" & Year(Now))
                    Debug.Print ("Beginning of Month: " & _
                        Format(FirstDate, "Short Date"))
                    Debug.Print ("End of Month: " & Format(LastDate, _
                        "Short Date"))
                Case "I"          'Integer
                    IntegerData = CInt(StringData)
                    Debug.Print IntegerData
            End Select
        Next
    End If
End Sub
```

VB .NET

```vbnet
'Declaring and Using Variables in VB .NET
'Copyright (c)2001 by Bischof Systems, Inc.

Module Module1
    Sub Main()
        ProcessScript("D1,Btrue,bfalse,I4453")
        Console.ReadLine()
    End Sub

    Private Sub ProcessScript(ByVal Script As String)
        'Declare an array and automatically populate its values
        Dim DaysOfMonth() As Integer = New Integer() {31, 28, 31, 30, 31, _
            30, 31, 31, 30, 31, 30, 31}
        'Both date variables are declared as a Date
        Dim FirstDate, LastDate As Date
        Dim IntegerData As Integer, StringData As String, BooleanData As _
            Boolean
        Dim Command As Char
        Dim Scripts() As String
        Dim ScriptCount As Integer
        If Not Script = "" Then
            Console.WriteLine("The script is: {0}", Script)
            'Split the string into a string array using a comma seperator
            Scripts = Script.Split(","c)
            For ScriptCount = 0 To UBound(Scripts)
                Command = Scripts(ScriptCount).ToUpper.Chars(0)
                StringData = Scripts(ScriptCount).Substring(1)
                Select Case Command
                    Case "B"c           'Boolean
                        If StringData.ToUpper = "TRUE" Then
                            BooleanData = True
                        Else
                            BooleanData = False
                        End If
                        Console.WriteLine(BooleanData.ToString)
                    Case "D"c           'Date
                        FirstDate = CDate(StringData & "/1/" & Today.Year())
                        LastDate = CDate(StringData & "/" & DaysOfMonth( _
                            CInt(StringData) - 1) & "/" & Today.Year())
                        Console.WriteLine("Beginning of Month: {0}", _
                            FirstDate.ToShortDateString)
                        Console.WriteLine("End of Month: {0}", _
                            LastDate.ToShortDateString)
```

```
                    Case "I"c        'Integer
                        IntegerData = CInt(StringData)
                        Console.WriteLine(IntegerData)
                End Select
            Next
        End If
    End Sub
End Module
```

C#

```
//Declaring and Using Variables in C#
//Copyright (c)2001 by Bischof Systems, Inc.

using System;

namespace C_DataTypes_Variables
{
    class Class1
    {
        [STAThread]
        static void Main(string[] args)
        {
            ProcessScript("D1,Btrue,bfalse,I4453");
            Console.ReadLine();
        }

        private static void ProcessScript(string Script)
        {
            //Declare an array and automatically populate its values
            int[] daysOfMonth = new int[] {31, 28, 31, 30, 31, 30, 31, 31, 30,
                                    31, 30, 31};
            //Both date variables are declared as a DateTime
            DateTime firstDate, lastDate;
            int integerData;
            string stringData;
            bool booleanData;
            char command;
            string[] scripts;
            int scriptCount;
```

```
                    if (Script != "")
                    {
                        Console.WriteLine("The script is: {0}", Script);
                        //Split the string into a string array based upon the comma
                        //seperator
                        scripts = Script.Split(',');
                        for (scriptCount = 0; scriptCount < scripts.Length;
                            scriptCount++)
                        {
                            command = char.Parse(scripts[scriptCount].Substring(0,1).
                                ToUpper());
                            stringData = scripts[scriptCount].Substring(1);
                            switch(command){
                                case 'B':        //Boolean
                                    if (stringData.ToUpper() == "TRUE")
                                    {
                                        booleanData = true;
                                    }
                                    else
                                    {
                                        booleanData = false;
                                    }
                                    Console.WriteLine("{0}",booleanData.ToString());
                                    break;
                                case 'D':        //Date
                                    firstDate = DateTime.Parse(stringData + "/1/" +
                                        DateTime.Today.Year);
                                    lastDate = DateTime.Parse(stringData + "/"
                                        + daysOfMonth[int.Parse(stringData) - 1]
                                        + "/" + DateTime.Today.Year);
                                    Console.WriteLine("Beginning of Month: {0}",
                                        firstDate.ToShortDateString());
                                    Console.WriteLine("End of Month: {0}",
                                        lastDate.ToShortDateString());
                                    break;
                                case 'I':        //Integer
                                    integerData = int.Parse(stringData);
                                    Console.WriteLine(integerData);
                                    break;
                            } //switch
                        } //for
                    } //if
                } //ProcessScript
            } //class
        }
```

Example 3-1 Output

```
The script is: D1,Btrue,bfalse,I4453
Beginning of Month: 1/1/2001
End of Month: 1/31/2001
True
False
4453
```

Example 3-2. Using Enumerators to Print Employee Information

This example prints the position and department of an employee at a company. It uses the Flags attribute of the enumerated class so that this information can be stored as bit values. The first two bits store the user's position and the next two bits store the users department. Bit manipulation is used to determine the employee's position or department by doing an AND with the two bits that apply to each. Printing the string equivalent of an enumerated entry is demonstrated using the Console.WriteLine() method.

VB .NET

```
'Using Enumerators to Print Employee Info in VB .NET
'Copyright (c)2001 by Bischof Systems, Inc.

Module Module1
    <Flags()> Enum EmpRecord
        'The "&H" prefix specifies a hexidecimal constant
        Staff = &H1
        Manager = &H2
        Accounting = &H4
        Advertising = &H8
    End Enum

    Sub Main()
        Dim employee As EmpRecord
        'Create a variable representing a manager in the accounting dept.
        'Use a binary OR to add them together
        employee = EmpRecord.Manager Or EmpRecord.Accounting
        'Display that person's information
        ShowInfo("Joe Jones", employee)
        'Create a variable representing a manager in the accounting dept.
        'Use a binary OR to add them together
        employee = EmpRecord.Staff Or EmpRecord.Advertising
```

```
            'Display that person's information
            ShowInfo("Mary Jane", employee)
            Console.ReadLine()
        End Sub


    Sub ShowInfo(ByVal Name As String, ByVal Employee As EmpRecord)
        Dim position, department As EmpRecord
        Dim allPositions, allDepartments As EmpRecord
        'Use a binary OR to get the bits that represent a
        'Position or Department
        allPositions = EmpRecord.Staff Or EmpRecord.Manager
        allDepartments = EmpRecord.Accounting Or _
            EmpRecord.Advertising
        'Use binary AND to filter out the bits in the other area
        position = Employee And allPositions
        department = Employee And allDepartments
        'Print out the name and the employee info
        Console.WriteLine()
        Console.WriteLine("Employee: {0}", Name)
        Console.Write("Position: ")
        Console.WriteLine(position.ToString());
        Console.Write("Department: ")
        Console.WriteLine(department.ToString());
    End Sub
End Module
```

C#

```
//Using Enumerators to Print Employee Info in C#
//Copyright (c)2001 by Bischof Systems, Inc.

using System;

namespace C_Enum
{
    class Class1
    {
        [Flags] enum EmpRecord
        {   //The "0x" prefix specifies a hexidecimal constant
            Staff = 0x01,
            Manager = 0x02,
            Accounting = 0x04,
            Advertising = 0x08
        }
```

```csharp
[STAThread]
static void Main(string[] args)
{
    EmpRecord employee;
    //Create a variable representing a manager in the accounting dept.
    //Use a binary OR to add them together
    employee= EmpRecord.Manager | EmpRecord.Accounting;
    //Display that person's information
    ShowInfo("Joe Jones", employee);
    //Create a variable representing a manager in the accounting dept.
    //Use a binary OR to add them together
    employee = EmpRecord.Staff | EmpRecord.Advertising;
    //Display that person's information
    ShowInfo("Mary Jane", employee);
    Console.ReadLine();
}

static void ShowInfo(string Name, EmpRecord Employee)
{
    int position, department;
    EmpRecord allPositions, allDepartments;
    //Use a binary OR to get the bits that represent a
    //Position or Department
    allPositions = EmpRecord.Staff | EmpRecord.Manager;
    allDepartments = EmpRecord.Accounting | EmpRecord.Advertising;
    //Use binary AND to filter out the bits in the other area
    position = Employee & allPositions;
    department = Employee & allDepartments;
    //Print out the name and the employee info
    Console.WriteLine();
    Console.WriteLine("Employee: {0}", Name);
    Console.Write("Position: ");
    Console.WriteLine(position.ToString());
    Console.Write("Department: ");
    Console.WriteLine(department.ToString());
}
}
}
```

Example 3-2 Output

```
Employee: Joe Jones
Position: Manager
Department: Accounting

Employee: Mary Jane
Position: Staff
Department: Advertising
```

Example 3-3. Comparing Boolean Operators

This example shows the differences between the Boolean operators. You pass
the procedure two Boolean constants and they are then passed to two functions.
An `If` statement calls these two functions. Each function will print whether it
returns `True` or `False`. The output of the program indicates which functions were
called by the `If` statement. Depending on the values passed to the function, the
`If` statements that use short-circuited logic will only call the first function. Thus,
there will only be one line outputted for these statements. The `If` statements that
don't use short-circuited logic always call both functions. Notice that VB 6.0 and
C# have fewer Boolean operators than VB .NET.

VB 6.0

```
'Comparing Boolean Operators in VB6
'Copyright (c)2001 by Bischof Systems, Inc.

Sub Main()
    Comparisons False, True
    Comparisons True, False
End Sub

'Show how each logical operator works on two boolean variables
Private Sub Comparisons(ByVal Condition1 As Boolean, ByVal Condition2 As
Boolean)
    Debug.Print "Conditions Tested: " & Condition1 & "," & Condition2
    'Test the And operator
    Debug.Print "Operator: And"
    If FirstComparison(Condition1) And SecondComparison(Condition2) Then
        Debug.Print "  Result: True"
    Else
        Debug.Print "  Result: False"
    End If
```

```
        'Test the Or operator
        Debug.Print " Operator: Or"
        If FirstComparison(Condition1) Or SecondComparison(Condition2) Then
            Debug.Print "  Result: True"
        Else
            Debug.Print "  Result: False"
        End If
        Debug.Print "---------------"
        Debug.Print
End Sub


'Show that the first comparison was performed
Private Function FirstComparison(ByVal Condition As Boolean) As Boolean
        Debug.Print "  First Comparison is: " & Condition
        FirstComparison = Condition
End Function


'Show that the second comparison was performed
Private Function SecondComparison(ByVal Condition As Boolean) As Boolean
        Debug.Print "  Second Comparison is: " & Condition
        SecondComparison = Condition
End Function
```

VB 6.0 Output

```
Conditions Tested: False,True
Operator: And
  First Comparison is: False
  Second Comparison is: True
  Result: False
Operator: Or
  First Comparison is: False
  Second Comparison is: True
  Result: True
---------------

Conditions Tested: True,False
Operator: And
  First Comparison is: True
  Second Comparison is: False
  Result: False
Operator: Or
  First Comparison is: True
  Second Comparison is: False
  Result: True
---------------
```

VB .NET

```
'Comparing Boolean Operators in VB .NET
'Copyright (c)2001 by Bischof Systems, Inc.

Module Module1

    Sub Main()
        Comparisons(False, True)
        Comparisons(True, False)
        Console.ReadLine()
    End Sub

    'Show how each logical operator works on two boolean variables
    Private Sub Comparisons(ByVal Condition1 As Boolean, ByVal Condition2 _
        As Boolean)
        Console.WriteLine("Conditions Tested: {0}, {1}", _
            Condition1.ToString, Condition2.ToString)
        'Test the And operator
        Console.WriteLine("Operator: And")
        If FirstComparison(Condition1) And SecondComparison(Condition2) Then
            Console.WriteLine("  Result: True")
        Else
            Console.WriteLine("  Result: False")
        End If
        'Test the AndAlso operator
        Console.WriteLine("Operator: AndAlso")
        If FirstComparison(Condition1) AndAlso _
            SecondComparison(Condition2) Then
            Console.WriteLine("  Result: True")
        Else
            Console.WriteLine("  Result: False")
        End If
        'Test the Or operator
        Console.WriteLine("Operator: Or")
        If FirstComparison(Condition1) Or SecondComparison(Condition2) Then
            Console.WriteLine("  Result: True")
        Else
            Console.WriteLine("  Result: False")
        End If
```

```
        'Test the OrAlso operator
        Console.WriteLine("Operator: OrElse")
        If FirstComparison(Condition1) OrElse _
            SecondComparison(Condition2) Then
            Console.WriteLine("  Result: True")
        Else
            Console.WriteLine("  Result: False")
        End If
        Console.WriteLine("--------------")
        Console.WriteLine()
    End Sub

    'Show that the first comparison was performed
    Private Function FirstComparison(ByVal Condition As Boolean) As Boolean
        Console.WriteLine("  First Comparison is: {0}", Condition.ToString)
        Return Condition
    End Function

    'Show that the second comparison was performed
    Private Function SecondComparison(ByVal Condition As Boolean) As Boolean
        Console.WriteLine("  Second Comparison is: {0}", Condition.ToString)
        Return Condition
    End Function
End Module
```

VB .NET Output

```
Conditions Tested: False, True
Operator: And
  First Comparison is: False
  Second Comparison is: True
  Result: False
Operator: AndAlso
  First Comparison is: False
  Result: False
Operator: Or
  First Comparison is: False
  Second Comparison is: True
  Result: True
Operator: OrElse
  First Comparison is: False
  Second Comparison is: True
  Result: True
--------------
```

```
Conditions Tested: True, False
Operator: And
  First Comparison is: True
  Second Comparison is: False
  Result: False
Operator: AndAlso
  First Comparison is: True
  Second Comparison is: False
  Result: False
Operator: Or
  First Comparison is: True
  Second Comparison is: False
  Result: True
Operator: OrElse
  First Comparison is: True
  Result: True
---------------
```

C#

```csharp
//Comparing Boolean Operators in C#
//Copyright (c)2001 by Bischof Systems, Inc.

using System;

namespace C_DataTypes_Operators
{
    class Class1
        {
        [STAThread]
        static void Main(string[] args)
        {
            Comparisons(false, true);
            Comparisons(true, false);
            Console.ReadLine();
        }
        private static void Comparisons(bool Condition1, bool Condition2)
        {
            Console.WriteLine("Conditions Tested: {0}, {1}",
                Condition1.ToString(), Condition2.ToString());
            //Test the & operator
            Console.WriteLine("Operator: &");
            if (FirstComparison(Condition1) & SecondComparison(Condition2))
            {
                Console.WriteLine("  Result: True");
            }
```

```csharp
    //Test the && operator
    Console.WriteLine("Operator: &&");
    if (FirstComparison(Condition1) && SecondComparison(Condition2))
    {
        Console.WriteLine("  Result: True");
    }
    else
    {
        Console.WriteLine("  Result: False");
    }
    //Test the | operator
    Console.WriteLine("Operator: |");
    if (FirstComparison(Condition1) | SecondComparison(Condition2))
    {
        Console.WriteLine("  Result: True");
    }
    else
    {
        Console.WriteLine("  Result: False");
    }
    //Test the || operator
    Console.WriteLine("Operator: ||");
    if (FirstComparison(Condition1) || SecondComparison(Condition2))
    {
        Console.WriteLine("  Result: True");
    }
    else
    {
        Console.WriteLine("  Result: False");
    }
    Console.WriteLine("--------------");
    Console.WriteLine();
}

//Show that the first comparison was performed
private static bool FirstComparison(bool Condition)
{
    Console.WriteLine("  First Comparison is: {0}",
        Condition.ToString());
    return Condition;
}
```

```
            //Show that the second comparison was performed
            private static bool SecondComparison(bool Condition)
            {
                Console.WriteLine("  Second Comparison is: {0}",
                    Condition.ToString());
                return Condition;
            }
        }
}
```

C# Output

```
Conditions Tested: False, True
Operator: &
  First Comparison is: False
  Second Comparison is: True
  Result: False
Operator: &&
  First Comparison is: False
  Result: False
Operator: |
  First Comparison is: False
  Second Comparison is: True
  Result: True
Operator: ||
  First Comparison is: False
  Second Comparison is: True
  Result: True
---------------

Conditions Tested: True, False
Operator: &
  First Comparison is: True
  Second Comparison is: False
  Result: False
Operator: &&
  First Comparison is: True
  Second Comparison is: False
  Result: False
Operator: |
  First Comparison is: True
  Second Comparison is: False
  Result: True
Operator: ||
  First Comparison is: True
  Result: True
```

CHAPTER 4
Program Flow

Table 4-1. Program Flow Equivalent Chart

VB 6.0	VB .NET	C#

If condition Then
…
Else
…
End If
	If condition Then
	…
	Else
	…
	End If
		if condition
		{…}
		else
		{…}

Select Case variable
Case expression1
…
Case expression2
…
Case Else
…
End Select
	Select Case variable
	Case expression1
	…
	Case expression2
	…
	Case Else
	…
	End Select
		switch (variable) {
		case expression1:
		…
		 goto case expression2;
		case expression2:
		…
		 break;
		default:
		…
		 break;
		}

For var = start To end
…
Next
	For var = start To end
	…
	Next
		for (var=start; var<end; var++){
		…
		}

For var = start To end Step value
…
Next
	For var = start To end Step value
	…
	Next
		for (var=start; var<=end;
		var+=value){
		…
		}

While condition
…
Wend
	While condition
	…
	End While
		while (condition) {
		…
		}

Do While/Until condition … Loop	Do While/Until condition … Loop	
Do … Loop While/Until condition	Do … Loop While/Until condition	do { … } while (condition);

Table 4-1. Program Flow Equivalent Chart (Continued)

VB 6.0	VB .NET	C#

For Each var In array/collection
 	
...
 	
Next
	For Each var In array/collection
	
	...
	
	Next
		foreach (type var in array/
		collection) {
		
		...
		
		}

Exit	Exit	break;
		continue;

Overview

Program flow statements are very similar in all languages. With the exception of the Select Case/switch statement, the biggest difference between VB and C# is the fact that VB uses Begin..End blocks and C# uses curly braces. The program flow statement types consist of the following: If Else, Select Case/switch, For loops, While loops, Do loops, and For Each loops.

Testing Conditions with the If Statement

The If statement tests an expression and executes certain code depending on the result of that test. If the expression returns True, it executes the If block. If the expression returns False, it executes the Else block. A major change in .NET is that it's possible that not all expressions in the If statement will be tested. An expression can be rendered unnecessary by previously tested conditions. This is called *short-circuited logic*. For example, in VB 6.0 if a condition includes two expressions separated by the And keyword, both expressions are always executed. If the first expression is false, obviously the entire statement will be false, but VB 6.0 will still process the second expression anyway. VB .NET does away with this problem by adding the operators AndAlso and OrElse. These operators only evaluate as many tests as necessary until the condition is determined to be true or false. Depending on the expression called, this can affect performance if it is a time-intensive procedure. In C#, the && and || use short-circuited logic. See the "Using Logical Operators" section in Chapter 3 for a thorough discussion.

VB 6.0/VB .NET
The If keyword is followed by a condition. If the condition is true, the If code block is executed. If it is false, the Else code block is executed.

```
'Do a single test
If a>b Then
    ...
Else
    ...
EndIf
'Do a nested test
If a>b Then
    ...
ElseIf a>c Then
    ...
EndIf
```

C#

The if keyword is followed by a condition. If the condition is true, the If code block is executed. If it is false, the else code block is executed.

```
//Do a single test
if (a>b)
{
    ...
}
else
{
    ...
}
//Do a nested test
if (a>b)
{
    ...
}
else if (a>c)
{
    ...
}
```

Select Case/switch

The Select Case/switch statement is an alternative for the If statement because it provides a clearer format for testing a variable for multiple expressions. The same functionality can be implemented using a large tree of nested If statements, but the readability isn't nearly as clear. There are two major differences between VB and C#: the statement syntax, and how the compiler chooses which code to execute.

Both VB 6.0 and VB .NET use the `Select Case` statement to define which variable to test. The `Case` statement matches the proper expression. C# uses the `switch` statement to define which variable to test and the `case` statement to match the proper expression.

VB 6.0 and VB .NET differ from C# on how to use the `Case` statement for determining which code block to execute. VB allows multiple expressions with one `Case` statement to be evaluated. If any of the expressions match, the code block following that `Case` statement is executed. C# only allows one constant-expression per `case` statement, but it allows a single code block to be executed by multiple `case` statements. In other words, both languages allow you to test multiple conditions and then execute a certain code block. VB allows all the tests to be with one `Case` statement and C# requires that each test be with a separate `case` statement.

A major difference between VB and C# is that VB has a variety of ways to test the variable against an expression and C# can only test the variable against a single constant-expression. For example, in VB you can test the variable using a single constant-expression such as "3"; you can use an expression range such as "1 to 5"; you can use a relational expression such as "Is > 5"; or you can use any combination of these by separating them with a comma. VB 6.0 and VB .NET also enable you to use variables as well as constants. C# only allows you to use a single constant-expression such as "3." This really hinders the `switch` statement's practicality in C#. Many times you are better off using a nested `if` statement.

Let's look at how this can impact a C# program by writing a code snippet that takes an integer between 1 and 6 and prints whether the number is less than four or greater than three.

```
switch (value){
    case 1:
    case 2:
    case 3:
        Console.WriteLine("Less than four");
        break;
    case 4:
    case 5:
    case 6:
        Console.WriteLine("Greater than three");
        break;
}
```

The Select Case statement in VB is much more concise.

```
Select Case Value
    Case Is < 4
        Console.WriteLine("Less than four")
    Case Is > 3
        Console.WriteLine("Greater than three")
End Select
```

As you can see from this simple example, switch statements using constant-expressions that span a large range of numbers are not practical. If statements are a better choice.

In VB, you can exit the Select Case block using the Exit Select statement. In C#, you must exit the switch block using the break statement. This is required for case statements that have code in them. If you want a case statement to drop into the following case statement, do not include any code for it and don't use the break statement.

VB 6.0/VB .NET

The Select Case statement uses Case statements to compare expressions against a single variable. A Case statement can use multiple constant-expressions so that one code block can be executed for many expressions. If a variable doesn't match any constant-expressions, the code block in the Case Else statement will be executed. If no Case Else statement is provided, the program will drop out of the Select Case block without executing any code.

```
Select Case variable
    Case expression1, expression2
        ...
    Case expression3
        ...
        Exit Select
    Case Else
        ...
End Select
```

C#

The switch statement uses a maximum of one constant-expression per case statement. You can have multiple case statements execute the same code block by using the goto statement. We all know the goto statement is a very bad thing. But in this situation, Microsoft designed the switch statement with the expectation that the goto statement would be used regularly. If a case statement doesn't have any lines of code, a goto statement is not necessary because the program will automatically drop into the next `case` statement with code. If a variable doesn't match any constant-expressions, the code block for the default statement will be executed. If no `default` statement is provided, the program will drop out of the `switch` block without executing any code.

```
switch (variable) {
    case value1:
        ...
        goto case value2;
    case value2:
        ...
        break;
    default:
        ...
}
```

For Loops

The `For` loop is based on initializing a counter and looping for a set number times. The difference between VB and C# is that VB is more strict on the syntax used for this loop. It is required that an initial value and final value be specified. C# is very flexible because each part of the loop criteria is optional. C# will allow you to not specify any of the parameters of the loop and instead put all the logic within the code block. But this isn't recommended because it would be very cryptic.

In VB you can exit for a `For` loop using the `Exit For` statement. In C# you can exit the `for` loop using the `break` statement. C# also gives you the ability to skip certain lines in a `for` loop. Use the `continue` statement to skip to the end of the loop and then keep looping.

VB 6.0/VB .NET

The `For` loop is constructed by defining an initial value and a final value. An optional step value can be specified to have the loop count backward or use an increment different from the default of 1.

```
For counter = initialvalue To finalvalue Step increment
    ...
Next
'Demonstrate a standard loop
For var = 0 to 10
    ...
Next
```

```
'Demonstrate looping with even numbers
For var = 2 to 10 Step 2
    ...
Next
```

C#

The for loop is constructed by using an initializer to set the starting value of the variable, specifying a looping condition, and setting an iterator for incrementing the loop variable. Each of these can be thought of as a separate line of code that is independent of the others. Each item is optional because they can be placed outside of the for loop. For example, the initializer is optional because the variable's value could have already been set before entering the loop. The looping condition is optional because you can use a break statement within the code block to exit the loop. The iterator is optional because that line of code could be put within the loop's code block and have the same result. Even though these items are optional, you should specify each as the syntax suggests so that your code is readable and maintainable.

Use the continue statement to skip to the end of the loop and continue processing the loop. Use the break statement to exit the loop.

It is common practice to declare and initialize the iterator within the for statement. Once the for statement completes, the iterator will go out of scope. This prevents it from being misused outside of the loop. You can also declare, initialize, and iterate multiple variables.

```
for (initializer; looping condition; iterator)
{
    ...
    break;    //exit the loop
    ...
    continue;  //skip to the end of the loop
    ...
}
//Demonstrate a standard loop
for (int var=0; var<=10; var++)
{
    ...
}
//Demonstrate looping with even numbers
for (int var=2, string myString="default"; var<=10; var+=2)
{
    ...
}
```

```
//Demonstrate using two variables in a for loop
for (int a=0, b=0; a<=10 & b<=10; a++, b++)
{
    ...
}
```

While Loops

The While loop is based on testing a condition prior to executing the code block. All three languages work the same.

In VB you exit a While block using the Exit While statement. In C# you exit the while block using the break statement.

VB 6.0

The While statement always has the condition appear before the code block. Close the block with the Wend statement.

```
While condition
    ...
Wend
```

VB .NET

The While statement always has the condition appear before the code block. Enclose the condition in a parentheses pair. Close the block with the End While statement.

```
While condition
    ...
End While
```

C#

The while statement always has the condition appear before the code block. Enclose the condition in a parentheses pair.

```
while (condition)
{
    ...
}
```

Do Loops

Do loops are very different between the VB languages and the C# language. Within VB, you have a lot of flexibility on how to organize the loop. C# is much more rigid and only has one way of working with it.

VB gives you a lot more flexibility with the Do loop for two reasons. First, you can put the loop condition either before or after the code block. Second, the loop condition can be specified by using either the While keyword or the Until keyword. C# requires that the loop condition always be placed after the closing bracket and it must use the while keyword.

Where you put the loop condition determines if the code block is executed or not. If the loop condition is before the code block, the condition must succeed for the code to be executed. If it fails, the code block will be skipped and the program will continue at the first line after the code block. If the condition is after the code block, the code block will be executed before the condition is tested. Thus, the code block will always be executed at least once. In both cases, as long as the condition succeeds, the code block will continue to be executed repeatedly.

The While statement and the Until statement are exact opposites. The While statement succeeds and executes the code block when the condition is True. The Until statement succeeds and executes the code block when the condition is False.

In VB, the Do While loop is equivalent to the While…End While loop.

In C#, a do loop requires the condition to be after the code block. If you want to put the condition before the code block, use a while loop. The Until keyword is not part of the C# language. The equivalent is to negate the condition.

In VB you exit a Do loop using the Exit Do statement. In C# you exit the do loop using the break statement.

VB 6.0/VB .NET

The Do statement can use the While keyword or the Until keyword. Both keywords can appear either before the code block or after it.

```
Do While/Until condition
    ...
Loop

Do
    ...
Loop While/Until condition
```

C#

The do statement pairs the test condition with a while statement. The while statement is after the code block. Enclose the condition in a parentheses pair.

```
do
{
    ...
} while (condition);
```

For Each Loops

A For Each loop lets you loop through an array or collection object and work with each item. The benefit of this looping construct is that programmers don't have to know the bounds of the array or collection. Nor do they have to worry about tracking the index. In VB 6.0, the For Each statement works with arrays and collections. In .NET it works with arrays, collections, and any object that implements the IEnumerable interface. The details of implementing the IEnumerable interface are not within the scope of this book.

If you look over all the changes between VB 6.0 and VB .NET, it appears that a lot of the new improvements to the VB language are coding changes that already existed in C++. Hence, C++ programmers may be reading this book and thinking that they've "been there, done that." This time, however, VB beat them to the punch. For Each loops were first implemented in VB 4.0 when Microsoft added the collection class to the language. For Each loops have been used extensively by VB programmers since then. Now that Microsoft has created C#, For Each loops are available to both languages.

C# uses a single keyword because it doesn't have a space between the for and each. This keyword is called foreach.

In VB you can exit for a For Each loop using the Exit For statement. In C# you can exit the foreach loop using the break statement.

VB 6.0/VB .NET

The For Each statement can only be used with collections and arrays. VB .NET can use any object that implements the IEnumerable interface. The code block is closed using the Next statement.

```
For Each variable In array/collection
    ...
Next
```

C#

The foreach statement can be used with arrays, collections, or any object that implements the IEnumberable interface. Notice it is required that you state the data type in front of the variable. Thus, you can't define this variable outside of the foreach loop.

```
foreach (type variable in array/collection)
{
    ...
}
```

Example 4-1. Logging In a User and Looping Through a Collection

This example demonstrates having a user log in with their ID and password. The ID is required to have a length of more than three characters. After a valid ID has been entered, a password is asked for (use "Delphi"). The While/Until loops are used to do this. An If statement tests the user ID length and displays an error message if necessary. A user's ID determines his or her employee category. A Select Case/switch statement determines the category and displays it. Lastly, the user's ID is broken down by each digit and the text equivalent of each number is displayed. A For loop is used to process each digit in the ID. A For Each loop is used to determine the text equivalent of each digit.

VB 6.0

```
'Logging in a user in VB 6.0
'Copyright (c)2001 by Bischof Systems, Inc.

'Add a reference to the Microsoft Scripting Library to use the
'Dictionary object

Sub Main()
    Dim UserId As String, Password As String
    Dim UserIdIndex As Integer, CurrentNumber As String * 1
    Dim FirstDigit As Integer
    Dim NumberElement
    Dim Numbers As New Dictionary
    'Initialize the numbers collection
    Numbers.Add "0", "Zero": Numbers.Add "1", "One"
    Numbers.Add "2", "Two": Numbers.Add "3", "Three"
    Numbers.Add "4", "Four": Numbers.Add "5", "Five"
```

```
                Numbers.Add "6", "Six": Numbers.Add "7", "Seven"
                Numbers.Add "8", "Eight": Numbers.Add "9", "Nine"
                'Get the user id using the While...End While loop
                While Len(UserId) <= 3
                    UserId = InputBox("Please enter user id that is more than 3 digits")
                    'Test the user id length using an If Then statement
                    If Len(UserId) = 0 Then
                        MsgBox "You didn't enter a user id"
                    ElseIf Len(UserId) <= 3 Then
                        MsgBox "You didn't enter more than 3 digits"
                    Else
                        MsgBox "User id was entered successfully"
                    End If
                Wend

                'Get the password using Do...Loop Until
                Do
                    Password = InputBox("Please enter a password (Hint: it's Delphi)")
                Loop Until Password = "Delphi"
                'Display the user's employee level using the first number in the user id
                FirstDigit = CInt(Mid(UserId, 1, 1))
                Select Case FirstDigit
                    Case Is <= 3
                        MsgBox "You are a hard working Staff person"
                    Case 4 To 8
                        MsgBox "It's always good to have management logging in"
                    Case 9
                        MsgBox "Hey, it's the big shot"
                    Case Else
                        MsgBox "Invalid user id."
                End Select
                'Loop through the user id and display the text equivalants of the number
                MsgBox "Your user id numbers are:"
                For UserIdIndex = 1 To Len(UserId)
                    'Get the first digit of the user id
                    CurrentNumber = Mid(UserId, UserIdIndex, 1)
                    'Use a For Each loop to find the number that matches
                    For Each NumberElement In Numbers.Keys
                        If CurrentNumber = NumberElement Then
                            MsgBox Numbers(NumberElement)
                        End If
                    Next
                Next
            End Sub
```

VB .NET

```
'Logging in a user in VB .NET
'Copyright (c)2001 by Bischof Systems, Inc.

Module Module1

    Sub Main()
        Dim userId As String = "", password As String
        Dim userIdIndex As Integer, currentNumber As Integer
        Dim firstDigit As Integer
        Dim numbers As New Collections.Hashtable()
        Dim numberElement As DictionaryEntry
        'Initialize the numbers collection
        numbers.Add(0, "Zero") : numbers.Add(1, "One")
        numbers.Add(2, "Two") : numbers.Add(3, "Three")
        numbers.Add(4, "Four") : numbers.Add(5, "Five")
        numbers.Add(6, "Six") : numbers.Add(7, "Seven")
        numbers.Add(8, "Eight") : numbers.Add(9, "Nine")
        'Get the user id using the While...End While loop
        While (userId.Length <= 3)
            Console.WriteLine("Please enter user id that is more than 3 digits")
            userId = Console.ReadLine()
            'Test the user id length using an If Then statement
            If userId.Length = 0 Then
                Console.WriteLine("You didn't enter a user id")
            ElseIf userId.Length <= 3 Then
                Console.WriteLine("You didn't enter more than 3 digits")
            Else
                Console.WriteLine("User id was entered successfully")
            End If
        End While
        'Get the password using the Do...Loop Until
        Do
            Console.WriteLine("Please enter a password (Hint: it's Delphi)")
            password = Console.ReadLine()
        Loop Until password = "Delphi"
        'Display the user's employee level using the first number in the user id
        firstDigit = Integer.Parse(userId.Chars(0))
```

```vbnet
        Select Case firstDigit
            Case Is <= 3
                Console.WriteLine("You are a hard working Staff person")
            Case 4 To 8
                Console.WriteLine("It's always good to have management " & _
                    "logging in")
            Case 9
                Console.WriteLine("Hey, it's the big shot")
            Case Else
                Console.WriteLine("Invalid user id.")
        End Select
        'Loop through the user id and display the text equivalants of the number
        Console.WriteLine("Your user id numbers are:")
        For userIdIndex = 0 To userId.Length - 1
            'Get the first digit of the user id
            currentNumber = Integer.Parse(userId.Chars(userIdIndex))
            'Use a For Each loop to find the number that matches
            For Each numberElement In numbers
                If currentNumber.Equals(numberElement.Key) Then
                    Console.WriteLine(numberElement.Value)
                End If
            Next
        Next
        Console.ReadLine()
    End Sub
End Module
```

C#

```csharp
//Logging in a user in C#
//Copyright (c)2001 by Bischof Systems, Inc.

using System;

namespace C_ProgramFlow
{
    class Class1
    {
        [STAThread]
        static void Main(string[] args)
        {
            string userId = "", password;
            int userIdIndex, currentNumber;
            int firstDigit;
            System.Collections.Hashtable numbers = new
                System.Collections.Hashtable();
```

```
//Initialize the numbers collection
numbers.Add(0, "Zero"); numbers.Add(1, "One");
numbers.Add(2, "Two"); numbers.Add(3, "Three");
numbers.Add(4, "Four"); numbers.Add(5, "Five");
numbers.Add(6, "Six"); numbers.Add(7, "Seven");
numbers.Add(8, "Eight"); numbers.Add(9, "Nine");
//Get the user id using the While...End While loop
while (userId.Length <= 3)
{
    Console.WriteLine("Please enter user id that is more " +
        "than 3 digits");
    userId = Console.ReadLine();
    //Test the user id length using an If Then statement
    if (userId.Length == 0)
        Console.WriteLine("You didn't enter a user id");
    else if (userId.Length <= 3)
        Console.WriteLine("You didn't enter more than 3 digits");
    else
        Console.WriteLine("User id was entered successfully");
}
//Get the password using the Do...While loop
do
{
    Console.WriteLine("Please enter a password " +
        "(Hint: it's Delphi)");
    password = Console.ReadLine();
} while (password != "Delphi");
//Display the user's employee level using the first number
//in the user id
firstDigit = int.Parse(userId.Substring(0,1));
switch (firstDigit)
{
    case 1:
    case 2:
    case 3:
        Console.WriteLine("You are a hard working Staff person");
        break;
    case 4:
    case 5:
    case 6:
    case 7:
```

```
                    case 8:
                        Console.WriteLine("It's always good to have " +
                            "management logging in");
                        break;
                    case 9:
                        Console.WriteLine("Hey, it's the big shot");
                        break;
                    default:
                        Console.WriteLine("Invalid user id.");
                        break;
                }
                //Loop through the user id and display the text equivalants
                //of the number
                Console.WriteLine("Your user id numbers are:");
                for (userIdIndex = 0; userIdIndex < userId.Length; userIdIndex++)
                {
                    //Get the first digit of the user id
                    currentNumber = int.Parse(userId.Substring(userIdIndex,1));
                    //Use a For Each loop to find the number that matches
                    foreach (System.Collections.DictionaryEntry numberElement
                                in numbers)
                    {
                        if (currentNumber.Equals(numberElement.Key))
                        {
                            Console.WriteLine(numberElement.Value);
                        }
                    }
                }
                Console.ReadLine();
            }
        }
}
```

Example 4-1 Output

This is the output for each language. One thing to note is that because VB 6.0 doesn't have a console window, the InputBox() and MsgBox() statements are used to get and send data to the user.

```
Please enter a user id that is more than 3 digits
5139
User id was entered successfully
Please enter a password (Hint: it's Delphi)
delphi
```

Please enter a password (Hint: it's Delphi)
Delphi
It's always good to have management logging in
Your user id numbers are:
Five
One
Three
Nine

CHAPTER 5

Exception Handling

Table 5-1. Exception Class Syntax Conversion Chart

VB 6.0	.NET	DESCRIPTION
Err.Number		The error number.
Err.Description	E.Message	A description of the error.
Err.Source	E.TargetSite	The method declaration that triggered the exception.
	E.StackTrace	A trace of the calls made prior to the exception.
	E.ToString()	A full description of the error.
	E.Source	The application name where the exception occurred.
	E.InnerException	When you throw a new exception in response to another exception, this lets you save the original exception information.
Err.HelpFile	E.HelpLink	The filename/URL that has Help information.
Err.HelpContext		The context number of the Help file.

Overview

Thorough exception handling is an essential part of every robust program. Every programming language has some form of error handling, and some are better than others. Visual Basic has always used the On Error Goto structure of error handling. Although this is acceptable to most programmers, it certainly isn't ideal. Exception handling is vastly improved in .NET.

There are four aspects of exception handling: using the exception class, Structured Exception Handling, throwing exceptions, and creating custom exception objects.

Using the Exception Class

When an exception is thrown, VB 6.0 uses the `Err` object to let the programmer determine the current error number, description, and other miscellaneous information. .NET uses the `Exception` class to define the methods and properties of the current exception. The `Exception` class is part of the .NET Framework and is accessible by VB .NET and C#.

Table 5-1 compares the properties of the VB 6.0 `Err` object with the .NET `Exception` class. It's interesting to note that VB 6.0 uses the `Err.Number` property to identify an error, but .NET doesn't have an equivalent property. This is because the .NET Framework uses a class hierarchy to identify errors. This is much more useful because it lets programmers categorize errors by relevance. For example, there is now a general `IOException` class to catch file I/O errors. There are also classes that are derived from the `IOException` class that can trap specific file I/O errors. A couple of these are the `FileNotFoundException` class and the `FileLoadException` class. If you are trying to open a file and you are getting an error, you have the option of trapping for all file errors with the `IOException` class or you could have a specific catch for the `FileNotFoundException` class. This isn't possible with VB 6.0 because all you can do is trap for different error numbers. A simple number scheme such as this doesn't have the capability to manage the complex exception hierarchy found in .NET.

As you can see from Table 5-1, the `Exception` class in .NET provides a lot more information about the current error. This lets you write more robust and informative error-handling code.

Handling Errors

.NET implements Structured Exception Handling in both VB .NET and C# using the `Try...Catch...Finally` keywords. This is similar to the error handling in C++.

A major problem with the `On Error Goto` method of error handling found in VB 6.0 is that within a single procedure, there can only be one type of error handling turned on at any given time. For example, it is common to have an `On Error Goto ErrHandler` statement at the beginning of a procedure. Any errors that occur during execution will all be forced to the `ErrHandler` block. Within the `ErrHandler` block you would write a myriad of tests to see which error occurred and how to handle it. After handling the error you would call a `Goto` statement to perform cleanup code. This error-handling mechanism is a very generic method that results in code that jumps around a lot.

Structured Exception Handling makes it easy to have multiple error handlers inside the same procedure. In fact, error handling can be nested within error handling. This makes it possible to have a general error handler for the entire procedure and, where needed, add different error handling for certain sections of code within that procedure.

Structured Exception Handling consists of three code blocks: the Try block, the Catch block, and the Finally block.

The Try block is where you put the main implementation code. This is the code that may or may not have errors.

The Catch block is where you put the code to trap any errors and handle them. If no errors occur within the Try block, this block is skipped. There can be multiple Catch statements after a Try statement. Each Catch statement can be specific to a certain type of error or it can be very generic so that it traps many types of errors, if not all of them. Because a Catch statement can trap all types of errors, it is important to list the Catch statements starting with the most specific error first and then work down to the most generic type of error. .NET starts at the top of the Catch list and tests it to see if the current error matches it. If it doesn't, it moves down to the next error. You don't want to put the generic Catch statement first because every error will match it and the remaining Catch statements will never be tested.

If an error is triggered and there is no Catch statement within the current Try block, or if there is no Try block at all, the program goes to the calling procedure and looks for a Catch statement. The program continues to work its way up the calling chain until an appropriate Catch statement is found in the program. If there is none in your program, the system will use its internal Try-Catch statement that it wrapped around your program when it originally ran it.

The Finally block is where you put code to clean up any work done in the Try block. This code is always executed, regardless of whether or not there were any errors in the Try block. Most of the time this includes closing any open database connections or deleting any temporary files. If you don't have any cleanup code that needs to be called, the Finally block can be omitted. In VB 6.0, you often need to use a Goto statement after handling an error to make sure this cleanup work took place. The Finally block makes this task a thing of the past.

You can have a Try statement and not have a Catch statement or a Finally statement because they are optional. But you must have at least one of them because a Try statement can't be used by itself. If you have a Catch statement or a Finally statement, you must also have a Try statement. Table 5-2 shows what happens with the different variations of including or excluding each statement.

Table 5-2. Possible Try-Catch-Finally Scenarios

TRY	CATCH	FINALLY	WHAT HAPPENS WHEN AN ERROR OCCURS
No	No	No	Control is passed upward to the calling procedure to find a matching Catch statement.
Yes	No	No	This is invalid syntax and the compiler will not allow it.
Yes	Yes	No	Error is handled in the Catch block or passed upward if the error type doesn't match. No cleanup code is performed.
Yes	No	Yes	Cleanup code in the Finally block is called immediately. Control is then passed upward to find a matching Catch statement.
Yes	Yes	Yes	Error is handled in the Catch block. Cleanup code is called afterward.

It is interesting to notice in the following code samples that there is a difference between the VB .NET Try structure and the C# try structure. The VB .NET Try block encloses not only its own code, but also the Catch and Finally code blocks. C#, on the other hand, treats each code block separately. The try block is terminated before the catch block begins. The finally block is also separate from the try block. It's interesting that the Microsoft developers had the VB .NET compiler treat the Catch and Finally code blocks as being part of the Try block, but the C# compiler treats them all as separate. I think that the reason is that making it this way means that in VB .NET there isn't a need for End Catch and End Finally statements. Whatever the reason, it works for me!

VB 6.0

The error-handling code in VB 6.0 uses the On Error Goto statements. There are a variety of ways to use this structure to handle errors. However, the focus of this book is not to teach you how to use older error-handling techniques. There are examples showing this type of error handling at the end of the chapter. Note that VB .NET still allows the On Error Goto structure to be used. But as a result of the benefits of using Structured Exception Handling, it is expected that use of On Error Goto will fall out of grace.

```
Sub Procedure1()
  On Error Goto ErrHandler
  ...
  CleanUpCode:
  ...
  Exit Sub
ErrHandler:
  ...
  Goto CleanUpCode
End Sub
```

VB .NET

Handle possible errors by enclosing the code within `Try`...`End Try` statements.

The `Catch` statement has three options.

The first option is to use a `Catch` statement by itself and this will handle every error. This is a general error-trapping structure to catch all errors. This will also handle errors that are from components written with a non-CLS-compatible language.

```
Try
  ...
Catch
  ...
End Try
```

The second option is to list a variable and an exception class after the `Catch` statement. Normally, this variable is called `e`. The most specific exception class should be listed first.

```
Try
  ...
Catch e As FileNotFoundException 'a specific exception
  ...
Catch e as Exception ' a general exception
  ...
Catch      'catch non-CLS exceptions
  ...
End Try
```

The third option is to have a `When` clause after the `Catch` statement. Not only will the `Catch` statement have to be of the proper exception class, but the `When` clause must also be satisfied. If the `When` clause isn't satisfied, it goes to the next `Catch` statement.

```
Try
  ...
Catch e as Exception When Err.Number = 14
  ...
End Try
```

The `Finally` statement always comes after the last `Catch` statement, if one is used.

```
Try
  ...
Catch
  ...
Finally
  ...
End Try
```

C#

Handle possible errors within the `catch` block. It comes after the closing curly bracket of the `try` code block.

The catch comes after the `try` block and it has two options.

The first option is to use a `catch` statement by itself and this will handle every error. This is a general error-trapping structure to catch all errors. This will also handle errors that are from components written with a non-CLS-compatible language.

```
try
{
  ...
}
catch
{
  ...
}
```

The second option is to use a `catch` statement with an exception class and variable declared. Normally, this object variable is called `e`. If you don't need to reference the methods or parameters of the object variable, you can leave off the reference to the `e` variable. The most specific exception class should be listed first.

```
try
{
  ...
}
catch (FileNotFoundException e) //a specific exception
{
  ...
}
catch (Exception)// a general exception
{
  ...
}
catch // catch non-CLS exceptions
{
  ...
}
```

The `finally` statement always comes after the last `catch` block, if one is used.

```
try
{
  ...
}
catch
{
  ...
}
finally
{
  ...
}
```

Throwing Exceptions

Throwing an exception creates an exception object within a procedure and causes the program flow to jump to the currently applicable `Catch` statement for handling. You may want to throw exceptions for a few reasons.

- The user performed an action that is not allowed, but not necessarily an error. You can throw a custom exception to tell the calling procedure what the user is attempting to do.

- Your class may handle an exception and perform certain cleanup, but you still want the calling procedure to use its own error-handling mechanism.

- Your class may trap a certain type of generic error and you want to throw a custom exception that indicates to the calling procedure what specific action is being attempted.

You can throw an exception anywhere in your code, but it is normally done in two places. In the first situation in the preceding list, you throw an exception in a procedure where you detect that the user has performed an invalid action. Because this is a user error that isn't recognized by the system, you will probably throw a custom error class.

The remaining two situations in the list have an exception thrown within a Catch block because they are both done in response to an existing exception that you are currently handling. You want to throw it again (either in its original form or as a custom exception) so that the calling procedure can handle it. This is often done when writing components that are to be used by other programs. The programs that use your component normally have a predetermined method of handling and reporting exceptions, so you want to leave this responsibility to the calling program.

VB 6.0

Throwing an exception in VB 6.0 is referred to as *raising an error*. This is done using the Raise keyword. After the Raise keyword, list the parameters that you want to pass to the calling program.

```
Public Sub Proceudure1()
    On Error Goto ErrHandler

    ...
    Exit Sub
ErrHandler:
    'Cleanup code
    Raise ErrorNumber, SourceName, ErrorDescription, HelpFile, HelpContext
End Sub
```

VB .NET

Throw an exception by using the Throw keyword followed by the exception object. Because there is no reason to create an exception object anywhere else in your procedure, you should declare a new object within the Throw statement.

```
Throw New exceptionclass()
```

Every exception object can be initialized with a string message. This string message can be used by the Catch statement to retrieve, and possibly log, information specific to your program.

```
Throw New Exception("message")
```

You can omit the exception class if the Throw statement is within a Catch block. The Throw statement will rethrow the current exception that caused the program to go into the Catch block.

```
Try
   ...
Catch
   ...
   Throw
End Try
```

C#

You throw an exception by using the throw keyword followed by the exception object. Because there is no reason to create an exception object anywhere else in your procedure, you should declare a new object within the throw statement.

```
throw (new exceptionclass());
```

Every exception object can be initialized with a string message. This string message can be used by the catch statement to retrieve, and possibly log, information specific to your program.

```
throw (new Exception("generic message"));
```

You can omit the exception class if the throw statement is within a catch block. The throw statement will rethrow the current exception that caused the program to go into the catch block.

```
try
{
   ...
}
catch
{
   ...
   throw;
}
```

Creating Custom Exception Classes

Custom exception classes are useful when you want to throw an exception
that is unique to your class. This custom exception class is derived from the
ApplicationException class. In most cases it will implement the base class constructor with a string message. It is recommended that you name each custom
exception class with the word Exception appended to the end.

VB 6.0

Custom exception classes are not available in VB 6.0.

VB .NET

Create a new class that inherits the ApplicationException class.

```
Class CustomException
    Inherits ApplicationException
    Public Sub New(Message as  String)
        MyBase.New("Custom exception: " & Message)
    End Sub
End Sub
```

C#

Create a new class that inherits the ApplicationException class.

```
class CustomException: ApplicationException
{
    public CustomException(string message)
        : base("Custom exception :" + message)
        {}
}
```

Example 5-1. Copying a File

This example copies the contents of a text file to another text file.

The first Try block encloses all the logic within the Main() procedure. It
gets both filenames from the user and calls the CopyFile() procedure. The
CopyFile() procedure is where all the work is done. If there are any unhandled
exceptions thrown within the CopyFile() procedure, they will be handled by
the Catch statements in the Main() procedure.

The CopyFile() procedure first tries to open the source text file. It isn't in a
Try block because you want the Main() procedure to handle the "File Not
Found" error and ask the user to enter a new filename. After opening the

source text file there is a `Try` block. This `Try` block is used to wrap all the file access code. If any exception is thrown, you want to make sure that all open files are closed.

Within this `Try` block is another `Try` block that creates the destination file. If the file already exists, you will catch the exception and delete the file. Program execution will continue uninterrupted. Although this chapter doesn't cover file access techniques, it should be noted that it would be easier to use the `StreamWriter` class because it automatically overwrites the file if it already exists. The `FileStream` class throws an exception, which requires more work. However, I wanted to show how an `On Error Resume Next` statement in VB 6.0 would be done in .NET and I felt that the `FileStream` class was a good way of demonstrating this.

After creating the destination file, the copy process begins. The first line in the file is the header record and it tells how many lines are in the file. A `For Next` loop reads all the lines and saves them to the destination file. If a `null` is read (`Nothing` in VB .NET), that signifies that you reached the end of the file early. Hence, the header file is wrong. Because there are no exceptions in .NET to specify this, a custom exception is thrown. The `Catch` statement in the `Main()` procedure handles this.

After the copying is finished, the user is notified that everything is done.

C:\SourceFile.txt

```
3
First line of file
Second line of file
```

VB 6.0

```
'Copying a File sample application in VB 6.0
'Copyright (c)2001 by Bischof Systems, Inc.

Sub Main()
    Dim FinishedCopying As Boolean
    Dim SourceName, DestinationName As String
    FinishedCopying = True
    Do
        On Error GoTo ErrorHandler
        'Override value in case it failed last time
        FinishedCopying = True
        'Get the filenames and do the copy
        SourceName = InputBox("Enter source file: ")
        DestinationName = InputBox("Enter destination file: ")
        CopyFile SourceName, DestinationName
    Loop While (Not FinishedCopying)
```

```
Finished:
    Debug.Print "File copying is finished"
    Exit Sub
ErrorHandler:
    Select Case Err.Number
    Case 53      'File not found
        Debug.Print "The source file was not found: " + SourceName
        'Prompt the user for the filename again
        FinishedCopying = False
        Resume Next
    Case vbObjectError + 1
        Debug.Print Err.Description
    Case Else
        Debug.Print "Unexpected error: " + Err.Description
    End Select
    GoTo Finished
End Sub


'Copy from one file to another file
Private Sub CopyFile(ByVal SourceName As String, ByVal DestinationName _
    As String)
    Dim SourceFile As Integer
    Dim DestinationFile As Integer
    Dim DestinationFileReady As Boolean
    Dim LineCount As Integer
    Dim FileText As String
    Dim CurrentLine As Integer
    SourceFile = FreeFile
    Open SourceName For Input As #SourceFile
    DestinationFile = FreeFile
    Do
        On Error Resume Next
        'Open the destination file for output
        Open DestinationName For Output As #DestinationFile
        If Err = 0 Then
            'File open succeeded
            DestinationFileReady = True
        Else
            'The file already exists, so delete it
            File.Delete DestinationName
            Err.Clear
        End If
    Loop While (Not DestinationFileReady)
```

```
        'At this point anything that happens will involve open files.
        'So make sure we close files even if there is an error.
        On Error GoTo Finished
        'Both of the files are now open, so do the copy
        Input #SourceFile, LineCount
        Print #DestinationFile, LineCount
        For CurrentLine = 1 To LineCount
        Input #SourceFile, FileText
            If (FileText = "") Then
                Err.Raise vbObjectError + 1, , "Source File has an invalid header"
            End If
            Print #DestinationFile, FileText
        Next
Finished:
    'Close any open files
    Close #SourceFile
    Close #DestinationFile
    If Err <> 0 Then
        Select Case Err.Number
        Case 62
            Err.Raise vbObjectError + 1, , "Source File has an invalid header"
        Case Else
            Err.Raise Err.Number, , Err.Description
        End Select
    End If
End Sub
```

VB .NET

```
'Copying a File sample application in VB .NET
'Copyright (c)2001 by Bischof Systems, Inc.

Imports System.IO

Module Module1

    Sub Main()
        Dim finishedCopying As Boolean = True
        Dim sourceName, destinationName As String
        Do
```

```
            Try
                'Override value in case it failed last time
                finishedCopying = True
                'Get the filenames and do the copy
                Console.WriteLine("Enter source file: ")
                sourceName = Console.ReadLine()
                Console.WriteLine("Enter destination file: ")
                destinationName = Console.ReadLine()
                CopyFile(sourceName, destinationName)
            Catch e As FileNotFoundException
                Console.WriteLine("The source file was not found: " + _
                    sourceName)
                'Prompt the user for the filename again
                finishedCopying = False
            Catch e As InvalidHeaderException
                Console.WriteLine(e.Message)
            Catch e As Exception
                Console.WriteLine("Unexpected error: " + e.Message)
            End Try
        Loop While (Not finishedCopying)
        Console.WriteLine("File copying is finished")
        Console.ReadLine()
    End Sub


    'Copy from one file to another file
    Private Sub CopyFile(ByVal SourceName As String, ByVal DestinationName _
        As String)
        Dim sourceFile As StreamReader = Nothing
        Dim destinationFile As StreamWriter = Nothing
        Dim destinationFileStream As FileStream
        Dim destinationFileReady As Boolean
        Dim lineCount As Integer
        Dim fileText As String
        Dim currentLine As Integer
        'There is no error checking here because the calling procedure
        'is designed to handle the "File Not Found" error.
        'sourceName must be converted to string so that it isn't
        'misinterpreted by the compiler as a Stream
        sourceFile = New StreamReader(SourceName.ToString())
        'At this point anything that happens will involve open files.
        'Wrap everything in a try block to close the files when done
```

```
    Try
        Do
            Try
                'Open the destination file for output
                destinationFileStream = New FileStream(DestinationName, _
                    FileMode.CreateNew, FileAccess.Write)
                destinationFile = New StreamWriter(destinationFileStream)
                'File open succeeded
                destinationFileReady = True
            Catch
                'The file already exists, so delete it
                File.Delete(DestinationName)
            End Try
        Loop While (Not destinationFileReady)
        'Both of the files are now open, so do the copy
        lineCount = Integer.Parse(sourceFile.ReadLine())
        destinationFile.WriteLine(lineCount)
        For currentLine = 1 To lineCount
            fileText = sourceFile.ReadLine()
            If (fileText = Nothing) Then
                Throw New InvalidHeaderException()
            End If
            destinationFile.WriteLine(fileText)
        Next
    'There is no catch block so that all unhandled errors will
    'be passed to the calling procedure
    Finally
        'close any open files
        If (Not sourceFile Is Nothing) Then
            sourceFile.Close()
        End If
        If (Not destinationFile Is Nothing) Then
            destinationFile.Close()
        End If
    End Try
End Sub
```

```vb
        'custom exception class to handle a bad header record
    Public Class InvalidHeaderException
        Inherits ApplicationException
            Public Sub New()
                Me.New("")
            End Sub
            Public Sub New(ByVal message As String)
                MyBase.New("Source file had invalid header." + message)
            End Sub
        End Class
End Module
```

C#

```csharp
//Copying a File sample application in C#
//Copyright (c)2001 by Bischof Systems, Inc.

using System;
using System.IO;

namespace C_ExceptionHandling
{
    class Class1
    {
        [STAThread]
        static void Main(string[] args)
        {
            bool finishedCopying = true;
            string SourceName="", DestinationName="";
            do
            {
                try
                {
                    //Override value in case it failed last time
                    finishedCopying = true;
                    //Get the filenames and do the copy
                    Console.WriteLine("Enter source file: ");
                    SourceName = Console.ReadLine();
                    Console.WriteLine("Enter destination file: ");
                    DestinationName = Console.ReadLine();
                    CopyFile(SourceName, DestinationName);
                }
```

```
        catch (FileNotFoundException)
        {
            Console.WriteLine("The source file was not found: " +
                SourceName);
            //Prompt the user for the filename again
            finishedCopying = false;
        }
        catch (InvalidHeaderException e)
        {
            Console.WriteLine(e.Message);
        }
        catch (Exception e)
        {
            Console.WriteLine("Unexpected error: " + e.Message);
        }
    } while (!finishedCopying);
    Console.WriteLine("File copying is finished");
    Console.ReadLine();
}


//Copy from one file to another file
static void CopyFile(string SourceName, string DestinationName)
{
    StreamReader sourceFile = null;
    StreamWriter destinationFile = null;
    FileStream destinationFileStream;
    bool destinationFileReady = false;
    int lineCount;
    string fileText;
    //There is no error checking here because the calling procedure
    //is designed to handle the "File Not Found" error.
    //SourceName must be converted to string so that it isn't
    //misinterpreted by the compiler as a Stream
    sourceFile = new StreamReader(SourceName.ToString());
    //At this point anything that happens will involve open files.
    //Wrap everything in a try block to close the files when done
    try
    {
        do
        {
```

```csharp
        try
        {
            //Open the destination file for output
            destinationFileStream = new FileStream(DestinationName,
                FileMode.CreateNew, FileAccess.Write);
            destinationFile = new
                StreamWriter(destinationFileStream);
            //File open succeeded
            destinationFileReady = true;
        }
        catch (IOException)
        {
            //The file already exists, so delete it
            File.Delete(DestinationName);
        }
    } while (!destinationFileReady);

    //Both of the files are now open, so do the copy
    lineCount = int.Parse(sourceFile.ReadLine());
    destinationFile.WriteLine(lineCount);
    for (int currentLine = 1; currentLine <= lineCount;
        currentLine++)
    {
        fileText = sourceFile.ReadLine();
        if (fileText == null)
        {
            throw new InvalidHeaderException();
        }
        destinationFile.WriteLine(fileText);
    }
}
//There is no catch block so that all unhandled errors will
//be passed to the calling procedure
finally
{
    //close any open files
    if (sourceFile != null)
    {
        sourceFile.Close();
    }
    if (destinationFile != null)
    {
        destinationFile.Close();
    }
```

```
        }
      }
    }

    //Custom exception class to handle a bad header record
    public class InvalidHeaderException : ApplicationException
    {
          public InvalidHeaderException()
          : this("")
          {}
          public InvalidHeaderException(string message)
          : base("Source file had invalid header." + message)
          {}
    }
}
```

Example 5-1 Output

This example runs the program by first giving an invalid filename for the source file. On the second request the correct filename is entered.

```
Enter source file:
C:\NoFile.txt
Enter destination file:
c:\DestFile.txt
The source file was not found: C:\NoFile.txt
Enter source file:
C:\SourceFile.txt
Enter destination file:
C:\DestFile.txt
Source file had invalid header.
File copying is finished
```

CHAPTER 6

Classes

Table 6-1. Class Declaration Equivalent Chart

VB 6.0	VB .NET	C#
Public Class aClass	Public Class aClass	public class aClass
myObject_Initialize	Public Sub New()	public aClass()
myObject_Terminate	Public Sub Finalize()	public ~aClass()
Public myObject As New aClass	Public myObject As New aClass()	public aClass myObject = new aClass();
Public myObject As aClass Set myObject = New aClass	Public myObject As aClass Set myObject = New aClass()	aClass myObject; aClass = new myObject();
Public myObject As New aClass myObject.Init(var1, var2)	Public myObject As New _ aClass(var1, var2)	
	Public myObject As aClass = New _ aClass(var1, var2)	aClass myObject = new aClass(var1, var2);
	MyBase.variable = parameter	this.variable = parameter;

With myObject
   .Method()
End With
	With myObject
	   .Method()
	End With	

Overview

Classes have been rewritten for .NET to make them more sophisticated than their VB 6.0 counterparts. Microsoft introduced classes in VB 4.0 and with each new version of VB they made minor improvements to the implementation. .NET has made major improvements to all aspects of classes with a primary focus on adding more compliance to the object-oriented programming (OOP) requirements. The most requested change that programmers have been asking for is now possible: The .NET Framework supports inheritance.

Some people feel that these changes are the best part of .NET. This may be a little overhyped because the general population of VB programmers may not be able to immediately take full advantage of OOP. Because it wasn't available until now, most VB 6.0 programmers probably haven't spent much time using it and will probably have to take additional training to fully utilize its benefits. On the other hand, there are many other changes in .NET that are much easier to implement and take advantage of right from the start. These changes can have a big impact on a programmer's productivity without requiring as much effort as it will take to learn OOP.

Whether you want to learn OOP concepts or not, .NET programmers have to know how to use classes because both languages are heavily dependent on class hierarchies. This chapter focuses on creating classes and declaring instances of them.

Declaring Classes and Objects

Knowing how to declare a class and instantiate an object is essential for writing .NET programs. Just for the record, let's define two commonly misused words: *class* and *object*. It's easy to confuse these words because they are so similar. Many people often use them interchangeably without thinking about it. That may be fine when you're having a general discussion around the watercooler, but when you're learning a new language syntax it is important to know the difference. The following are some simple definitions, but if you have no prior experience with object-oriented concepts, there are entire books dedicated to them. I recommend that you read one of these books to fully understand object-oriented concepts and learn how to implement them.

- *Class*: A template that defines properties (variables) and methods (procedures). Once defined, it will not change because it doesn't have any local storage allocated for it.

- *Object*: An instance of a class. It gets space for it allocated in memory and therefore it can have its properties changed. Its methods will perform operations on the object based that are defined by the class.

A class is like a blueprint for a house. The blueprint defines what type of house is to be built and where the windows and doors belong. But you can't live in a blueprint. Instead, you have to set aside some land to build the house on. That house is built using the blueprint as a starting point, and then you get to decide the style of the windows and the type of door you want. Once a blueprint is finished, it probably won't change. But if multiple houses are built from the same blueprint, they can each have their own unique characteristics that help distinguish them from all the other houses that were built using that same blueprint.

A class defines certain functionality and the properties and methods that can be used to carry out that functionality. Just as no land is automatically set aside for a blueprint, no memory is set aside for the class.

Once a class is defined, programmers working with the class rely on it to remain the same. As objects are instantiated from a class, each object will have its own memory space to manage the properties associated with it.

Declaring the Class

Declaring the class requires deciding which properties and methods will be created to carry out its functionality.

VB 6.0

Each class is defined in a separate class module file. The class name is set in the Properties window.

```
'Create a class file and set its name property to the name of the class
Public Var As Integer
Public Sub Procedure1(Param1 As String)
    ...
End Sub
```

VB .NET

Declare a class using the Class keyword followed by the name of the class. Within the Class and End Class keywords, declare the properties and methods of the class.

```
Public Class aClass
    Public Var As Integer
    Public Sub Procedure1(Param As String)
        ...
    End
End Class
```

C#

Declare a class using the Class keyword followed by the name of the class. Within the curly brackets, declare the properties and methods of the class.

```
public class myClass{
    public int Var;
    void Procedure1(string Param){
    ...
    }
}
```

Using Shared/static Members

A variable declared as Shared (VB .NET) or static (C#) will only have one copy of itself in memory for your application.

The fact that VB .NET and C# use two different names for these attributes makes them very confusing to discuss. In addition to the different names, VB .NET also has a Static attribute, but it is totally different and can only be used with functions (see Chapter 2). To try to avoid confusion, this section will refer to these types of variables as shared variables for both languages. Although not technically accurate for the C# language, it does convey the concept. Hopefully, this won't upset any C-sharpers.

A variable that isn't declared as a shared variable is called an *instance* variable. Normally, every object declared in your program will get its own copy of all instance variables declared in the class. These are separate from each other and cannot overlap. This is not the case with shared variables. Regardless of how many objects are instantiated from a class, there will always be just one copy of the variable. This makes it possible to have data that is shared among multiple objects.

In addition to declaring shared variables, you can also declare shared methods.

Using shared variables and methods is not dependent upon creating an instance of the class. You reference them using the class name.

Shared members are not allowed to access instance members. In other words, a shared variable can only reference other shared variables. A shared method can only call shared methods and reference shared variables. This is a result of the way that shared members work. Because they can be referenced just by using their class name, you can't be certain that an object of that class has been instantiated yet. If you can't guarantee that an object exists yet, you certainly can't reference members of that object. If you create a class and try to have shared members access instance members, the compiler will give you an error.

In VB .NET, your program can reference a shared member by using the class name or any object of that class. In C#, static variables can only be accessed using the class name. You cannot reference a static variable through an object variable.

Creating a class with only shared members is the equivalent of creating a global module in VB 6.0. Just like global modules, you don't have to create an instance of it to use it.

VB .NET

Declare shared methods and variables using the Shared attribute. Shared members are not allowed to access instance members.

```
'Demonstrate creating a class with shared and instance members
Public Class aClass
    Public Shared value1 As Integer = 5 'This is a shared member
    Public value2 As Integer = 10  'This is an instance member
    Public Shared Function Multiply(Num As Integer) As Integer
        Return Value1 * Num
        'This line would give a compiler error if you uncommented it
        'because you can't access instance members from a shared method
        'Return value2 * Num
    End Function
End Class
```

Your program can call shared members using either the class name or the object name.

```
Dim myObject As New aClass()
Dim var As Integer = 3
'All of these statements are valid (but they really don't do much)
var = aClass.Multiply(var)
var = myObject.value1
var = myObject.value2
```

C#

Declare shared methods and variables using the static attribute. Shared members are not allowed to access instance members.

```
//Demonstrate creating a class with shared and instance members
public class aClass
{
    public static int value1 = 5; //This is a shared member
    public int value2 = 10;  //This is an instance member
    public static int Multiply(int Num)
    {
        return value1 * Num;
        //This line would give a compiler error if you uncommented it
        //because you can't access instance members from a shared method
        //return value2 * Num;
    }
}
```

Your program can call shared members using only the class name.

```
int var = 3;
var = aClass.Multiply(var);
```

Your program can't call shared members using the object name.

```
aClass myObject = new aClass();
int var = 3;
//These statements will give a compiler error.
var = myObject.value1;
var = myObject.Multiply(var);
```

Initializing the Class with Constructors

A *constructor* is a class method that is automatically called when an object is instantiated. When an object is instantiated from a class, it is often necessary to have a way to set default values of the object as well as to set its environment before it is used. For example, if you create an object that makes changes to a database, you may want to initialize a variable with the name of the database server and have it open a connection to the database. This is implemented by creating a constructor method that has code to initialize the class based upon the parameters passed to it. The way this is performed is different for each language.

Initializing classes has been dramatically improved in VB .NET with the ability to initialize a class using constructors. Constructors are much more flexible than the Class_Initialize() method in VB 6.0 because they can now accept parameters and they can be overridden. A constructor in VB .NET uses the New keyword and C# has you create a method with the same name as the class.

Constructors in .NET allow a programmer to have a lot of flexibility when creating a class. There are a variety of ways that constructors can be written:

- If no constructors are declared, the compiler will supply a default constructor with no parameters.

- A constructor can have parameters that are used to initialize variables within the class. This ensures that all variables are initialized before any methods are called.

- Constructors can be overridden so that there are multiple ways to initialize a class.

- If at least one constructor with parameters is created, the compiler won't supply a default constructor without parameters. This means that if you want the client code to have the option of instantiating the class either with or without parameters, a constructor without parameters must also be defined. If you want to force the client code to always pass a parameter(s) when instantiating the class, make sure that every constructor has at least one parameter.

VB 6.0

VB 6.0 automatically creates an `Initialize` method for each class. Put any initialization code in this method. If you want to set any default values, you can create a separate method that is called by the client code before using the class. I always create a method called `Init()`.

```
'Create a class file and set its name property to the name of the class
Private Sub aClass_Initialize()
    ...
End Sub

Public Sub Init(Param As Integer)
    ...
End Sub
```

VB .NET

Initializing a class uses the `New` constructor. It can have parameters to initialize the properties of the class. Note that although inheritance hasn't been discussed yet, it should be mentioned that when a class inherits another class, the constructor method can't be inherited. Defining a new constructor is optional. If you don't define a constructor, a default constructor is implicitly created by the compiler that calls the base class constructor.

```
Public Class aClass
    Public Sub New(Param As String)
        ...
    End Sub
End Class
```

C#

C# constructors use the name of the class. Right after declaring the class, create a procedure with the same name as the class. This procedure can have parameters to initialize the properties of the class. I discuss this more in Chapter 8.

```
public class aClass{
    public aClass(string Param){
        ...
    }
}
```

Shared/static Constructors

As discussed earlier, Shared variables in VB .NET are similar to static variables in C#. The same applies to constructors. Shared constructors are used to initialize shared variables and these are the only variables it can access. No reference to instance variables is allowed. .NET keeps these variables in memory during the life of the class. Thus, when the class is instantiated for the first time in the program, its shared variables are also created. A shared constructor is used to set the default values of these variables.

An interesting aspect of this constructor is that it isn't called directly by any client code. It is executed one time by the system when the first object of a given class is instantiated. Because it isn't called directly by client code, there are no parameters that can be passed to it.

VB .NET

Use the Shared keyword before the New keyword. Do not specify any parameters.

```
Public Class aClass
    Shared Sub New()
        ...
    End Sub
End Class
```

C#

Use the static keyword before the method name. Do not specify any parameters.

```
public class aClass{
    static aClass(){
        ...
    }
}
```

Declaring Methods

Methods are responsible for implementing the functionality in the class. It is important to decide which methods should be exposed to external clients and which ones should be hidden. You generally hide certain methods if they perform underlying functionality to support the primary functionality of the class. Setting the access modifiers of the method declarations does this.

Shared methods can also be declared using these access modifiers. Shared methods were discussed earlier in this chapter.

The following access modifiers determine the rules for when an object's methods can be called.[1]

- The Public modifier allows a method to be accessed from any object instance. There are no restrictions. VB .NET uses this as the default modifier if you don't specify one.

- The Private modifier only allows a method to be accessed from within the object itself. Even classes that are derived from it can access the method. C# uses this as the default modifier if you don't specify one.

- The Friend (VB .NET) and internal (C#) modifiers allow a method to be accessed from an object variable that is an instance of the class as long as it is within the same program.

Declaring Properties

Properties provide you with a way to control access to a variable. Properties can be used in many ways: They can set a variable to be read-only, check the bounds of a variable before assigning it, and format a variable when you assign it a value.

VB 6.0 uses three types of properties: Let, Set, and Get. The Let and Set properties are used for assigning a value to class variable. The Set property has to be used when working with objects. The Get property is used for retrieving a value from a class variable.

The .NET Framework also has properties. It uses the Set and Get properties. Because every variable is considered an object in .NET, there is no reason to have a Let property.

VB 6.0 structures each property separately. Consequently, each property can have a different scope. For example, you can define the Get property as Public and the Let property as Private. This lets a property be read-only for external clients, but methods within the class are allowed to change it. This isn't possible in .NET. .NET groups the properties together and thus both properties will have the same scope.

In VB 6.0, the Get property acts as a function. You return data to the external client by assigning a value to the property name. The Set property uses a parameter to assign data to the class variable.

The VB .NET Get property also acts as a function. Use the Return statement to pass data to the external client. The Set property also uses a parameter to assign data to the class variable.

---

1. Additional modifiers are discussed in Chapter 8.

C# passes data between the external clients differently than VB. In C# the get property also acts like a function and uses the `return` statement. The `set` property uses a predefined variable, `value`, to assign data to the class variable. It is a built-in keyword and you can't rename it.

Using a `Get` property without a `Let` or `Set` property creates read-only properties in VB 6.0. A write-only property is the opposite—use a `Let` or `Set` property without using a `Get` property.

Oddly enough, VB .NET doesn't follow the VB 6.0 structure, but C# does. VB .NET requires read-only properties to use the `ReadOnly` keyword in the declaration *and* only use the `Get` property. Write-only properties have to use the `WriteOnly` keyword in the declaration *and* only use the `Set` property. This is obviously redundant, and I have no idea why it is implemented like this. C#, on the other hand, doesn't use extra keywords. Just like VB 6.0, a read-only property is defined by only using the get property, and a write-only property is defined by only using the set property.

VB 6.0

Declare a `Private` variable to store the data. Declare a public `Get` property for accessing the variable. Declare a public `Let` or `Set` property to assign a value to the variable.

```
Private var As type
Public Property Get myProperty() As type
    myProperty = var
End Property
Public Property Let myProperty(ByVal vNewValue As type)
    vNewValue = var
End Property
```

A read-only property only uses the `Get` property.

```
Public Property Get myProperty() As type
    myProperty = var
End Property
```

A write-only property only uses the `Let` or `Set` property.

```
Public Property Let myProperty(ByVal vNewValue As type)
    vNewValue = var
End Property
```

VB .NET

VB .NET uses the Property keyword to declare a property. Specify the Get and Set properties within this code block.

```
Private var As type
Public Property myProperty() As type
    Get
        Return var
    End Get
    Set(ByVal Value As type)
        var = Value
    End Set
End Property
```

A read-only property uses the ReadOnly keyword and only the Get property.

```
Public ReadOnly Property myProperty() As type
    Get
        Return var
    End Get
End Property
```

A write-only property uses the WriteOnly keyword and only the Set property.

```
Public WriteOnly Property myProperty() As type
    Set(ByVal Value As type)
        var = Value
    End Set
End Property
```

C#

In C# you declare a property the same way you would declare a standard variable. But you also need to add a code block after it that uses either the set or get property. The value variable is implied and you do not have to declare it.

```
private type var;
public type myProperty
{
    get
    {
        return var;
    }
```

```
    set
    {
        var = value;
    }
}
```

A read-only property only uses the `get` property.

```
public type myProperty
{
    get
    {
        return var;
    }
}
```

A write-only property only uses the `set` property.

```
public type myProperty
{
    set
    {
        var = value;
    }
}
```

Shadowing Variables

Shadowing a variable consists of having a variable declared within the scope of a class and also declaring it within a method in that same class or as a method parameter. The duplicate variable names create a naming conflict between the variables within a class. Normally, this naming conflict meant that you could only access the variable that had the most local scope (the variable in the current method). In .NET it is possible to resolve a naming conflict by explicitly stating which variable belongs to the class. This is done in VB .NET by using the Me keyword and in C# by using the this keyword.

VB .NET

When there is a naming conflict with a class variable, use the Me keyword to identify the variable belonging to the class.

```
Public Class aClass
    Private Var As Integer
    Public Sub Method(Var As Integer)
        Me.Var = Var
    End Sub
End Class
```

C#

When there is a naming conflict with a class variable, use the this keyword to identify the variable belonging to the class.

```
public class aClass
{
    private int var;
    public void Method(int var)
    {
        this.var = var;
    }
}
```

Shadowing variables helps you code more clearly and efficiently because it fixes the problem of having to spend time making up creative variable names. As an example, let's say you have a class variable representing a person's last name. You call it lastName. You also create a method where one of the parameters can be used to set the last name. You want to call the parameter something descriptive, but you don't want to create a naming conflict. So after thinking about it, you decide to call it userLastName. This is perfectly acceptable, but another programmer reading your code may wonder if there is some slight difference between the lastName variable and the userLastName parameter. .NET lets you avoid the "creative variable names" problem because you can now call both of them lastName. Within the method where there is a naming conflict, refer to the class level variable as either Me.lastName (VB .NET) or this.lastName (C#). Refer to the method parameter as lastName.

Destroying the Class with Finalizers

Finalizers are methods within your class definition designed to perform any necessary cleanup work before the object is released. For example, temporary files should be deleted and any open database connections should be closed. The Finalizer() method is automatically called by the system when the object is destroyed. In C#, the equivalent to the Finalizer() method is to declare a method with the class name and prefix it with a tilde (~).

VB 6.0 destroys an object when all references to it are set to `Nothing`. .NET has changed this implementation because it is no longer the programmer's responsibility to release the object. An object reference is automatically released when the object variable goes out of scope. When all references to an object have been released, the object can be destroyed.

Garbage collection in .NET is a very important concept to learn because it completely deviates from VB 6.0. In VB 6.0, you know that when all references to an object are set to `Nothing`, the code in the `Terminate` event is called. .NET changes this because now when you clear all references to an object, the object isn't immediately removed from memory. The object is destroyed when the garbage collector is run, and this is determined by the .NET runtime. There is no way for a programmer to know when an object will be destroyed.

Garbage collection is a great concept because it eliminates the problem of a programmer forgetting to release object references (and causing memory problems). The downfall of the garbage collector is that because the system is now in charge of determining when to release an object, it needs to be smart enough to know when the best time is to do this. The system is smart, but not smart enough. If an object created references to resource-intensive objects, such as database connections, you want to release them immediately. Waiting for the garbage collection process to run isn't acceptable. To resolve this problem, implement the `IDisposable` interface in your class and define a `Dispose()` method to put the cleanup code in. You can also inherit the `System.ComponentModel.Component` class and override its `Dispose()` method.

Any methods that create a reference to your object need to call the `Dispose()` method when they are done using it. This ensures that resources are released immediately.

Within the `Dispose()` method, you should call the `GC.SuppressFinalize()` method. This prevents the garbage collection from calling the `Finalize()` method of the object. This helps performance.

An alternative is to waiting for garbage collection is to call the method `System.GC.Collect()`. This isn't recommended because it may hinder your application's performance if called at a nonadvantageous time. It is usually best to let the system determine when to run the garbage collector.

VB 6.0

A `Terminate` method is automatically created for each class. Put cleanup code that needs to run before an object is destroyed in this method. It is called when the object is set to `Nothing`.

```
'Create a class file and set its name property to the name of the class
Private Sub aClass_Terminate()
    ...
End Sub
```

VB .NET

Because there is no way to guarantee when the object is removed from memory, create a `Dispose()` method that will be called when the object is no longer needed.

```
Public Class aClass
    Implements IDisposable
    Public Overridable Sub Dispose() Implements IDisposable.Dispose
        ...
        GC.SuppressFinalize(Me)
    End Sub
    Protected Overrides Sub Finalize()
        ...
    End Sub
End Class
```

C#

Because there is no way to guarantee when the object is removed from memory, create a `Dispose()` method that will be called when the object is no longer needed. The finalizer is created by declaring a method with the class name and prefixing it with a tilde (~).

```
public class aClass : IDisposable
{
    public void Dispose(){
        ...
        GC.SuppressFinalize(this);
    }
    ~aClass()
    {
        ...
    }
}
```

Overloading Class Methods

Method overloading allows a class to have the same function name used with different sets of parameters. Method overloading is a feature that C++ programmers are very familiar with, but VB 6.0 programmers have only heard about. .NET brings it to both worlds because VB .NET and C# support method overloading.

For example, you could create a procedure called `LogError` that saves error information. You have the option of only passing the error description or passing the error description along with extra information that may help debug the problem. In VB 6.0 you have to create a procedure with the second parameter declared as Optional. Note that in VB you can use the Optional keyword with any procedure, regardless of whether it is part of a class or not. With .NET you can create the same function multiple times and use different parameters each time. If the class is inheriting from another class, use the Overloads keyword. When you call the method, the compiler will look at the parameters being passed to the function and determine which one to use.

When you overload methods, each method declaration must have a different parameter list; otherwise, the compiler won't be able to determine which one to use. Functions are allowed to have different return types, as long as their parameter list is different from the other functions that are being overloaded.

VB .NET

Simply repeat the method declaration with different parameters. Only use the Overloads keyword if the class is inheriting another class.

```
Public Class aClass
    Public Sub LogError(errMessage As String)
        ...
    End Sub

    Public Sub LogError(errMessage As String, extraInfo As String)
        ...
    End Sub
End Class
```

C#

Simply repeat the method declaration with different parameters.

```
public class aClass{
    public void LogError(string errMessage){
        ...
    }

    public void LogError(string errMessage, string extraInfo){
        ...
    }
}
```

Instantiating Objects

Now that you have seen at all the details of writing a class, here is what you need to use your classes: objects. An object is an instance of a class. That means that you have a variable set aside in memory that represents the class. Now you can change its properties and call its methods.

.NET added three major changes to working with objects. The first change is that the Set keyword is no longer used, the second is how the New keyword is used, and the third major change is the addition of constructors. I've already discussed constructors, so let's look at the Set keyword and the New keyword.

The Set keyword has been dropped from the .NET syntax. In VB 6.0 you have to use the Set keyword when instantiating a new object or assigning an object variable to another object. This is necessary to differentiate between assigning object references and assigning the default value of an object. In VB .NET you simply treat an object variable just like any other variable and you don't use the Set keyword.

Regarding use of the New keyword, in VB 6.0 you can declare an object using the New keyword, or you can use the New keyword on a separate line. From a coding standpoint, it is easier to declare the variable and call the New function on the same line (less typing). But this has performance drawbacks because the compiler doesn't know when the code really needs the object to be created. So every time your code uses the object, the application has to check if the object has been created yet. If it hasn't been created, it goes ahead and creates it. Having the application check if the object exists every time it is referenced creates a lot of unnecessary overhead. This isn't the case if you call the New function on a separate line because now you are telling the compiler exactly when you need the object created. The application doesn't have to keep checking if you created the object or not. So the tradeoff for less typing is that you get slower performance. Not a good deal.

VB 6.0

Use the New keyword to instantiate an object. This can be done with the object declaration or separately.

```
'Creating the object on one line is not efficient
Public myObject As New aClass

'Create the object on a line different from the declaration - efficient
Public myObject As aClass
Set myObject = New aClass
```

```
'Create the object and set its initial properties
Public myObject As aClass
Set myObject = New aClass
myObject.Init var1, var2
```

.NET still allows you to have the option of declaring and instantiating the object variable on a single line or on two lines. But now the implementation has the same performance for both options. When you use the New statement on the same line as the declaration statement, the object will be created right away. There isn't any performance overhead for checking if the object exists because it is created immediately. Note that in VB 6.0, if you set the object to Nothing in the middle of the procedure and then try to use it again, the object will be created again. In .NET this will raise an error because the application will only create the object when the New keyword is used.

VB .NET

Use the New keyword to instantiate an object. This can be done with the object declaration or separately. If the class has a parameterized constructor, pass it the parameters when instantiating it.

```
 'Create the object on one line - efficient
Public myObject As New aClass()
```

```
'Create the object on a line different from the declaration - also efficient
Public myObject As aClass
myObject = New aClass()
```

```
'Create the object and set its initial properties with a constructor
Public myObject As New aClass(Var1, Var2)
```

Or

```
Public myObject As aClass = New aClass(Var1, Var2)
```

C#

Use the new keyword to instantiate an object. This can be done with the object declaration or separately. If the class has a parameterized constructor, pass it the parameters when instantiating it.

```
//Create the object on one line - efficient
public aClass myObject = new aClass();
```

```
//Create the object on a line different from the declaration - also efficient
public aClass myObject;
myObject = new aClass();

//Create the object and set its initial properties with a constructor
public aClass myObject = new aClass(Var1, Var2);
```

Using With Statements

The With statement is used in VB as a way to shorten the amount of code you have to type when using objects. You specify the name of an object with the With statement and inside that code block you can reference members of the object without using the object name. The compiler identifies these "orphaned" members and makes them reference the object identified in the With statement.

With statements can be nested within each other. However, only one object can be active at a time. The compiler associates an orphaned member will the most current object.

C# does not have an equivalent to the With statement.

VB 6.0/VB .NET
Use the With statement and the name of the object. All methods of that object are prefixed with a dot operator (.) to signify that they belong to the object. End the code block with the End With statement.

```
With object
    .Method1()
    .Method2()
End With
```

Using Structs

A *struct* is a lightweight class. It gives you the benefits of a class, and you get better performance. In VB .NET, you declare a struct using the Structure keyword. In C#, use the struct keyword.

Structs are treated like built-in data types. When you declare a variable using a struct, you don't have to use the New keyword. Every struct has a default constructor that is parameterless. If you define a constructor for your struct, it must have at least one parameter.

If structs are so great, why bother using classes? Structs have limitations that make them impractical for anything but the simplest of tasks. Some of the limitations of structs are as follows:

- Structs can't inherit from another class or another struct. However, they can implement interfaces.

- Variables in a struct can't be initialized within the struct definition. Use a constructor to do this.

- Structs are designed to represent simple data types.

- If a struct gets very large or uses non-simple data types, it loses its performance edge over classes.

VB .NET

Declare a struct using the Structure keyword. Finish the code block with the End Structure statement.

```
Public Structure myStruct
    Public var As type
    'Constructors must have at least one parameter
    Public Sub New(Param As type)
        ...
    End Sub
    Public Sub Method()
        ...
    End Sub
End Structure
```

C#

Declare a struct using the struct keyword.

```
public struct myStruct
{
    public type var;
    //Constructors must have at least one parameter
    public myStruct(type param)
    {
        ...
    }
    public void Method()
    {
    }
}
```

Example 6-1. Writing to a Log File

This example demonstrates a program that manages someone's checking account. A user can deposit or withdraw money from his or her account by calling the Deposit and Withdraw methods of the CCheckingAccount class. The status of each transaction is saved to a text file called "Logfile.txt". The Logfile.txt file will confirm that the transaction took place as well as when there are insufficient funds. If a user tries to withdraw more money than is in his or her account, the transaction fails. Saving to a text file is used to illustrate opening the file in the class initialization and closing the file when the class is destroyed.

The CheckingAccount class uses a shared constructor to ensure that the text file is opened before anyone tries to access it.

VB 6.0

```
'Write to a log file sample application using VB 6.0
'Copyright (c)2001 by Bischof Systems, Inc.

Option Explicit

Private Sub Main()
    Dim CheckingAccount As CCheckingAccount
    Set CheckingAccount = New CCheckingAccount
    CheckingAccount.Init
    CheckingAccount.Deposit 500
    CheckingAccount.Withdraw 400
    CheckingAccount.Withdraw 75
    CheckingAccount.Withdraw 50
    Set CheckingAccount = Nothing
End Sub


'CCheckingAccount class
Private m_CurrentBalance As Double
Private LogFile As Integer
Const m_MinimumBalance = 100
Public Sub Init(Optional BeginningBalance As Double)
    m_CurrentBalance = BeginningBalance
End Sub
'Deposit money into the checking account
Public Sub Deposit(Amount As Double)
    m_CurrentBalance = m_CurrentBalance + Amount
    Write #LogFile, "Deposited $" & Amount & "; Current balance is $" & _
        m_CurrentBalance
End Sub
```

```
'Withdraw money from the checking account
Public Sub Withdraw(Amount As Double)
    'Check to make sure the balance won't go below zero
    If (m_CurrentBalance - Amount) >= 0 Then
        m_CurrentBalance = m_CurrentBalance - Amount

        'Log that the transaction took place
        Write #LogFile, "Withdrew $" & Amount & "; New Balance is $" & _
            m_CurrentBalance
        'Check if the minimum balance was reached
        If m_CurrentBalance < m_MinimumBalance Then
            'Log that it went below the minimum balance
            Write #LogFile, "You are below the minimum balance of $" & _
                m_MinimumBalance
        End If
    Else
        'Log that there weren't enough funds
        Write #LogFile, "Insufficient funds - $" & Amount & " was not " & _
            "withdrawn"
    End If

End Sub


Private Sub Class_Initialize()
    LogFile = FreeFile
    Open "C:\Logfile.txt" For Output As #LogFile
End Sub

Private Sub Class_Terminate()
    Close #LogFile
End Sub
```

VB .NET

```
'Write to a log file sample application using VB .NET
'Copyright (c)2001 by Bischof Systems, Inc.

Module Module1

    Sub Main()
        Classes()
        Console.ReadLine()
    End Sub
```

```vb
Public Sub Classes()
    Dim CheckingAccount As New CCheckingAccount()
    CheckingAccount.Deposit(500)
    CheckingAccount.Withdraw(400)
    CheckingAccount.Withdraw(75)
    CheckingAccount.Withdraw(50)
    CheckingAccount.Dispose()
    CheckingAccount = Nothing
End Sub


Public Class CCheckingAccount
    Shared MinimumBalance As Double = 100
    Private LogFile As IO.StreamWriter
    Private CurrentBalance As Double
    'The constructor will open the file for output
    Public Sub New()
        LogFile = New IO.StreamWriter("C:\Logfile.txt")
    End Sub
    'Deposit money into the checking account
    Public Sub Deposit(ByVal Amount As Double)
        CurrentBalance += Amount
        LogFile.WriteLine("Deposited ${0}; New Balance is ${1}", _
            Amount, CurrentBalance)
    End Sub
    'Withdraw money from the checking account
    Public Sub Withdraw(ByVal Amount As Double)
        'Check to make sure it isn't below zero
        If (CurrentBalance - Amount) >= 0 Then
            CurrentBalance -= Amount
            'Log that the transaction took place
            LogFile.WriteLine("Withdrew ${0}; New Balance is ${1}", _
                Amount, CurrentBalance)
            'Check if the minimum balance was reached
            If CurrentBalance < MinimumBalance Then
                'Log that it went below the minimum balance
                LogFile.WriteLine("You are below the minimum balance " & _
                    "of ${0}", MinimumBalance)
            End If
        Else
            'Log that there weren't enough funds
            LogFile.WriteLine("Insufficient funds - ${0} was not " & _
                "withdrawn", Amount)
        End If
    End Sub
```

```
            Public Sub Dispose()
                LogFile.Close()
                GC.SuppressFinalize(Me)
            End Sub
            Protected Overrides Sub Finalize()
                LogFile.Close()
            End Sub
        End Class
End Module
```

C#

```
//Write to a log file sample application using C#
//Copyright (c)2001 by Bischof Systems, Inc.

using System;

namespace C_Classes
{
    class Class1
    {
        [STAThread]
        static void Main(string[] args)
        {
            RunCheckingAccount();
            Console.ReadLine();
        }
        static void RunCheckingAccount()
        {
            CCheckingAccount CheckingAccount = new CCheckingAccount();

            CheckingAccount.Deposit(500);
            CheckingAccount.WriteCheck(400);
            CheckingAccount.WriteCheck(75);
            CheckingAccount.WriteCheck(50);
            CheckingAccount.Dispose();
            CheckingAccount = null;
        }
```

```csharp
public class CCheckingAccount
{
    static double MinimumBalance = 100;
    private double CurrentBalance;
    private System.IO.StreamWriter LogFile;
    //The constructor will open the file for output
    public CCheckingAccount()
    {
        LogFile = new System.IO.StreamWriter(@"C:\LogFile.txt");
    }
    //Deposit money into the checking account
    public void Deposit(double Amount)
    {
        CurrentBalance += Amount;
        LogFile.WriteLine("Deposited ${0}; New Balance is ${1}",
            Amount, CurrentBalance);
    }
    //Withdraw money from the checking account
    public void WriteCheck(double Amount)
    {
        //Check to make sure it isn't below zero
        if ((CurrentBalance - Amount) > 0)
        {
            CurrentBalance -= Amount;
            //Log that the transaction took place
            LogFile.WriteLine("Withdrew ${0}; New Balance is ${1}",
                Amount, CurrentBalance);
            if (CurrentBalance < MinimumBalance)
            {
                //Log that they are below the minimum balance
                LogFile.WriteLine("You are below the minimum " +
                    "balance of ${0}", MinimumBalance);
            }
        }
        else
        {
            //Log that there weren't enough funds
            LogFile.WriteLine("Insufficient funds - ${0} was not " +
                "withdrawn", Amount);
        }
    }
```

```
public void Dispose()
{
    LogFile.Close();
    GC.SuppressFinalize(this);
}
~CCheckingAccount()
{
    LogFile.Close();
}
        }
    }
}
```

Output to File Logfile.txt

```
"Deposited $500; Current balance is $500"
"Withdrew $400; New Balance is $100"
"Withdrew $75; New Balance is $25"
"You are below the minimum balance of $100"
"Insufficient funds - $50 was not withdrawn"
```

CHAPTER 7

Class Interfaces

Table 7-1. Class Interface Equivalent Chart

VB 6.0	VB .NET	C#

(a class module called IInterface)
Public Sub Method()
	Public Interface IInterface
	    Public Sub Method()
	End Interface
		public interface IInterface{
		    public void Method();
		}

(a class module called aClass) Implements IInterface	Public Class aClass Implements IInterface	public class aClass : IInterface

(a class module called aClass)
Implements IInterface1
Implements IInterface2
	Public Class aClass
	    Implements IInterface1
	    Implements IInterface2
		public class aClass :
		IInterface1, IInterface2

Sub IInterface1_Method() Sub IInterface2_Method()	Sub Procedure1() Implements _ IInterface1.Method Sub Procedure2() Implements _ IInterface2.Method	void IInterface1.Method() void Iinterface2.Method()
Dim myObject1 As New aClass Dim myObject2 As IInterface Set myObject2 = myObject1	myObject2 = CType(myObject1, _ IInterface)	IInterface myObject2 = (IInterface)myObject1;
myObject2.Method()	myObject2.Method()	((IInterface)myObject2).Method();

Overview

An *interface* is a group of methods, properties, and events that can be implemented by a class. Although an interface defines different methods and properties, it doesn't have any code to provide the functionality for the methods. Its purpose is to define a set a characteristics that can be implemented by other classes. Using an interface enables you to standardize the public methods and properties of multiple classes.

When you write a new class or interface, you can implement multiple interfaces. When you create a new class using inheritance, you can only inherit from one other class. Using interfaces is a way of working around this restriction.

Defining an Interface

An interface must be defined before it can be implemented by the classes in a program. Defining an interface consists of creating the interface file and defining the members that belong to the interface.

Declaring the interface is different in VB 6.0 than in .NET. In VB 6.0 every class must be in its own file. Thus, the name of an interface is the name of the class as set in the Properties window. .NET allows multiple classes to be declared in the same file, so they have to have a line of code to declare them. In .NET, an interface is declared using the `Interface` keyword.

Within the interface, each member that will be available is declared, but no code is associated with the method. This is because the interface doesn't implement the functionality of its members. The class is responsible for implementing the functionality of the interface it is based on.

VB 6.0

Creating an interface in VB 6.0 is very similar to creating a class. You add a new class module to the program and declare the necessary methods and properties. The difference between a class and an interface is that with an interface you don't write any implementation code for the methods. In this way, it can't do any work by itself and it must be implemented by another class. Hence, it now meets the definition of an interface. Even though the file is class module, the naming convention is that you place a capital *I* at the beginning of the name. This is done in the Properties window for the class.

```
'Create a class file and set its name property to the name of the interface
'to IInterface1
'Declare the method
Public Sub Method(Param1 As Integer)
```

VB .NET

Use the `Interface` and `End Interface` keywords to declare an interface block.

```
Public Interface IInterface
 Sub Method(param1 As Integer)
End Interface
```

C#

Use the `interface` keyword and curly brackets to declare an interface block.

```
public interface IInterface
{
  void Method(int param1);
}
```

Implementing an Interface

Implementing an interface consists of declaring a class that is based on the interface and implementing the methods defined by the interface. An interface is a contract that states which members belong in a class. This requires that the class have declarations for every member that is in the interface. For each method defined in the interface, the class will have implementation code associated with it. If a class is based on an interface that has implemented another interface, the class automatically must implement all the members of every interface.

VB 6.0

Use the `Implements` keyword at the beginning of the class module. Each method that is based on of one of the interface members will be declared using the notation "Interface_Method()." Methods based on the interface are declared as `Private`. This is because objects that use the class don't access methods defined by an interface via the class declaration. Instead, they use the interface declaration to access the methods of that interface. This is shown in detail in the section "Applying Interfaces."

```
'Create a class file and set its name property to the name of the class
Implements IInterface
'Declare the method
Private Sub IInterface_Method(Param1 As Integer)
  ...
End Sub
```

VB .NET

Use the `Implements` keyword after the class declaration and also use it after each method declaration. You are allowed to use member names that are different than the interface member they are based off of. This isn't allowed in the other languages. Note that even though the member names can be different, they still need to have the same parameter list.

```
Public Class aClass
   Implements IInterface
   'Use the same name As the interface
   Public Sub Method(param1 As Integer) Implements IInterface.Method
      ...
   End Sub
   'Demonstrate using a different name than what is declared in the interface
   Public Sub Method2(param1 As Integer) Implements _
      IInterface.Method
      ...
   End Sub
End Interface
```

C#

Use a colon (:) after the class name to designate its interface. Using the interface name in the method declaration is optional. This is usually done when there are multiple interfaces and you need to resolve the name conflict. That is described in the next section, "Implementing Multiple Interfaces."

```
public class aClass : IInterface{
   //Don't use the interface name in the declaration
   public void Method(int param1){
      ...
   }
}
```

```
public class aClass2 : IInterface{
   //Demonstrate using the interface name in the declaration
   public void IInterface.Method(int param1){
      ...
   }
}
```

Implementing Multiple Interfaces

Implementing multiple interfaces simply requires that you list the other interfaces in the class declaration. You must use caution with multiple interfaces because there can be naming conflicts with the methods from different interfaces. This is handled differently by each language. In VB 6.0 you can only implement a method from a class by referencing one of the interfaces. The interface you reference determines which method will be accessed. In VB .NET you resolve the conflict by declaring the methods with different names and mapping each one to a different interface. C# allows you to declare both methods using the same name, but when you reference them you must specify which interface you intend to use.

VB 6.0

For each interface use the Implements keyword on a separate line. This examples assumes that there is an Interface2 that declares a method Method2(Param1 As Integer).

```
'Create a class file and set its name property to the name of the class
Implements IInterface1
Implements Iinterface2
'Declare the method
Private Sub IInterface1_Method1(Param1 As Integer)
  ...
End Sub
Private Sub IInterface2_Method2(Param1 As Integer)
  ...
End Sub
```

VB .NET

For each interface use the Implements keyword on a separate line.

```
Public Class aClass
  Implements IInterface1
  Implements IInterface2

  Public Sub Method1(param1 As Integer) Implements IInterface1.Method1
    ...
  End Sub
  Public Sub Method2(param1 As Integer) Implements IInterface2.Method2
    ...
  End Sub
End Class
```

C#

Use a colon (:) after the class name to designate an interface. Separate each interface with a comma.

```csharp
public class aClass : IInterface1, IInterface2{
  void IInterface1.Method1(int param1){
    ...
  }
  void IInterface2.Method2(int param1){
    ...
  }
}
```

Applying Interfaces

Creating an object variable based off of a standard class is relatively simple compared to basing it off a class that is based off of an interface. Each language handles this differently.

When working with a class, you need to know how to test which interface and methods it supports. This can get complicated when you work with multiple interfaces.

VB 6.0

If you look back at the "Implementing an Interface" section, you will see that the methods within the class are declared as `Private`. This is because objects based off of a class do not use the class declaration to access its methods. Instead, the interface declaration is used to determine which methods a class supports. This is done in multiple steps. First, declare an object variable of the proper class. Second, create an instance of the object. Third, declare an object variable from the interface. Then assign that variable to the first object and access its methods. Sound complicated? It's a good thing that .NET cleans up this process.

```vb
'Demonstrate applying multiple interfaces
Dim oMain As CInterface
Dim oInterface1 As IInterface1
Dim oInterface2 As IInterface2

'Instantiate the object from the class
Set oMain = New CInterface
'Access the methods from IInterface1
Set oInterface1 = oMain
```

```
Call oInterface1.Method()
'Access the methods from IInterface2
Set oInterface2 = oMain
Call oInterface2.Method()
```

VB .NET

There is nothing unusual about declaring an object from a class that uses interfaces. Simply declare it like you would declare any other class. If a class is derived from multiple interfaces and there is a name conflict that isn't resolved, use casting to specify which interface is to be used.

You can test if an object supports a given interface using the TypeOf statement. If an object does support an interface, you can reference that interface by using an explicit cast. VB .NET uses the CType() statement to cast an object as new class or interface. The first parameter is the object variable and the second parameter is the class or interface name.

```
'Declare an object using an explicit cast
Dim myBaseClass As New aClass()
Dim myNewClass As IInterface
myNewClass = myBaseClass

'Test if an object supports an interface
If TypeOf myObject Is IInterface Then ...

'Cast an object variable using the CType() function
Dim myObject As New aClass()
Dim myNewClass As IInterface
myNewClass = CType(myObject, IInterface)

'Demonstrate using an object based off of a class that uses multiple interfaces.
'The class is defined in the section "Implementing Multiple Interfaces".

Dim myObject As New aClass()
Dim var As Integer
'Use IInterface1
myObject.Method1(var)
'Use IInterface2
myObject.Method2(var)
```

C#

Declaring an object from a class that uses interfaces is the same as declaring any object.

You can test if a class supports a given interface using the `is` operator. You can reference the class as a given interface by either using an explicit cast or using the `as` operator. Note that if a class doesn't support the interface, an error will be raised.

```
//Declare an object based off an existing object using the "as" operator
IInterface myNewClass = myBaseClass as IInterface;

//Declare an object based off an existing object using an explicit cast
IInterface myNewClass = (IInterface)myBaseClass;

//Test if a class supports an interface
if (aClass is IInterface) {}


/*Demonstrate using an object based off of a class that uses multiple interfaces.
The class is defined in the section "Implementing Multiple Interfaces." Note
that the member "Method" is declared in both interfaces and this naming conflict
must be resolved.
Call methods of an interface using an explicit cast
Note the use of parentheses. The interface cast is within a set of parentheses
so that the method will be called on the resulting object reference */
aClass myObject = new aClass();
((Interface1)myObject).Method();
((Interface2)myObject).Method();
```

Example 7-1. Managing a Checking Account

The following example demonstrates a program that manages someone's checking account. A user can deposit or withdraw money from his or her account by calling the `Deposit` and `Withdraw` methods of the `CCheckingAccount` class. The status of each transaction is displayed on the console. This will confirm that the transaction took place as well as notify the user when there are insufficient funds. If a user tries to withdraw more money than is in his or her account, the transaction fails.

An interface is created for `ICredit` and `IDebit`. The class `CChecking` account implements both of these interfaces. The `StatusMessage` method is defined in both interfaces and must be resolved.

VB 6.0

```
'Manage a checking account using VB 6.0
'Copyright (c)2001 by Bischof Systems, Inc.

Private Sub Main()
    Dim CheckingAccount As CCheckingAccount
    'These objects are used to reference each interface method in CheckingAccount
    Dim oCredit As ICredit
    Dim oDebit As IDebit
    Set CheckingAccount = New CCheckingAccount
    Set oCredit = CheckingAccount
    Set oDebit = CheckingAccount
    'Run the checking account batch
    CheckingAccount.Init
    oCredit.Deposit 500
    oDebit.WriteCheck 400
    oDebit.WriteCheck 75
    oDebit.WriteCheck 50
    Set CheckingAccount = Nothing
End Sub


'ICredit interface
Public Sub Deposit(Amount As Double)
End Sub
Public Sub StatusMessage(Message As String)
End Sub


'IDebit interface
Public Sub WriteCheck(Amount As Double)
End Sub
Public Sub StatusMessage(Message As String)
End Sub


'CCheckingAccount class
Implements ICredit
Implements IDebit
Private m_CurrentBalance As Double
Const m_MinimumBalance = 100
Public Sub Init(Optional BeginningBalance As Double)
    m_CurrentBalance = BeginningBalance
End Sub
```

```
'Deposit money into the checking account
Private Sub ICredit_Deposit(Amount As Double)
    m_CurrentBalance = m_CurrentBalance + Amount
    ICredit_StatusMessage "Deposited $" & Amount & "; Current balance is $" & _
        m_CurrentBalance
End Sub
Private Sub ICredit_StatusMessage(Message As String)
    Debug.Print Message
End Sub
Private Sub IDebit_StatusMessage(Message As String)
    Debug.Print Message
End Sub
'Withdraw money from the checking account
Private Sub IDebit_WriteCheck(Amount As Double)
    'Check to make sure the balance won't go below zero
    If (m_CurrentBalance - Amount) >= 0 Then
        m_CurrentBalance = m_CurrentBalance - Amount
        'Log that the transaction took place
        IDebit_StatusMessage "Withdrew $" & Amount & "; New Balance is $" & _
            m_CurrentBalance
        'Check if the minimum balance was reached
        If m_CurrentBalance < m_MinimumBalance Then
            'Log that it went below the minimum balance
            IDebit_StatusMessage "You are below the minimum balance of $" & _
                m_MinimumBalance
        End If
    Else
        'Log that there weren't enough funds
        IDebit_StatusMessage "Insufficient funds - $" & Amount & _
            " was not withdrawn"
    End If
End Sub
```

VB .NET

```
'Manage a checking account using VB .NET
'Copyright (c)2001 by Bischof Systems, Inc.

Module Module1
    Sub Main()
        'Run the checking account batch
        Dim CheckingAccount As New CCheckingAccount()
        CheckingAccount.Deposit(500)
        CheckingAccount.Withdraw(400)
```

```
        CheckingAccount.Withdraw(75)
        CheckingAccount.Withdraw(50)
        Console.ReadLine()
End Sub
Public Interface ICredit
    Sub Deposit(ByVal Amount As Double)
    Sub StatusMessage(ByVal Message As String)
End Interface
Public Interface IDebit
    Sub WriteCheck(ByVal Amount As Double)
    Sub StatusMessage(ByVal Message As String)
End Interface

Public Class CCheckingAccount
    Implements IDebit
    Implements ICredit
    Shared MinimumBalance As Double = 100
    Shared LogFile As IO.StreamWriter
    Private CurrentBalance As Double
    'Standard constructor
    Public Sub New()
    End Sub
    'Deposit money into the checking account
    Public Sub Deposit(ByVal Amount As Double) Implements ICredit.Deposit
        CurrentBalance += Amount
        StatusMessage(String.Format("Deposited ${0}; New Balance is " & _
            "${1}", Amount, CurrentBalance))
    End Sub
    'Withdraw money from the checking account
    Public Sub Withdraw(ByVal Amount As Double) Implements IDebit.WriteCheck
        'Check to make sure it isn't below zero
        If (CurrentBalance - Amount) >= 0 Then
            CurrentBalance -= Amount
            'Log that the transaction took place
            StatusMessage(String.Format("Withdrew ${0}; " & _
                "New Balance is ${1}", Amount, CurrentBalance))
            'Check if the minimum balance was reached
            If CurrentBalance < MinimumBalance Then
                'Log that it went below the minimum balance
                StatusMessage(String.Format("You are below the " & _
                    "minimum balance of ${0}", MinimumBalance))
            End If
```

```
            Else
                'Log that there weren't enough funds
                StatusMessage(String.Format("Insufficient funds - ${0} " & _
                    "was not withdrawn", Amount))
            End If
        End Sub
        'This demonstrates using one method to implement two different interfaces
        Public Sub StatusMessage(ByVal Message As String) _
            Implements ICredit.StatusMessage, IDebit.StatusMessage
            Console.WriteLine(Message)
        End Sub
    End Class
End Module
```

C#

```
//Manage a checking account using C#
//Copyright (c)2001 by Bischof Systems, Inc.

using System;

namespace C_Interfaces
{
    class Class1
    {
        [STAThread]
        static void Main(string[] args)
        {
            RunCheckingAccount();
            Console.ReadLine();
        }
        //Run the checking account batch
        static void RunCheckingAccount()
        {
            CCheckingAccount CheckingAccount = new CCheckingAccount();
            CheckingAccount.Deposit(500);
            CheckingAccount.WriteCheck(400);
            CheckingAccount.WriteCheck(75);
            CheckingAccount.WriteCheck(50);
        }
```

```
public interface IDebit
{
    void WriteCheck(double Amount);
    void StatusMessage(string Message);
}
public interface ICredit
{
    void Deposit(double Amount);
    void StatusMessage(string Message);
}

public class CCheckingAccount: IDebit, ICredit
{
    static double MinimumBalance = 100;
    private double CurrentBalance;
    //Standard constructor
    public CCheckingAccount()
    {}
    //Deposit money into the checking account
    public void Deposit(double Amount)
    {
        CurrentBalance += Amount;
        StatusMessage(String.Format("Deposited ${0}; New Balance is " +
            "${1}", Amount, CurrentBalance));
    }
    //Withdraw money from the checking account
    public void WriteCheck(double Amount)
    {
        //Check to make sure it isn't below zero
        if ((CurrentBalance - Amount) > 0)
        {
            CurrentBalance -= Amount;
            //Log that the transaction took place
            StatusMessage(String.Format("Withdrew ${0}; New Balance " +
                "is ${1}", Amount, CurrentBalance));
            if (CurrentBalance < MinimumBalance)
            {
                //Log that they are below the minimum balance
                StatusMessage(String.Format("You are below the " +
                    "minimum balance of ${0}", MinimumBalance));
            }
        }
```

```
                else
                {
                    //Log that there weren't enough funds
                    StatusMessage(String.Format("Insufficient funds - ${0} " +
                        "was not withdrawn", Amount));
                }
            }
            public void StatusMessage(string Message)
            {
                Console.WriteLine(Message);
            }
        }
    }
}
```

Example 7-1 Output

```
Deposited $500; Current balance is $500
Withdrew $400; New Balance is $100
Withdrew $75; New Balance is $25
You are below the minimum balance of $100
Insufficient funds - $50 was not withdrawn
```

CHAPTER 8
Class Inheritance

Table 8-1. Class Inheritance Equivalent Chart

VB .NET	C#
MyBase	base
Overridable	virtual
Overrides	override
MustInherit	abstract
NotInheritable	sealed
Public Class derivedClass Inherits myBaseClass	public class derivedClass: myBaseClass

Public Sub New()
    MyBase.New()
	public derivedClass():
	    base()

Overview

Class inheritance is the process of a class deriving all the functionality of another class. Thus, the derived class now has the methods and properties of the base class. This is very similar to implementing a class interface, with the exception that the interface doesn't have any functionality built into it. An *interface* is a set of public method signatures that must be implemented by a class.

Inheritance is a very complex topic and it is not the purpose of this chapter to teach proper inheritance techniques. This chapter covers the syntax requirements for using inheritance.[1]

Inheriting a Class

There are two steps involved with inheriting a class: writing the base class and writing the derived class so that it refers to the base class. The details of writing

---

1. The VB 6.0 language doesn't implement class inheritance. Thus, VB 6.0 will not be referenced in this chapter.

a class are discussed in Chapter 6. This chapter focuses on the changes to a class so that another class can inherit it.

Let's define a simple base class and derive a new class from it. Notice that the derived class here doesn't do anything other than state that it inherits from BaseClass. Although this doesn't serve much of a purpose, it is perfectly acceptable because a derived class will inherit all the functionality of its base class. Thus, the derived class can do anything that the base class does, even though the derived class has no code. This isn't possible when you are implementing an interface.

VB .NET

```
Public Class myBaseClass
    Public Var As Integer
    Public Function MethodName(Param1 as String) As String

        ...
    End Function
End Class


Public Class DerivedClass
    Inherits myBaseClass
End Class
```

C#

```
public class myBaseClass
{
    public int var;
    public string MethodName(string Param1)
    {
        ...
    }
}

public class DerivedClass: myBaseClass
{
}
```

Extending the Base Class with New Methods

You can extend the functionality of the base class by adding new methods to the derived class.

The syntax for adding methods that are not in the base class is the same as adding a method in a standard class. You declare and implement the method as you normally would. The modifiers `Public`, `Private`, and `Friend`/`internal` are available, as well as `Protected` and `Protected Friend`/`internal`.

The scope modifiers for method declarations need to be looked at to see how they affect derived classes. These modifiers also apply to writing the base class.

- The `Private` modifier only allows a method to be accessed from within its own class. Not even classes that are derived from it can access the method.

- The `Protected` modifier is similar to `Private`, but it allows a method to be accessed from a derived class. Object variables that reference an instance of the class cannot access the method.

- The `Friend`/`internal` modifier allows a method to be accessed from an object variable that is an instance of the class as long as it is within the same program.

- The `Protected Friend`/`internal` modifier is a combination of the two. It can be accessed in the following ways: from a derived class and from within an instance of it in the same program. But it can't be accessed from anywhere outside the program.

VB .NET

This is a standard method declaration. The method modifiers are placed before the `Sub`/`Function` keyword. After the method declaration, use the `Inherits` keyword followed by the name of the base class.

```
Public Class DerivedClass
    Inherits myBaseClass
    Protected Friend Sub Method2()
        ...
    End Sub
End Class
```

C#

This is a standard method declaration. The method modifiers are placed before the data type of the method. After the method declaration, use a colon (:) followed by the name of the base class.

```
public class DerivedClass: myBaseClass
{
    protected internal void Method2()
    {
        ...
    }
}
```

Overriding Existing Methods

Overriding an existing method in the base class allows you to either add or replace the functionality of the method. When implementing the method in the derived class, you are allowed to call the same method in the parent class. Thus, you are using the method in the parent class and adding more functionality to it. You can replace the functionality in the parent class by overriding the method and not calling the parent's implementation of it.

Overriding a method consists of two steps. The first step is to declare the method in the base class with a modifier so that the compiler knows that it can be overridden. VB .NET uses the Overridable modifier and C# uses the virtual modifier. The second step is to declare the method in the derived class with a modifier so that the compiler knows it will override the parent's method. VB .NET uses the Overrides modifier and C# uses the override modifier. You add functionality to the method by calling the parent class' implementation of it. VB .NET does this using the MyBase keyword. C# uses the base keyword. You can determine when the parent method is implemented by calling it either at the beginning or at the end of the method.

The benefit of overriding methods is that when you declare a generic object variable as a base class and assign a derived class to that variable, calling the methods of the object variable will implement functionality in the derived class. For example, let's say you want to write a method that has a parameter that can be one of many derived classes. You create the method with a parameter declared as the base class. An external client can call it and pass it any derived class. The method will implement the functionality in the derived class. Even though the method declares the parameter to be of the base class, the derived class functionality will be what is implemented. This is demonstrated in Example 8-1 at the end of the chapter.

VB .NET

The method declaration in the base class uses the `Overridable` modifier. The method in the derived class uses the `Overrides` modifier.

```
Pubic Class myBaseClass
    Public Overridable Sub Method()
        ...
    End Sub
End Class

Public Class DerivedClass
    Inherits myBaseClass
    Public Overrides Sub Method()
        MyBase.Method()
        ...
    End Sub
End Class
```

C#

The method declaration in the base class uses the `virtual` modifier. The method in the derived class uses the `override` modifier. Static and abstract methods cannot be declared as virtual.

```
public class myBaseClass
{
    public virtual void Method()
    {
        ...
    }
}

public class DerivedClass: myBaseClass
{
    public override void Method()
    {
        base.Method();
        ...
    }
}
```

Inheriting Constructors

Constructor methods are unique because they can't be inherited. As stated earlier, when a class inherits another class, it automatically inherits all its methods and properties, but this isn't the case with constructors. You must redeclare them.

By default, a parameterless constructor is created by the compiler for each class if you didn't do so. However, if you want to declare a constructor in your base class and have all the derived classes use it, you must declare it in each derived class. Once you declare it in the derived class, you can have it call the constructor in the base class and its functionality will also be implemented. If a constructor has parameters, you can pass these parameters to the base class constructor. If you want to implement additional functionality, call the base class constructor first to ensure that all base instance variables are initialized by their variable initializers before any statements that have access to the instance are executed.

VB .NET

When you declare a constructor in a derived class, use the `MyBase` keyword to call the base class constructor.

```
Public Class DerivedClass
    Inherits myBaseClass
    Public Sub New()
        MyBase.New()
    End Sub
    Public Sub New(Param1 as String)
        MyBase.New(Param1)
    End Sub
End Class
```

C#

When you declare a constructor in a derived class, use the `base` keyword to call the base class constructor. It has to appear immediately after the constructor declaration and before the curly bracket.

```
public class DerivedClass: myBaseClass
{
    public DerivedClass()
    :base()
    {}
    public DerivedClass(string Param1)
    :base(Param1)
    {}
}
```

Forcing Inheritance

When you want to require a class to act as a base class, inheritance can be required. This means that an object variable can't be instantiated from this class—it must be instantiated from a derived class. This is similar to an interface except that the class implements functionality within its methods.

VB .NET

Use the `MustInherit` keyword to force inheritance.

```
Public MustInherit Class myBaseClass
```

C#

Use the `abstract` keyword to force inheritance.

```
public abtract class myBaseClass
```

Preventing Inheritance

Inheriting a class from a derived class can be prevented.

VB .NET

Use the `NotInheritable` keyword to prevent inheritance.

```
Public NotInhertiable Class myFinalClass
```

C#

Use the `sealed` keyword to prevent inheritance.

```
public sealed class myFinalClass
```

Example 8-1. Calculating the Price of Items for Sale

This example uses classes to calculate items for sale. The base class, `Item`, does two things: The constructor forces an item description to be all uppercase and the method `TotalPrice()` calculates the price to sell an item for. The `TotalPrice()` method is overloaded so that it will calculate the total price when passed the quantity sold and a unit price, or just the unit price.

The `Book` class inherits from the `Item` class. The constructor is written so that if it is initialized without a name, "Book" is assigned to it by default. The

`TotalPrice()` method is overridden so that it calls the base class method and then discounts the price by 25 percent.

The method `PrintInfo()` in `Main()` declares the `Product` object variable as type `Item`. When it is called by the `Main()` method, it is passed objects of type `Item` and `Book`. Because the `TotalPrice()` method is overridden, the `PrintInfo()` method will call the correct implementation of `TotalPrice()`.

VB .NET

```
'Calculate the price of items for sale using VB .NET
'Copyright (c)2001 by Bischof Systems, Inc.

Module Module1
    Sub Main()
        Dim Magazine As New Item("Magazine")
        Dim Bestseller As New Book()
        PrintInfo(Magazine, 10)
        PrintInfo(Bestseller, 5, 15)
        Console.ReadLine()
    End Sub
    Public Sub PrintInfo(ByVal Product As Item, ByVal Price As Double)
        Console.WriteLine("Price of 1 {0} is {1}", Product.Description, _
            Product.TotalPrice(Price))
    End Sub
    Public Sub PrintInfo(ByVal Product As Item, ByVal Qty As Integer, _
        ByVal Price As Double)
        Console.WriteLine("Price of {0} {1}S is {2}", Qty, _
            Product.Description, Product.TotalPrice(Qty, Price))
    End Sub

    Public Class Item
        Public Description As String
        'Constructor code - Force the item name to uppercase
        Public Sub New()
            Me.New("")
        End Sub
        Public Sub New(ByVal Description As String)
            Me.Description = Description.ToUpper()
        End Sub
        'Calculate the total price for all items - the quantity is optional
        Public Overridable Function TotalPrice(ByVal Price As Double) As Double
            Return Me.TotalPrice(1, Price)
        End Function
```

```
        Public Overridable Function TotalPrice(ByVal Qty As Integer, _
            ByVal Price As Double) As Double
            Return Qty * Price
        End Function
    End Class


    'This class calculates the price of books
    Public Class Book
        Inherits Item
        'Constructor code
        Public Sub New()
            'If no description is supplied, use the default of "Book"
            Me.New("Book")
        End Sub
        Public Sub New(ByVal Description As String)
            MyBase.New(Description)
        End Sub
        'Books are sold at a 25% discount
        Public Overloads Overrides Function TotalPrice(ByVal Qty As Integer, _
            ByVal Price As Double) As Double
            Dim Total As Double
            Total = MyBase.TotalPrice(Qty, Price)
            Total *= 0.75
            Return Total
        End Function
    End Class
End Module
```

C#

```
//Calculate the price of items for sale using C#
//Copyright (c)2001 by Bischof Systems, Inc.

using System;

namespace C_Inheritance
{
    class Class1
    {
        [STAThread]
        static void Main(string[] args)
```

```csharp
        {
            Item Magazine = new Item("Magazine");
            Book Bestseller = new Book();
            PrintInfo(Magazine, 10);
            PrintInfo(Bestseller, 5, 15);
            Console.ReadLine();
        }
        static void PrintInfo(Item Product, double Price)
        {
            Console.WriteLine("Price of 1 {0} is {1}", Product.Description,
                    Product.TotalPrice(Price));
        }
        static void PrintInfo(Item Product, int Qty, double Price)
        {
            Console.WriteLine("Price of {0} {1}S is {2}", Qty,
                Product.Description, Product.TotalPrice(Qty, Price));
        }
    }

    public class Item
    {
        public string Description;
        //Constructor code - Force the item name to uppercase
        public Item():
            this("")
        {}
        public Item(string Description)
        {
            this.Description = Description.ToUpper();
        }
        //Calculate the total price for all items - the quantity is optional
        public virtual double TotalPrice(double Price)
        {
            return this.TotalPrice(1, Price);
        }
        public virtual double TotalPrice(int Qty, double Price)
        {
            return Qty * Price;
        }
    }
```

```
//This class calculates the price of books
public class Book: Item
{
    //Constructor code
    public Book():
        this("Book")
    {} //If no description is supplied, use the default of "Book"
    public Book(string Description):
        base(Description)
    {}
    //Books are sold at a 25% discount
    public override double TotalPrice(int Qty ,double Price)
    {
        double Total;
        Total = base.TotalPrice(Qty, Price);
        Total *= 0.75;
        return Total;
    }
}
}
```

Example 8-1 Output

```
Price of 1 MAGAZINE is 10
Price of 5 BOOKS is 56.25
```

CHAPTER 9

Events

Table 9-1. Event Syntax Equivalent Chart

VB 6.0	VB .NET	C#
	`Public Delegate Sub myDelegate()`	`public delegate void myDelegate();`
`Public Event myEvent()`	`Public Event myEvent() As _` `myDelegate`	`public myDelegate myEvent;`
`RaiseEvent myEvent()`	`RaiseEvent myEvent()`	`myEvent();`
`Dim WithEvents myObject As _` `myEventClass`	`Dim WithEvents myObject As _` `myEventClass`	`myEventClass myObject;`
`Sub myObject_myEvent()`	`Sub myHandler() Handles _` `myObject.myEvent`	`void myHandler()` `{...}`

	`AddHandler myObject.myEvent, _`
	`AddressOf myHandler`
		`myObject.myEvent += new`
		`myEventClass.myDelegate`
		`(myHandler);`

	`RemoveHandler myObject.myEvent, _`
	`AddressOf myHandler`
		`myObject.myEvent -= new`
		`myEventClass.myDelegate`
		`(myHandler);`

Overview

Events are methods by which an object notifies another object that an action has occurred. Along with alerting the receiving object of the action, the sending object usually passes it some information about the action via the arguments in the parameter list. An example would be passing a string describing the status of the action.

Events are handled differently for each language. Regardless of which language you are using, declaring and handling events is a multistep process. VB 6.0 only has one way of working with events. Both of the .NET languages give you more options and flexibility when working with events. This allows you to optimize your programming code to match your needs. To show the details of how each language handles events, each step is broken out individually.

There are many steps for working with events. These steps are declaring an event, raising the event, handling the event, and linking the event to the event handler.

Declaring an Event

An event is a procedure that is triggered by an object. This trigger is in response to something happening. After being triggered, the event passes data to a receiving object through its parameter list. The parameter list is called its *signature*. It is the responsibility of the receiving object to take the information passed to it through the parameter list and process that information.

Declaring an event is very similar to declaring a class method, but there is a difference: Events don't have any code associated with them. The purpose of an event is to track a list of methods that should be called when the event is raised. When you call an event (raising it), the event goes through this list and calls each method. It passes the same data to each method. Calling the methods in the event list is handled automatically by the computer.

There are two ways to declare an event. The first way is to use the Event keyword to declare the event. Declaring it is the same as declaring any method with parameters. The second way is to use a delegate object. You should declare a delegate object when you have many events that use the same signature. This makes your code consistent and maintainable.

It is a common standard to declare the first parameter as an Object type. This is used for passing a reference to the object that raised the event. This is not required, and you can declare your events in whatever way best serves your purpose. However, when working with events raised by controls on a form, the .NET Framework always follows this convention. It is necessary in this circumstance because you often need a way to access the members of the control. Passing a reference to the control gives you this access. This chapter follows that standard as well.

Using the Event Keyword

Declaring an event is the same as declaring any other method, except that you use the Event keyword in the method declaration. C# doesn't have the Event keyword. Instead, you have to use delegates. Delegates are described next.

VB 6.0/VB .NET
Declare an event method using the Event keyword.

```
Public Event myEvent(ByVal obj As Object, ByVal Parameter As type)
```

Using a Delegate Object

Delegates are used with events as a way of defining a common signature. This delegate can be used when declaring one or more events.

In VB .NET, using delegates is optional. Delegates are beneficial when you have multiple events that use the same signature. For example, controls on a Windows Form have many events that are triggered by clicking the mouse. The .NET Framework has standardized these events by using a single delegate that passes mouse data. This ensures that events are consistent across different controls, which makes events easier to use.

After declaring the delegate, use the Event keyword to declare the event, but this time declare it as the delegate type.

C# requires that you use delegates when declaring an event. This is the case even if you only have one event that will use it.

VB. NET

Use the Delegate keyword and the event's signature to declare a delegate object.

```
Public Delegate Sub myDelegate(ByVal obj As Object, ByVal Parameter As type)
```

Declare the event using the Event keyword and the delegate name.

```
Public Event myEvent As myDelegate
```

C#

Use the delegate keyword and the event's signature to declare a delegate object.

```
public delegate void myDelegate(Object obj, type parameter);
```

Declare the event using the event keyword and the delegate name.

```
public event myDelegate myEvent;
```

Raising the Event

For an event to be used, it must be triggered with the data that is going to be passed to the event handler. This is done by calling the event from within the class it was declared and passing the appropriate data as parameters.

VB 6.0

Use the `RaiseEvent` keyword followed by the event name and the appropriate parameter data.

```
RaiseEvent myEvent (object, var)
```

VB .NET

Use the `RaiseEvent` keyword followed by the event name and the appropriate parameter data. Use the `Me` keyword to pass the current object.

```
RaiseEvent myEvent(Me, var)
```

C#

Call the event as you would any other procedure. Use the `this` keyword to pass the current object.

```
myEvent(this, var);
```

Handling the Event

The beginning of this chapter stated that events are used when an object alerts another object that an action took place. So far you have seen how to declare and raise the event from the sending object. This section shows you how to handle it with the receiving object.

To handle an event, write a method that takes the data passed by the event and process it. This method is located in the class that will be instantiated as the receiving object.

For data to be passed from the event to the method, the method and the event must have identical signatures. In other words, the arguments in their parameter lists must match. The argument names can be different, but the argument data types must be the same.

VB 6.0

VB 6.0 requires you to create a procedure by concatenating the name of the class and the event and separating them with an underscore. The naming convention is "class_event". Each event can only be handled by one procedure in a class.

```
Private Sub myObject_myEvent(ByVal obj As Object, ByVal param As type)
    ...
End Sub
```

VB .NET

Declare the procedure the same as you would declare any other procedure, but you can use any procedure name. You are not confined to using the "class_event" format that VB 6.0 imposes.

You also have to modify the procedure declaration by appending the Handles keyword at the end of the declaration along with the event name that the procedure will handle. This is described in the next section.

```
Private Sub myHandler(ByVal obj As Object, ByVal param As type) _
    Handles myObject.myEvent
  ...
End Sub
```

C#

Declare the procedure the same as you would declare any other procedure.

```
void myHandler(object obj, type param) {
  ...
}
```

Linking the Event to the Event Handler

So far you've seen how to write a class so that it can declare and raise an event, and you've seen how to write a class method to handle the event. But there is still one piece of the puzzle that is missing: how to link the event to the event handler. If the computer doesn't know that the method is supposed to handle the event, nothing will ever happen. As you might expect, each language does this differently.

VB 6.0 has a one-to-one relationship between an event and a class. Each class can only have one procedure to handle an event. In .NET this is not the case because it uses a *subscription model* for handling events. One event can be handled by multiple methods, and one method can handle multiple events. Each method has to add itself to the list of methods that the event will call. A method can also add itself to the list of many events. The only requirement is that the signature of each event must be identical.

VB 6.0 requires you to use the WithEvents keyword when declaring the object variable. This tells the compiler that the base class has one or more events declared in it. This allows you to select the event from the drop-down list in the code window.

VB .NET also uses the WithEvents keyword when declaring the object variable. In addition to that, you also have to tell the compiler which event a method will handle (subscribing to the event). Do this by using the `Handles` keyword at the end of the method declaration. A method can handle multiple events by listing all of them after the `Handles` keyword and separating them with commas.

One benefit of using the `WithEvents` keyword is that you can select an event from the drop-down list in the code editor and the `Handles` keyword is automatically added for you.

A second way to subscribe to an event in VB .NET is to use the `AddHandler` statement. Pass it the name of the event and the address of the method that will handle it. This method doesn't require declaring the object using the `WithEvents` keyword.

C# uses the `+=` operator to signify that a method is to be added to the event's list of methods to be called when the event is raised.

When using the `AddHandler` statement in VB .NET, and the `+=` operator in C#, you can't call these statements until an instance of the event object has been instantiated. If the program tries to execute these lines and the object hasn't been instantiated yet, a runtime error will occur.

If you have a complex program that uses multiple objects with an event and they are being instantiated and destroyed at different times, you should remove the event handlers manually. VB .NET uses the `RemoveHandler` statement. C# uses the `-=` operator.

You should know that just because a class declares an event, your object isn't required to use those events. For example, it's perfectly acceptable to declare the object as a class without using the `WithEvents` keyword. If you do this, the standard methods will operate as expected, but the object won't be notified of any events.

VB 6.0

Modify the class declaration to state that the class has an event. You do this by declaring the event class using the `WithEvents` keyword. This adds the class and its events to the drop-down list in the code window.

```
Private WithEvents myObject As myEventClass
```

VB .NET

There are two ways you can reference the event. The first way is to declare the event class using the `WithEvents` keyword. This adds the class and its events to the drop-down list in the code window. After you declare the object, modify the event handler by adding the `Handles` keyword at the end of the method declaration (this is the same code snippet from the last section).

```
Private WithEvents myObject As myEventClass
...
Private Sub EventHandler(ByVal param As type) _
    Handles myObject.myEvent
  ...
End Sub
```

The second way is to use the AddHandler statement. To use the AddHandler statement, write the class declaration without the WithEvents keyword. Then call the AddHandler statement by passing it the event name and the address of the method that handles the event.

```
Private myObject As myEventClass
...
AddHandler myObject.myEvent, AddressOf myHandler
```

Remove the event handler using the RemoveHandler statement. Pass it the event name and the address of the method that handles the event.

```
RemoveHandler myObject.myEvent, AddressOf myHandler
```

C#

Use the += operator to add the event-handling procedure to the class event's delegate list of procedures. This is similar to using the AddHandler statement in VB .NET.

```
myObject.myEvent += new myEventClass.myDelegate(myHandler);
```

Remove the event handler using the -= operator.

```
myObject.myEvent -= new myEventClass.myDelegate(myHandler);
```

Example 9-1. Managing a Checking Account

The following example demonstrates a program that manages someone's checking account. A user can deposit or withdraw money from his or her account by calling the Deposit and Withdraw methods of the CCheckingAccount class.

Two procedures are declared, TransactionConfirmation() and TransactionAlert(), and they handle the events from the CheckingAccount class. The CheckingAccount class declares the events Confirmation() and Alert(). After every transaction, the appropriate procedure will raise the Confirmation event and pass a descriptive string as a parameter. The TransactionConfirmation() procedure will handle the event and display a message. When the amount of money in the checking account gets below the minimum or is overdrawn, an `Alert` event is raised. The `TransactionAlert()` procedure will handle the event and display a message.

VB 6.0

```
'Managing a checking account in VB 6.0
'Copyright (c)2001 by Bischof Systems, Inc.

'Declare the class so that it can recognize the events
Dim WithEvents CheckingAccount As CCheckingAccount
Private Sub cmdExecute_Click()
    Set CheckingAccount = New CCheckingAccount
    CheckingAccount.Init 50
    CheckingAccount.Deposit 500
    CheckingAccount.Withdraw 400
    CheckingAccount.Withdraw 75
    CheckingAccount.Withdraw 50
    Set CheckingAccount = Nothing
End Sub
'Handle the Confirmation event
Private Sub CheckingAccount_Confirmation(Message As String)
    Debug.Print Message
End Sub
'Handle the Alert event
Private Sub CheckingAccount_Alert(Message As String)
    Debug.Print "Alert! " & Message
End Sub

'CCheckingAccount Class
'Declare the events that will be used
Public Event Confirmation(Message As String)
Public Event Alert(Message As String)
Private m_CurrentBalance As Double
Private m_MinimumBalance As Double
Public Sub Init(MinimumBalance As Double)
    m_MinimumBalance = MinimumBalance
End Sub
Public Property Get Balance() As Variant
    Balance = m_CurrentBalance
End Property
```

```
'Deposit money into the checking account
Public Sub Deposit(Amount As Double)
    m_CurrentBalance = m_CurrentBalance + Amount
    'Tell the user that the deposit was made
    RaiseEvent Confirmation("Deposited $" & Amount & "; Current balance is $" & _
        m_CurrentBalance)
End Sub
'Withdraw money from the checking account
Public Sub Withdraw(Amount As Double)
    'Check to make sure the balance won't go below zero
    If (m_CurrentBalance - Amount) >= 0 Then
        m_CurrentBalance = m_CurrentBalance - Amount
        'Tell the user that the withdrawal was made
        RaiseEvent Confirmation("Withdrew $" & Amount & "; New Balance is $" & _
            m_CurrentBalance)
        'Check if the minimum balance was reached
        If m_CurrentBalance < m_MinimumBalance Then
            'Raise the event that it went below the minimum balance
            RaiseEvent Alert("You are below the minimum balance of $" & _
                m_MinimumBalance)
        End If
    Else
        'Raise the event that there weren't enough funds
        RaiseEvent Alert("Insufficient funds - $" & Amount & " was not withdrawn")
    End If
End Sub
```

VB .NET

```
'Managing a checking account in VB .NET
'Copyright (c)2001 by Bischof Systems, Inc.

Module Module1
    'Declare the class so that it can recognize the events
    Private WithEvents CheckingAccount As CCheckingAccount

    Sub Main()
        CheckingAccount = New CCheckingAccount(100)
        'Subscribe to the Alert event using AddHandler statement
        AddHandler CheckingAccount.Alert, AddressOf TransactionAlert
        CheckingAccount.Deposit(500)
        CheckingAccount.Withdraw(400)
        CheckingAccount.Withdraw(75)
        CheckingAccount.Withdraw(50)
        Console.ReadLine()
    End Sub
```

```vb
'Handle the CheckingAccount.Alert event
Private Sub TransactionAlert(ByVal sender As Object, _
    ByVal Message As String)
    Console.WriteLine("Alert! {0}", message)
End Sub

'Subscribe to the Confirmation event and using Handles keyword
Private Sub TransactionConfirmation(ByVal sender As Object, _
    ByVal message As String) Handles CheckingAccount.Confirmation
    Console.WriteLine(message)
End Sub

Public Class CCheckingAccount
    'Declare the events that will be used
    Public Event Confirmation(ByVal sender As Object, _
        ByVal Message As String)
    Public Event Alert(ByVal sender As Object, ByVal Message As String)
    Private CurrentBalance As Double
    Private MinimumBalance As Double

    Public Sub New(ByVal MinimumBalance As Double)
        Me.MinimumBalance = MinimumBalance
    End Sub

    Public ReadOnly Property Balance(ByVal CurrentBalance As Double) _
        As Double
        Get
            Return Me.CurrentBalance
        End Get
    End Property

    'Deposit money into the checking account
    Public Sub Deposit(ByVal Amount As Double)
        CurrentBalance += Amount
        'Tell the user that the deposit was made
        RaiseEvent Confirmation(Me, String.Format("Deposited ${0}; " & _
            "New Balance is ${1}", Amount, CurrentBalance))
    End Sub
```

```vbnet
        'Withdraw money from the checking account
        Public Sub Withdraw(ByVal Amount As Double)
            'Check to make sure it isn't below zero
            If (CurrentBalance - Amount) >= 0 Then
                CurrentBalance -= Amount
                'Tell the user that the withdrawal was made
                RaiseEvent Confirmation(Me, String.Format("Withdrew ${0}; " & _
                    "New Balance is ${1}", Amount, CurrentBalance))
                'Check if the minimum balance was reached
                If CurrentBalance < MinimumBalance Then
                    'Raise the event that it went below the minimum balance
                    RaiseEvent Alert(Me, String.Format("You are below the " & _
                        "minimum balance of ${0}", MinimumBalance))
                End If
            Else
                'Raise the event that there weren't enough funds
                RaiseEvent Alert(Me, String.Format("Insufficient funds: " & _
                    "${0} was not withdrawn", Amount))
            End If
        End Sub
    End Class
End Module
```

C#

```csharp
//Managing a checking account in C#
//Copyright (c)2001 by Bischof Systems, Inc.

using System;

namespace C_Events
{
    class Class1
    {
        [STAThread]
        static void Main(string[] args)
        {
            //Create the object instance
            //Set the event reference for the TransactionAlert() method
            CCheckingAccount CheckingAccount = new CCheckingAccount(100);
            CheckingAccount.TransactionMessage +=
                new CCheckingAccount.AccountMessageHandler(TransactionAlert);
```

```csharp
            //Process transactions on the account
            CheckingAccount.Deposit(500);
            CheckingAccount.Withdraw(400);
            CheckingAccount.Withdraw(75);
            CheckingAccount.Withdraw(100);
            Console.ReadLine();
        }

        static void TransactionAlert(object sender, string Message)
        {
            Console.WriteLine(Message);
        }

        public class CCheckingAccount
        {
            public delegate void AccountMessageHandler(object sender,
                string message);
            public event AccountMessageHandler TransactionMessage;
            private double CurrentBalance;
            private double MinimumBalance;

            public CCheckingAccount(double MinimumBalance)
            {
                this.MinimumBalance = MinimumBalance;
            }
            public double Balance
            {
                get
                {
                    return CurrentBalance;
                }
            }
            //Deposit money into the checking account
            public void Deposit(double Amount)
            {
                CurrentBalance += Amount;
                //Tell the user that the deposit was made
                TransactionMessage(this, String.Format("Deposited ${0}; " +
                    "New Balance is ${1}", Amount, CurrentBalance));
            }

                //Withdraw money from the checking account
```

```
        public void Withdraw(double Amount)
        {
            //Check to make sure it isn't below zero
            if ((CurrentBalance - Amount) > 0)
            {
                CurrentBalance -= Amount;
                //Tell the user that the transaction took place
                Console.WriteLine("Withdrew ${0}; New Balance is ${1}",
                    Amount, CurrentBalance);
                //Check if the minimum balance was reached
                if (CurrentBalance < MinimumBalance)
                {
                    //Raise the event that they are below the minimum balance
                    TransactionMessage(this, "Warning: You are below the " +
                        "minimum balance of $" + MinimumBalance + ".");
                }
            }
            else
            {
                //Raise the event that there weren't enough funds
                TransactionMessage(this, "Insufficient Funds: $" + Amount +
                    " dollars was not withdrawn.");
            }
        }
    }
}
```

Example 9-1 Output

```
Deposited $500; Current balance is $500
Withdrew $400; New Balance is $100
Withdrew $75; New Balance is $25
Alert! You are below the minimum balance of $50
Alert! Insufficient funds - $80 was not withdrawn
```

CHAPTER 10
String Management

Table 10-1. *String Manipulation Equivalent Functions*

VB 6.0	SYSTEM.STRING	SYSTEM.STRINGBUILDER
		Append()
Asc, AscW	(int)'x' (C#)	
		Capacity
Chr	(char)n (C#)	
FormatCurrency, FormatDateTime, FormatNumber, FormatPercent	Format()	
GetChar	Chars() var[ ] (C# only)	Chars()
	Insert()	Insert()
InStr	IndexOf(), StartsWith(), EndsWith()	
InStrRev	LastIndexOf()	
Join	Join()	
LCase	ToLower()	
Left	SubString()	
Len	Length	Length
LSet	PadRight()	
LTrim	TrimStart()	
Mid	SubString()	
	Remove()	Remove()
Replace	Replace()	Replace()
Right	SubString()	
RSet	PadLeft()	
RTrim	TrimEnd()	
Space	String constructor	

Table 10-1. String Manipulation Equivalent Functions (Continued)

VB 6.0	SYSTEM.STRING	SYSTEM.STRINGBUILDER
Split	Split()	
StrComp	Compare()	
StrDup	String constructor	
StrReverse		
		ToString()
Trim	Trim()	
UCase	ToUpper()	

Table 10-2. System.Char Members[1]

MEMBER NAME	DESCRIPTION
IsControl()	Is it a control character?
IsDigit()	Is it a decimal digit?
IsLetter()	Is it a letter?
IsLetterOrDigit()	Is it a letter or a digit?
IsLower()	Is it a lowercase letter?
IsNumber()	Is it a decimal or hexadecimal digit?
IsPunctuation()	Is it a punctuation mark?
IsSeparator()	Is it a separator character?
IsSymbol()	Is it a symbol character?
IsUpper()	Is it an uppercase letter?
IsWhiteSpace()	Is it white space?
ToLower()	Convert it to lowercase.
ToUpper()	Convert it to uppercase.
ToString()	Convert it to a string.

---

1.   Source: MSDN Visual Studio .NET documentation. Use the index and type in **System.Char**.

Table 10-3. Standard Numeric Format Examples

FORMAT	ARGUMENT	OUTPUT
D or d	1234	1234
C or c	1234.5678	$1,234.57
E or e	1234.5678	1.234568e+003
F or f	1234.5678	1234.57
G or g	1234.5678	1234.5678
N or n	1234.5678	1,234.57
P or p	.123	12.30 %
X or x	10	a

Table 10-4. Custom Numeric Format Examples

FORMAT	ARGUMENT	OUTPUT
D6	1234	001234
C4	1234.5678	$1,234.5678
E4	1234.5678	1.2346e+003
F4	1234.5678	1234.5678
G4	1234.5678	1235
G6	1234.5678	1234.57
N4	1234.5678	1234.5678
N6	1234.5678	1234.567800
P4	.12345678	12.3457 %
X2	10	0a
000	1	001
###	1	1
0,000	1234	1,234
#,##0	1234	1,234
###,###.00	1234	1,234.00
00.00%	.1234	12.34%
#,##.00	-1234	-1,234.00
#,##.00;-;(#,##.00)	1234	1,234.00
#,##.00;-;(#,##.00)	0	

Table 10-4. Custom Numeric Format Examples (Continued)

FORMAT	ARGUMENT	OUTPUT
#,##.00;-;(#,##.00)	-1234	(1,234.00)
#,##.00;(#,##.00)	1234	1,234.00
#,##.00;(#,##.00)	0	0
#,##.00;(#,##.00)	-1234	(1,234.00)

Table 10-5. Standard DateTime Format Examples

FORMAT	ARGUMENT	OUTPUT
d	9/15/01	9/15/2001
D	9/15/01	Saturday, September 15, 2001
M or m	9/15/01	September 15
Y or y	9/15/01	September, 2001
s	9/15/01 8:59 PM	2001-09-15T20:59:00
f	9/15/01 8:59 PM	Saturday, September 15, 2001 8:59 PM
F	9/15/01 8:59 PM	Saturday, September 15, 2001 8:59:00 PM
g	9/15/01 8:59 PM	9/15/2001 8:59 PM
G	9/15/01 8:59 PM	9/15/2001 8:59:00 PM
t	8:59 PM	8:59 PM
T	8:59 PM	8:59:00 PM

Table 10-6. Custom DateTime Format Examples

FORMAT	ARGUMENT	OUTPUT
d/M/yy	9/1/01	9/1/01
dd/MM/yyyy	9/1/01	09/01/2001
dddd, MMMM dd, yyyy	9/01/01	Saturday, September 01, 2001
h:m:f t	9:08 PM	9:8:0 P
hh:mm:ff tt	9:08 PM	09:08:00 PM
HH:mm	9:08 PM	21:08

Overview

String manipulation consists of using different functions to modify the contents of a string. String manipulation in VB 6.0 and .NET is very similar. Although VB 6.0 uses built-in functions to modify a string and .NET uses the `System.String` class members, you can see from Table 10-1 that the functionality is almost identical between the two.

When you compare VB 6.0 to .NET, the biggest issue to be aware of is how the two languages differ when specifying the string that will be modified. VB 6.0 functions take an existing string as a parameter and return the new string. .NET uses a method of an existing string object and returns the modified string. Another important difference between VB 6.0 and the .NET classes is how you reference the first character in a string. The VB 6.0 and VB .NET built-in string functions assume the first character in a string is at index 1. The .NET classes assume the first character is at index 0.

This chapter focuses on summarizing the different string manipulation methods found in the `System.String` class and the `System.StringBuilder` class. It also points out important differences between VB 6.0 and .NET. If you are more comfortable using the functions in VB 6.0, you can still use them in .NET. VB .NET includes all the functions by default.[2] If you want to use them in C#, you need to include the library `Microsoft.VisualBasic.NET RunTime` in your project. The functions are in the `Strings` class.

Using the StringBuilder Class

One of the most important things to know about the `String` class in .NET is when not to use it. Chapter 3 explained that the drawback with using the `String` class is that it is immutable. This means that every time a change is made to a string, the system makes a copy of that string with the new data. This is not important if you are only making a few changes to a string. But if you are performing many modifications to the same string, this can adversely affect your program's performance. It is best to use the `StringBuilder` class because it will make modifications to the same memory space, which is much more efficient.

You will notice in Table 10-1 that the `StringBuilder` class doesn't have many members in it. This is because it is designed to specialize in making up for the deficiencies of the `String` class. Thus, it only needs to replace the functionality that impairs system performance. As a result of the fact that the members that have the same name as the `String` class implement the same

---

2. Although you can use all the VB 6.0 string functions in .NET, the areas dealing with VB .NET and C# will only make reference to the functionality found in the .NET namespace classes.

functionality, after this section this chapter will not make any special mention of the StringBuilder class.

The StringBuilder class works by allocating more memory than required when instantiating it. This lets the system add characters to it without having to reallocate more memory. You have the option of letting the system determine how much memory is needed for a variable, or you can call methods to manage this memory yourself. The capacity of a variable represents the total number of characters that a variable can hold without being resized. The length of a variable represents how many actual characters it currently stores. Because of this additional functionality, the StringBuilder class has some unique members that I discuss in this section.

Even though the StringBuilder class works with strings, you can't treat a StringBuilder variable as if it were a String variable. If you try to assign a string literal to it, you will get an error. To use its data with other classes, you must use the ToString() method to convert its data to a String type.

The StringBuilder class isn't a native data type in either VB .NET or C#, and therefore you need to instantiate it just like any other class. There are two primary ways to instantiate a StringBuilder object. The first way is to pass a string literal as a parameter, and this will set the initial value of the variable. The second way is to pass it an integer and this sets the capacity of the variable and initializes it to an empty string. If you don't pass the constructor anything, it will create an empty string with a capacity of 16 characters.[3] There are many more overloads for the constructor method, so you should reference MSDN for a complete list.[4]

The StringBuilder class is in the System.Text namespace.

VB .NET

Include the System.Text namespace to use the StringBuilder class. A String-Builder class can be instantiated with no parameters and it will initialize the variable to an empty string. Pass it an integer to set the initial size. Instantiate it with a string literal to set the initial value.

```
Imports System.Text
...
Dim var1 As StringBuilder = New StringBuilder()
Dim var2 As StringBuilder = New StringBuilder(10)
Dim var3 As StringBuilder
var3 = New StringBuilder("Initial String")
```

---

3. That is the default capacity as of the time this book was written. Of course, Microsoft might change the default capacity in future versions.

4. In the MSDN Help file, use the index and type in **System.StringBuilder**.

Because a `StringBuilder` object variable isn't the `String` data type, the following code *is not* valid and will cause a compiler error.

```
Dim var1 As StringBuilder = "Initial String"
Dim var2 As StringBuilder
var2 = "Initial String"
```

C#

Include the `System.Text` namespace to use the `StringBuilder` class. A `StringBuilder` class can be instantiated with no parameters and it will initialize the variable to an empty string. Pass it an integer to set the initial size. Instantiate it with a string literal to set the initial value.

```
using System.Text;
...
StringBuilder var1 = new StringBuilder(10);
StringBuilder var2 = new StringBuilder("Initial String", 50);
```

Because a `StringBuilder` object variable isn't the `String` data type, the following code *is not* valid and will cause a compiler error.

```
StringBuilder var1 = "Initial String";
StringBuilder var2;
var2 = "Initial String";
```

As a result of the fact that the `StringBuilder` class allocates more memory than immediately necessary to store a string, a few methods are unique to the `StringBuilder` class. The `Capacity` property indicates how many characters the variable can hold. The `Length` property indicates how many characters the current string uses. Once the length exceeds the capacity, additional memory is allocated and it will have additional capacity for more characters. If you are going to be making a lot of changes to a variable, you should declare an appropriate capacity in advance. My testing shows that the system only sets the capacity to be around ten characters more than the initial string length.

To add a string to the end of a variable, call the `Append()` method. The `Insert()` method inserts a string anywhere in the existing string. After working with a `StringBuilder` variable, you will need to convert it to a `String` so that it can be used with other .NET methods. Use the `ToString()` method to convert the `StringBuilder` data to a `String`.

VB .NET

The Capacity property indicates how many characters a variable can hold before being resized by the system. You can assign a value to it to change the capacity. The Length property indicates how many characters are in a string.

```
Console.WriteLine(var.Capacity)
var.Capacity = 100
Console.WriteLine(var.Length)
```

Concatenate strings at the end with the Append() method. Use the Insert() method to add a string anywhere in the existing string. The first parameter is the position to insert the new string, which is the second parameter.

```
var.Append("additional text")
var.Insert(2, "inserted text")
```

When you need to use a StringBuilder variable with other .NET objects that expect a string variable, convert it to a string using the ToString() method.

```
myString = var.ToString()
```

C#

The Capacity property indicates how many characters a variable can hold before being resized by the system. You can assign a value to it to change the capacity. The Length property indicates how many characters are in a string.

```
Console.WriteLine(var.Capacity);
var.Capacity = 100;
Console.WriteLine(var.Length);
```

Concatenate strings at the end with the Append() method.

```
var.Append("additional text");
```

Use the Insert() method to add a string anywhere in the existing string. The first parameter is the position to insert the new string, which is the second parameter.

```
var.Insert(2, "inserted text");
```

When you need to use a StringBuilder variable with other .NET objects that expect a string variable, convert it to a string using the ToString() method.

```
myString = var.ToString();
```

Working with Characters

Because a string is an array of characters, it is important to know how to manage the characters. It seems to me that knowing how to use characters is the most difficult part of using strings because every language I've programmed in handles them differently. Of course, VB 6.0 and the .NET languages are no exception. VB .NET has one way of handling characters and C# has another. However, in both languages the data type that handles characters is Char.

VB 6.0 makes working with characters easy. This is because it treats characters as strings of length 1. Hence, a one-character string is simply a character. If you want to find out the ASCII equivalent, call the Asc() function. To convert an integer to a character, use the Chr() function.

VB .NET doesn't let you assign a one-character string to the Char data type. It considers Char and String to be different data types and requires you to convert between the two. To assign a character literal to a Char variable, surround it by double quotes and put a lowercase *c* after the last quote. If you want to find the ASCII equivalent, use the Asc() function. Convert an integer to a character using the Chr() method. The Asc() and Chr() functions are built-in functions. The System.String class doesn't have equivalent methods.

C# also considers the char data type to be different from strings. To assign a character literal to a variable, surround it with single quotes. If you want to find the ASCII equivalent, cast it as an int data type. To convert an integer to a character, cast it as a char data type.

The System.Char namespace has some great functionality for analyzing characters. The methods use a naming convention of To followed by a description. Table 10-2 lists the different members of the Char class. Because these methods have a parameter of a single Char variable and their names are self-explanatory, I won't discuss them in detail. But it is important to be aware of them because they can eliminate a lot of coding you would otherwise be required to write for analyzing a character.

VB 6.0

A character is defined as a string of length 1.

```
Dim var As String
var = "x"
```

Use the Asc() function to convert a character to its ASCII equivalent.

```
Asc("x")
```

Use the `Chr()` function to convert an integer to a character.

```
Chr(var)
```

VB .NET

A character literal is assigned to a `Char` variable by surrounding it with double quotes and adding a *c* at the end.

```
Dim var As Char
var = "x"c
```

Use the `Asc()` function to convert a character to its ASCII equivalent.

```
Asc("x"c)
```

Use the `Chr()` function to convert an integer to a character.

```
Chr(num)
```

Call the `Is__()` methods by passing a character variable as the parameter. It returns `True` or `False` depending on whether or not the character matches the description.

```
If Char.IsNumber(var) Then
    ...
End If
```

C#

A character literal is assigned to a `char` variable by surrounding it with single quotes.

```
char var;
var = 'x';
```

To convert a character to its ASCII equivalent, cast the character as an `int`.

```
(int)var;
```

To convert an integer to a character, cast the integer as a `char`.

```
(char)num;
```

Call the Is__() methods by passing a character variable as the parameter. It returns true or false depending on whether or not the character matches the description.

```
if Char.IsLower(var)
{
    ...
}
```

Using String Functions

The String class provides nearly identical functionality that exists with the built-in functions in VB 6.0. This section provides an overview of the methods so you can see how they work. Each method has many overrides that you can use with it. This chapter shows you the most common ways of using each method. Consult MSDN for a complete listing of each method override.[5]

Filling a String with a Character

Filling a string with a character consists of initializing a string with the same character. This can be useful when you are using strings for formatting output and filling in a string with spaces so that it can be a consistent length.

VB 6.0 uses the Space() function to return a certain number of spaces and it uses the StrDup() function to enable you to duplicate a character other than a space. .NET uses the constructor of the String class to do this. The first parameter is the character to use and the second parameter is an integer specifying how many times to repeat it.

You can insert a certain quantity of the same character before or after a string by using concatenation. However, this requires you to do some calculations using the current string length and the new string length. There are two functions in VB 6.0 that make this easy. LSet() shifts the string to the leftmost position and fills the right portion of the string with spaces. RSet() works the same way except that the string is shifted to the rightmost position. .NET uses the PadRight() method to shift a string to the left and pad the right side with a character. PadLeft() shifts the string to the right and pads the left side with a character.

---

5.   In the MSDN Help file, use the index and type in **System.String class**.

VB 6.0

The `Space()` function requires an integer that specifies the size of the string. `StrDup()` requires an integer and the character to duplicate.

```
var1 = Space(integer)
var2 = StrDup(integer, "x")
```

The `LSet()` and `RSet()` functions both require the original string and the length of the new string.

```
var1 = LSet("string data", integer)
var2 = RSet(var3, integer)
```

VB .NET

The constructor of the `String` class is used to initialize a string variable to a certain length and fill it with a default character. Pass it a character as the first parameter and an integer as the second parameter.

```
Dim var As String = New String("x"c , integer)
```

The `PadLeft()` and `PadRight()` functions operate on an existing string variable. Pass an integer to specify the total length of the string. Pass a character as the second parameter if you don't want to use the default space character.

```
var = var.PadLeft(integer)
var = var.PadRight(integer, "x"c)
```

C#

The constructor of the `string` class is used to initialize a string variable to a certain length and fill it with a default character. Pass it a character as the first parameter and an integer as the second parameter.

```
string var = new String('c', integer);
```

The `PadLeft()` and `PadRight()` methods operate on an existing string variable. Pass an integer to specify the total length of the string. Pass a character as the second parameter if you don't want to use the default space character.

```
var = var.PadLeft(integer);
var = var.PadRight(integer, 'c');
```

Trimming a String

Trimming a string is the opposite of filling it: You are removing a certain character from the beginning or the end of a string. This can be useful when you are saving or printing data and you don't want to waste space.

VB 6.0 uses three functions to trim characters. LTrim() and RTrim() remove spaces from either the left side or the right side of a string. Trim() removes spaces from the beginning and the end of a string.

.NET has identical functionality to VB 6.0. TrimStart() and TrimEnd() remove white space from either the beginning or the end of a string.[6] Trim() removes white space from both sides. Instead of trimming white space, you can specify one or more characters and it will remove any occurrences of these characters from the string. Of course, this only applies to the beginning and/or end of a string as defined by the method definition.

VB 6.0

All the Trim() functions work by passing them a string. They return the modified version.

```
var1 = LTrim(var2)
var3 = RTrim("string data          ")
var4 = Trim("     string data     ")
```

VB .NET

All the Trim() functions modify an existing string. You can specify the character to trim instead of using the default white space. To trim more than one character, pass each one as a separate parameter.

```
var1 = var1.TrimStart()
var2 = var2.TrimEnd()
var3 = var3.Trim("x"c)
'Demonstrate trimming any comma and period from the both sides of the string
var4 = "..,..,.string data...,.."
var4 = var4.Trim("."c, ","c)
'var4 is now "string data"
```

---

6. You may think that white space only refers to the single space character (ASCII 32). However, MSDN Visual Studio .NET documentation defines white space characters as hexadecimal 0x9(TAB), 0xA(LF), 0xB(VT), 0xC(FF), 0xD(CR), 0x20(Space), 0xA0, 0x2000, 0x2001, 0x2002, 0x2003, 0x2004, 0x2005, 0x2006, 0x2007, 0x2008, 0x2009, 0x200A, 0x200B, 0x3000, and 0xFEFF.

C#

All the `Trim` functions modify an existing string. You can specify the character to trim instead of using the default white space. To trim more than one character, pass each one as a separate parameter.

```
var1 = var1.TrimStart();
var2 = var2.TrimEnd();
var3 = var3.Trim();
//Demonstrate trimming the number 1 from only the left side of the string
var4 = "1111string 1 data 1 1";
var4 = var4.TrimStart("1");
//var4 is now "string 1 data 1 1"
```

Modifying the String Contents

You can modify a string by changing the characters within a string. In the beginning of this chapter, I stated that making modifications to a string variable is not as efficient as using the `StringBuilder` class. However, if you are only making a few changes, instantiating a new `StringBuilder` class isn't worth the additional overhead. You should use the methods of the `String` class instead.

There are a variety of ways to modify the characters of a string. The most basic way is to concatenate two strings together. VB 6.0 and VB .NET both let you use either the & operator or the + operator to concatenate two strings. C# only allows the use of a + operator.

All languages allow you to replace a certain string with another string using the `Replace()` function. You have to specify the string to find and the string to replace it with. The .NET language has a `Remove()` method that lets you specify a substring to find and it deletes it. The other characters are left in the string. This same result can be achieved by calling the `Replace()` method and specifying an empty string as the replacement string. You can insert a string anywhere in an existing string with the .NET `Insert()` method.

You can also convert a string to uppercase or lowercase. VB 6.0 uses the `UCase()` and `LCase()` functions to convert a string to uppercase or lowercase. .NET uses the methods `ToUpper()` and `ToLower()`.

VB 6.0

Concatenate two strings together by separating them with either the & operator or the + operator.

```
var1 = "string1" & "string2"
var2 = "string1" + "string2"
```

The `Replace()` function returns a new string when given the original string, the string to delete, and a replacement string.

```
var = Replace(myString, "StringToDelete", "ReplacementString")
```

Convert a string to uppercase with the `UCase()` function and to lowercase with the `LCase()` function.

```
var1 = UCase("stringdata")
var2 = LCase("STRINGDATA")
```

VB .NET

Concatenate two strings together by separating them with either the & operator or the + operator.

```
var1 = "string1" & "string2"
var2 = "string1" + "string2"
```

The `Replace()` method works on an existing string. Pass it the string to delete and a replacement string.

```
var = var.Replace("StringToDelete", "ReplacementString")
```

The `Insert()` method works on an existing string. Pass it an integer representing where it should start (0 is the beginning) and the string to insert.

```
var = var.Insert(integer, "NewString")
'Demonstrate inserting a string at the beginning
var = var.Insert(0, "NewString")
```

C#

Concatenate two strings together by separating them with the + operator.

```
var = "string1" + "string2";
```

The `Replace()` method works on an existing string. Pass it the string to delete and a replacement string.

```
var = var.Replace("StringToDelete", "ReplacementString");
```

The `Insert()` method works on an existing string. Pass it an integer representing where it should start (0 is the beginning) and the string to insert.

```
var = var.Insert(integer, "NewString");
//Demonstrate appending a string at the end
var = var.Insert(var.Length, "NewString");
```

Converting Strings to and from a String Array

You can convert a single string to an array of strings and back by using a character in the string as a delimiter. This is an enormous help when you're doing string parsing and when you're reading comma-delimited text from a flat file.

Both VB 6.0 and .NET use `Split()` to convert a single string into an array of strings using a certain character as the delimiter. You can specify multiple delimiters with .NET. `Join()` is used to convert a string array back into a single string and the individual string elements are delimited with the specified character. .NET lets you delimit the new string with any other string, not just a single character.

An interesting function found in VB 6.0 but not included in the .NET String class is the `Filter()` function. Pass it a single dimension string array and a filter string. It will return all the elements of the array that have the filter string in them. You can also tell it to return all the elements that don't have the filter string in them.

VB 6.0

Convert a string into an array of strings using the `Split()` function. Convert the string array back into a single string with the `Join()` function. Both functions require you to pass the delimiter character to the function.

```
myArray = Split(myString, ",")
myString = Join(myArray, ",")
'Demonstrate splitting a string into an array using "," as a delimiter.
Dim myString As String
Dim myArray() As String
myString = "1,2,3"
myArray = Split(myString, ",")
Debug.Print myArray(0) 'Displays "1"
Convert it back to a single string using "+" as a delimiter.
myString = Join(myArray, "+")
Debug.Print myString 'Displays "1+2+3"
```

The Filter() function is passed a string array, a filter string, and a Boolean specifying if the function should return the elements that match the filter.

```
'Demonstrate the Filter() function
Dim MyString(2) As String
MyString(0) = "string1"
MyString(1) = "string2"
MyString(2) = "data"
Debug.Print "Matching: " & (Join(Filter(MyString, "string", True)))
'Prints "Matching: string1 string2"
Debug.Print "Not Matching: " & (Join(Filter(MyString, "string", False)))
'Prints "Not Matching: data"
```

VB .NET

Convert a string into an array of strings using the Split() method. You can pass one or more characters as the delimiter. Convert the string array back into a single string with the Join() method. You can pass any string as the delimiter. The Split() method works with an existing string object and the Join() method is called using the String class name.

```
Dim myArray() As String
Dim myString As String

myArray = myString.Split(myString, ","c)
myString = String.Join(","c , myArray)
'Demonstrate splitting a string into an array using "," and "+" as delimiters.
Dim myString As String = "1,2+3"
Dim myArray() As String
myArray = myString.Split(","c, "+"c)
Console.WriteLine(myArray(0)) 'Displays "1"
'Convert it back to a single string using "==" as the delimiter.
myString = String.Join("==", myArray)
Console.WriteLine(myString) 'Displays "1==2==3"
```

C#

Convert a string into an array of strings using the Split() method. You can pass one or more characters as the delimiter. Convert the string array back into a single string with the Join() method. You can pass any string as the delimiter. The Split() method works with an existing string object and the Join() method is called using the string class name.

```
myArray = myString.Split(myString, ',');
myString = string.Join(myArray, ',');
//Demonstrate splitting a string into an array using "," and "+" as delimiters
string myString = "1,2+3";
string[] myArray;
myArray = myString.Split(',', '+');
Console.WriteLine(myArray[0]) 'Displays "1"
//Convert it back to a single string using "==" as the delimiter
myString = string.Join("==", myArray);
Console.WriteLine(myString); //Displays "1==2==3"
```

Analyzing a String

It is often necessary to analyze the contents of string. This is useful when you're deciding how to modify a string and when you're testing the validity of user input.

VB 6.0 uses the Len() function to determine how many characters are in a string. The .NET equivalent is the Length() method.

You can compare two strings based upon an alphabetic sort. An integer is returned specifying which string comes first in the sort order. See Table 10-7 for a listing of the return results. VB 6.0 uses the StrComp() function and .NET uses the Compare() method.

Table 10-7. The Return Value of the Compare() Method

RESULT	DESCRIPTION
−1	The first string sorts before the second string.
0	The strings are equivalent.
1	The second string sorts before the first string.

A string can be searched to determine if it contains a substring. You can do this by starting at the left of the string and going to the right using the InStr() function in VB 6.0 and the IndexOf() method in .NET. You can search in the opposite direction with the InStrRev() function in VB 6.0 and with the LastIndexOf() method in .NET. If you just want to see if a string is at the start or the end of another string, .NET lets you call the StartsWith() and EndsWith() methods. VB 6.0 doesn't have an equivalent function. As an alternative you can compare a string using the Right() and Left() functions.

You can extract part of a string with the Mid() function in VB 6.0 and the SubString() method in .NET. VB 6.0 has two additional functions not found in

.NET: `Left()` and `Right()`. These functions return a specified number of characters starting from either the left side or the right side of the string.

VB 6.0

`StrComp()` is passed two strings and it returns a value representing which string is first in the sort order.

```
Debug.Print StrComp(string1, string2)
```

The `InStr()` and `InStrRev()` functions are both passed a string to search and the substring to find. An option is to specify an integer as the first parameter; this tells it which character to start searching from. The return value is the position of the first character matching the substring.

```
var1 = InStr(integer, string, substring)
var2 = InStr(string, substring)
var3 = InStrRev(integer, string, substring)
var4 = InStrRev(string, substring)
```

The `Mid()` function is passed a string, a starting position, and the number of characters to return. If the number of characters isn't passed to it, it returns the remaining part of the string.

```
var1 = Mid(string, starting position, length)
var2 = Mid(string, starting position)
```

The `Left()` and `Right()` functions are a passed a string and the number of characters to return. They return a substring that starts at either the leftmost or the rightmost character.

```
var1 = Left(string, length)
var2 = Right(string, length)
```

VB .NET

`Compare()` compares two strings and returns a value representing which string is first in the sort order.

```
Console.WriteLine(String.Compare(string1, string2))
```

The `IndexOf()` and `LastIndexOf()` methods work with an existing string. Pass them a substring to find and they return the position of the first character matching the substring. You can pass an integer as the second parameter to specify where to start searching.

```
var1 = myString.IndexOf(substring, integer)
var2 = myString.IndexOf(substring)
var3 = myString.LastIndexOf(substring, integer)
var4 = myString.LastIndexOf(substring)
```

The StartsWith() and EndsWith() methods return a Boolean if the first or last characters match the specified substring.

```
var = myString.StartsWith(substring)
var = myString.EndsWith(substring)
```

The SubString() method works with an existing string. Pass it a starting position and the number of characters to return. If the number of characters isn't passed to it, it returns the remaining part of the string.

```
var1 = myString.SubString(starting position, length)
var2 = myString.SubString(starting position)
```

C#

Compare() compares two strings and returns a value representing which string is first in the sort order.

```
Console.WriteLine(string.Compare(string1, string2));
```

The IndexOf() and LastIndexOf() methods work with an existing string. Pass them a substring to find and they return the position of the first character matching the substring. You can pass an integer as the second parameter to specify where to start searching.

```
var1 = myString.IndexOf(substring, integer);
var2 = myString.IndexOf(substring);
var3 = myString.LastIndexOf(substring, integer);
var4 = myString.LastIndexOf(substring);
```

The StartsWith() and EndsWith() methods return a bool if the first or last characters match the specified substring.

```
var = myString.StartsWith(substring);
var = myString.EndsWith(substring);
```

The SubString() method works with an existing string. Pass it a starting position and the number of characters to return. If the number of characters isn't passed to it, it returns the remaining part of the string.

```
var1 = myString.SubString(starting position, length);
var2 = myString.SubString(starting position);
```

Formatting Output

Formatting the contents of a variable enables you to customize the way it will be displayed. This is useful when you display text to the user or when you print reports.

Formatting data in .NET can be performed with any class that implements the IFormatter interface. The functionality described in this chapter is found in a lot of classes in .NET because many of them implement the IFormatter interface.

The ToString() method of the .NET data types takes a format string as the only parameter and it returns a string representing that data in the specified format.

The String.Format() method and the Console output methods take a format string and multiple arguments and they return a single string representing all the arguments in the specified format. Each of these methods uses the same parameter list. The first parameter is a string representing the output characters and a placeholder where each argument should be positioned. A placeholder looks like this:

```
{0:###.00}
```

The syntax is to put curly brackets around the argument number, which is followed by a colon (:), which is in turn followed by the output format. The remaining parameters are the arguments that are to be displayed.

Tables 10-3 through 10-6 give examples of the different format strings and the output they produce.

VB .NET
Pass the format string to the ToString() method of the variable to convert.

```
var1 = var2.ToString("format")
'Demonstrate using the basic numeric format
var3 = 5000
myString = var3.ToString("n")
'Returns "5,000.00"
```

Pass the `String.Format()`, `Console.Write()`, and `Console.WriteLine()` methods an output string and the arguments to display.

```
myString = String.Format("{arg:format}", var)
'Demonstrate printing a user's account number and account balance
Console.WriteLine("Account Number: {0:D4} Balance: {1:c}", 1234, 1023.56)
'Prints "Account Number: 1234, Balance: $1,023.56"
```

C#

Pass the format string to the `ToString()` method of the variable to convert.

```
var1 = var2.ToString("format");
```

Pass the `String.Format()`, `Console.Write()`, and `Console.WriteLine()` methods an output string and the arguments to display.

```
myString = String.Format("{arg:format}", var);
//Demonstrate printing a single value with no formatting
Console.WriteLine("{0}", 23};
//Prints "23"
```

Example 10-1. Manipulating an Input String

This example demonstrates ways of using the string methods. The user is asked to input a string to work with. After entering a string, the user chooses menu options to modify the string. The `Replace()` method demonstrates replacing any occurrence of a string with another string. The `Remove()` method demonstrates finding a substring within another string and then removing it. The other two menu options convert the string to uppercase or lowercase.

VB 6.0

```
'Manipulating an input string using VB 6.0
'Copyright (c)2001 by Bischof Systems, Inc.

Sub Main()
    Dim menuItem, startPos, numChars As Integer
    Dim myString, input1, input2 As String
    Debug.Print "String Management Functions"
```

```
        Do
            Debug.Print
            Debug.Print "Current String: ", myString
            Debug.Print "1. Enter new string"
            Debug.Print "2. Replace text"
            Debug.Print "3. Remove text"
            Debug.Print "4. Convert to uppercase"
            Debug.Print "5. Convert to lowercase"
            Debug.Print "0. Exit"
            menuItem = "0" & InputBox("Selection: ")
            Select Case (menuItem)
                Case 1 'Enter a new string
                    myString = InputBox("Enter new string: ")
                Case 2 'Replace characters
                    input1 = InputBox("Text to replace: ")
                    input2 = InputBox("New text: ")
                    myString = Replace(myString, input1, input2)
                Case 3 'Remove text
                    input1 = InputBox("Text to remove: ")
                    'Find the starting position
                    startPos = InStr(myString, input1)
                    myString = Replace(myString, input1, "")
                Case 4 'Convert to uppercase
                    myString = UCase(myString)
                Case 5    'Convert to lowercase
                    myString = LCase(myString)
            End Select
        Loop While (menuItem <> 0)
End Sub
```

VB .NET

```
'Manipulating an input string using VB .NET
'Copyright (c)2001 by Bischof Systems, Inc.

Module Module1

    Sub Main()
        Dim menuItem, startPos, numChars As Integer
        Dim myString, input1, input2 As String
        Console.WriteLine("String Management Functions")
```

```vbnet
            Do
                Console.WriteLine()
                Console.WriteLine("Current String: {0}", myString)
                Console.WriteLine("1. Enter new string")
                Console.WriteLine("2. Replace text")
                Console.WriteLine("3. Remove text")
                Console.WriteLine("4. Convert to uppercase")
                Console.WriteLine("5. Convert to lowercase")
                Console.WriteLine("0. Exit")
                Console.Write("Selection: ")
                menuItem = Integer.Parse("0" & Console.ReadLine())
                Select Case (menuItem)
                    Case 1 'Enter a new string
                        Console.Write("Enter new string: ")
                        myString = Console.ReadLine()
                    Case 2 'Replace characters
                        Console.Write("Text to replace: ")
                        input1 = Console.ReadLine()
                        Console.Write("New text: ")
                        input2 = Console.ReadLine()
                        myString = myString.Replace(input1, input2)
                    Case 3 'Remove text
                        Console.Write("Text to remove: ")
                        input1 = Console.ReadLine()
                        'Find the starting position
                        startPos = myString.IndexOf(input1)
                        If (startPos >= 0) Then
                            numChars = input1.Length
                            'Remove the characters at the starting position
                            myString = myString.Remove(startPos, numChars)
                        End If
                    Case 4 'Convert to uppercase
                        myString = myString.ToUpper()
                    Case 5     'Convert to lowercase
                        myString = myString.ToLower()
                End Select
            Loop While (menuItem <> 0)
        End Sub
    End Module
```

C#

```
//Manipulating an input string using C#
//Copyright (c)2001 by Bischof Systems, Inc.

using System;
using System.Text;

namespace C_Strings
{
    class Class1
    {
        [STAThread]
        static void Main(string[] args)
        {
            int menuItem, startPos, numChars;
            string myString="", input1="", input2="";
            Console.WriteLine("String Management Functions");
            do
            {
                Console.WriteLine();
                Console.WriteLine("Current String: {0}", myString);
                Console.WriteLine("1. Enter new string");
                Console.WriteLine("2. Replace text");
                Console.WriteLine("3. Remove text");
                Console.WriteLine("4. Convert to uppercase");
                Console.WriteLine("5. Convert to lowercase");
                Console.WriteLine("0. Exit");
                Console.Write("Selection: ");
                menuItem = int.Parse("0" + Console.ReadLine());
                switch (menuItem)
                {
                    case 1:     //Enter a new string
                        Console.Write("Enter new string: ");
                        myString = Console.ReadLine();
                        break;
                    case 2:     //Replace characters
                        Console.Write("Text to replace: ");
                        input1 = Console.ReadLine();
                        Console.Write("New text: ");
                        input2 = Console.ReadLine();
                        myString = myString.Replace(input1, input2);
                        break;
```

```
            case 3:      //Remove text
                Console.Write("Text to remove: ");
                input1 = Console.ReadLine();
                //Find the starting position
                startPos = myString.IndexOf(input1);
                if (startPos>=0)
                {
                    numChars = input1.Length;
                    //Remove the characters at the starting position
                    myString = myString.Remove(startPos, numChars);
                }
                break;
            case 4:      //Convert to uppercase
                myString = myString.ToUpper();
                break;
            case 5:      //Convert to lowercase
                myString = myString.ToLower();
                break;
        }
    } while (menuItem!=0);
        }
    }
}
```

Example 10-1 Output

```
String Management Functions

Current String:
1. Enter new string
2. Replace text
3. Remove text
4. Convert to uppercase
5. Convert to lowercase
0. Exit
Selection: 1
Enter new string: aabbcc

Current String: aabbcc
1. Enter new string
2. Replace text
3. Remove text
4. Convert to uppercase
5. Convert to lowercase
0. Exit
```

```
Selection: 2
Text to replace: b
New text: d

Current String: aaddcc
1. Enter new string
2. Replace text
3. Remove text
4. Convert to uppercase
5. Convert to lowercase
0. Exit
Selection: 3
Text to remove: dd

Current String: aacc
1. Enter new string
2. Replace text
3. Remove text
4. Convert to uppercase
5. Convert to lowercase
0. Exit
Selection: 4

Current String: AACC
1. Enter new string
2. Replace text
3. Remove text
4. Convert to uppercase
5. Convert to lowercase
0. Exit
Selection: 5

Current String: aacc
1. Enter new string
2. Replace text
3. Remove text
4. Convert to uppercase
5. Convert to lowercase
0. Exit
Selection: 0
```

CHAPTER 11
Windows Form Applications

Table 11-1. Common Control Members

VB 6.0	.NET
Appearance	BorderStyle
Enabled	Enabled
Visible	Visible
Top	Location.Y
Left	Location.X
Width	Size.Width
Height	Size.Height
Index	
Name	Name
BackColor	BackColor
ForeColor	ForeColor
Font	Font
Tag	Tag
TabIndex	TabIndex
CausesValidation	CausesValidation
Validate	Validating()
ToolTipText	ToolTip (a separate control)
DragMode	DoDragDrop
DragIcon	
Click	Click()
DblClick	DoubleClick()
DragDrop	DragDrop()

Table 11-1. Common Control Members (Continued)

VB 6.0	.NET
DragOver	DragOver()
	DragEnter()
	DragLeave()
	AllowDrop
GotFocus	Enter()[1]
LostFocus	Leave()
SetFocus	Focus
KeyPress	KeyPress()
KeyUp	KeyUp()
KeyDown	KeyDown()
MouseDown	MouseDown()
MouseUp	MouseUp()
Paint	Paint()
Resize	Resize()
Terminate	Dispose()
Validate	Validated()

Table 11-2. Form Members

VB 6.0	.NET
Caption	Text
Command.Default	AcceptButton
Command.Cancel	CancelButton
StartUpPosition	StartPosition
WindowState	WindowState
BorderStyle	FormBorderStyle
Icon	Icon
	IsMdiContainer

---

1. .NET controls also have the GotFocus() and LostFocus() events. However, according to MSDN, the Enter and Leave events should be used instead.

Table 11-2. Form Members (Continued)

VB 6.0	.NET
MDIChild	MdiParent = parent
Caption	Caption
ActiveControl	ActiveControl()
Hide	Hide()
Show	Show()
Show vbModal	ShowDialog()
Activate	Activated()
Deactivate	Deactivate()
Unload	Closing()

Table 11-3. Label Members

VB 6.0	.NET
Caption	Text
AutoSize	AutoSize
Alignment	TextAlign
WordWrap	

Table 11-4. TextBox Members

VB 6.0	.NET
Text	Text
AutoSize	AutoSize
PasswordChar	PasswordChar
ScrollBars	ScrollBars
MultiLine	MultiLine
Locked	ReadOnly
Change	TextChanged()
SelLength	SelectedLength
SelStart	SelectedStart
SelText	SelectedText
WordWrap	WordWrap

Table 11-5. Button Members

VB 6.0	.NET
Cancel	Form.CancelButton
Default	Form.AcceptButton
Caption	Text
Picture	Image
	ImageAlign

Table 11-6. CheckBox and RadioButton Members

VB 6.0	.NET
Value	CheckState
	Checked
	ThreeState

Table 11-7. ListBox and ComboBox Members

VB 6.0	.NET
AddItem	Items.Add(), Items.Insert()
RemoveItem	Items.RemoveAt()
Clear	Items.Clear()
List()	Items()
ItemData()	
MultiSelect	SelectionMode
Sorted	Sorted
Style	DropDownStyle

Table 11-8. Image/PictureBox Members

VB 6.0	.NET
Picture	Image
Stretch	SizeMode

Table 11-9. Clipboard Members

VB 6.0	.NET
	GetDataPresent()
	GetDataObject()
Text, GetData	GetData()
SetText, SetData	SetDataObject()

Overview

Creating a Windows application, now referred to as a Windows Form in .NET, is the standard way of writing desktop solutions. The .NET Framework provides many new controls to explore and it enhances many of the existing controls. Although all these new enhancements may seem overwhelming at first, you will find that many of the things that you did on a daily basis when writing a Windows application are very similar. The new tricks added to .NET will certainly make your application more feature-rich, but you will still rely upon the basic event-driven skills you already know. This chapter focuses on showing you how to perform the common tasks needed every day for writing Windows Form applications. The other features are left for you to explore in MSDN.

Default Windows Form Source Code

When you open a new Windows Application project, the IDE automatically displays an empty form on the screen and creates a corresponding source code template. Although it is easy to add and delete controls on the form just by using the mouse, you will need to modify the default source code to create a useful program. It is a good idea to get familiar with this template.

Each template consists of visible code and hidden code. The visible code is the area that you will make changes to as you develop your application. The hidden code is the area that the IDE modifies as you add controls and set their properties. The hidden code is within a region called "Windows Form Designer generated code." It is shown in the code with a plus sign (+) to the left of it. When you click the plus sign, the code expands. Most of the time you will not have to edit the hidden code.

The VB .NET visible code only creates an empty Form class. As you develop your application, you will put your methods in this class. The C# code, on the other hand, creates a new namespace (as discussed in Chapter 2) with a new Form class in it. VB .NET also creates a namespace, but it is only visible within the Project Properties dialog box. Within the C# class is the Dispose() method for disposing of any controls created on the form and the Main() method for starting the program. This is much more extensive than the VB .NET visible code.

The size of the hidden code is inversely proportional to the size of the visible code that is shown by default. VB .NET only has a few lines of code shown by default and the hidden code is huge by comparison. C# shows many lines of code by default and the hidden code is only a dozen lines of code.

If you look at the entire code block for each language, you will see that they both do the same thing. The difference is that the IDE hides the details from the VB .NET programmer and shows the details to the C# programmer.

As you add controls to a form and link them, the IDE puts the code to instantiate the controls into these hidden regions. This saves you from having to look at the details of how your form is built. Of course, you can always open this region to learn more about your application.

Using the Visual Studio IDE

The Visual Studio IDE is very similar to the VB 6.0 IDE. By default, you are given a blank form to work with. On the left side is the Toolbox, which contains the controls you can place on the form. On the right side is the Solution Explorer, which lists the files you are working with. Below the Solution Explorer is the Properties window. The IDE layout is so similar to VB 6.0 that after installing Visual Studio, you should be able to immediately start creating projects. Rather than teaching you how to use the IDE, this section focuses on the things that have changed from VB 6.0.

Renaming a Control

In VB 6.0, a good rule of thumb to follow when adding controls is to rename them before you add any code to their events. This is because event handlers follow a naming convention where the event name is prefixed with the control name. For example, the Click event of a command button called Command1 would be named as follows:

```
Command1_Click
```

If you later decide to give the command button a better name, such as cmdOK, the event will no longer be associated with the control because the naming convention doesn't match. Controls in .NET don't have this problem.

There are two reasons for this. First, the method name that handles a control event doesn't have any special naming restrictions, because a method in .NET has to subscribe to an event handler. The compiler no longer parses the method name to determine which event it handles. Second, when you modify the name of a control, the IDE automatically changes your code so that your method will subscribe to the event with the new control name.[2] This feature makes it easy for you to change your mind about a control name without having to go back and track down "lost event code."

Although it is now easy to change the name of a control, it still isn't recommended. Because the procedure names that were generated by the IDE stay the same, there may be some confusion about determining which event a procedure is written for.

As an example, let's say that you created an event handler for the Click event of Button1. It is created automatically by the IDE and is named Button1_Click(). You later change the control name to OkButton. You know that the IDE will make sure that the event handler will still work even though it is still called Button1_Click(). However, if you (or another programmer) are reading your code, it will not be obvious which control that event handler belongs to. Immediately naming new controls helps keep your code maintainable.

Adding Event Handlers

Most of the controls added to a form need some code associated with their events so that they can be functional. When you double-click a control, you are taken to the code window. The IDE automatically generates the code to handle the default event of the control you clicked. This is the same functionality found in VB 6.0.

The VB .NET interface is very similar to the VB 6.0 code editor. Above your code are two drop-down boxes. The leftmost drop-down box lists the controls on the form. The rightmost drop-down box lists all the possible events for the control currently selected. Events that have code associated with them are in bold. When you click an event that is bold, you go to the code associated with the event. If you click an event that isn't bold, an empty event handler is automatically generated so that you can add code to it. This makes it easy to see what events are associated with each control and add code to them.

The code editor in C# is very different. The leftmost drop-down box only lists the current form. None of the controls on the form are listed. The rightmost box lists the methods in the form and you can quickly go to one by clicking it. You can have the IDE automatically generate an event handler for a control in C# from the View Designer. Click the control that you want to add

---

2. As of the time of this writing, there was an interesting situation where if you had more than one procedure subscribing to the same control event, and you changed the name of the control, the IDE would delete the references to the event for all but one of the procedures. Of course, this might be a bug that is fixed in future versions.

an event to. Then click the Events button at the top of the Properties window. It changes the list from a list of all the properties into a list of all the events available for that control. Double-click the event name and you will be taken to the Code window. The event-handling code has been automatically generated for you by the IDE. You only have to add the code within the handler. To add more events automatically, you have to switch back to the View window and click the event list again.

Using Common Controls

The controls in VB 6.0 are very similar to the controls in .NET. While the functionality has been carried forward from VB 6.0, .NET has changed some of the property names and improved their features.

The controls in .NET are based off the same base class. Thus, they have many properties and events in common. Table 11-1 lists the common properties, methods, and events in VB 6.0 and how they are now used in .NET.

To completely cover every feature of every control in the .NET Framework would require rewriting the MSDN Help file. Rather than do that, this section focuses on helping you quickly learn how to migrate the functionality found in VB 6.0 controls to the .NET environment.

Table 11-1 lists the common members for most of the controls.

Using DoEvents()

The DoEvents() method in VB 6.0 tells Windows to process other event messages. This is useful when you are performing a long loop and you want the screen to be able to refresh itself. In the .NET Framework, the DoEvents() method is part of the Application class. Use the fully qualified name to call it.

VB .NET
Use the Application.DoEvents() method to tell Windows to process other event messages.

```
Application.DoEvents()
```

C#
Use the Application.DoEvents() method to tell Windows to process other event messages.

```
Application.DoEvents();
```

Using Message Boxes

The MsgBox statement in VB 6.0 is the standard way of displaying short messages to the user. .NET has replaced it with the MessageBox class. Call the Show() method to display a message to the user. It works the same as the MsgBox statement.

VB .NET

Use the MessageBox.Show() method to display a short message to the user.[3]

```
MessageBox.Show("Hello, World")
```

C#

Use the MessageBox.Show() method to display a short message to the user.

```
MessageBox.Show("Hello, World");
```

Locking Controls

In VB 6.0, it is possible to lock the position of all the controls on a form so that you can't accidentally move them with your mouse. Go to the Format menu item and choose Lock Controls to do this. In .NET each control can be locked individually. There is a new property called Locked that you can set to True. It locks a control's position on the form layout.

Resizing and Repositioning Controls

Every control has properties to determine its location and size on the form. In VB 6.0, these are called Top, Left, Height, and Width. You can modify these properties in your program and immediately see the effect.

.NET controls also have properties to determine the location and size of a control. Unlike in VB 6.0, each of these properties is an object. The Location property is derived from the System.Drawing.Point class. It has the properties X and Y. The Size property is derived from the System.Drawing.Size class. It has the properties Height and Width. The System.Drawing library is included in the Windows Form template for both VB .NET and C#.

The properties of both classes are read-only. You can examine the current location and size of a control, but you can't modify it directly. To change these properties, you have to create new instances of each class and assign it to the control.

---

3. I wouldn't be able to forgive myself if I didn't have a "Hello, World" example in this book.

VB .NET

Use the Location and Size properties to get the coordinates of a control.

```
'Demonstrate printing the location and size of the current form
MessageBox.Show(String.Format("Location X:{0} Y:{1}", _
    Me.Location.X, Me.Location.Y))
MessageBox.Show(String.Format("Height:{0} Width:{1}", _
    Me.Size.Height, Me.Size.Width))
```

To change the Location and Size properties, create new instances of the Point and Size classes.

```
'Demonstrate moving a button to the right
Button1.Location = New Point(Button1.Location.X + 100, Button1.Location.Y)
'Demonstrate increasing the height of a button
Button1.Size = New Size(Button1.Size.Width, Button1.Size.Height + 50)
```

C#

Use the Location and Size properties to get the coordinates of a control.

```
MessageBox.Show(String.Format("Location X:{0} Y:{1}", this.Location.X,
    this.Location.Y));
MessageBox.Show(String.Format("Height:{0} Width:{1}",
    this.Size.Height, this.Size.Width));
```

To change the Location and Size properties, create new instances of the Point and Size classes.

```
button1.Location = new Point(button1.Location.X + 100,
    button1.Location.Y);
button1.Size = new Size(button1.Size.Width,
    button1.Size.Height + 100);
```

Changing a Control's Font

Changing a control's Font property involves the same issues as changing a control's Size and Location properties. You can view the member values, but you can't change them directly. You have to instantiate a new Font object and assign it to the control's Font property.

The Font class has numerous overloads for its constructor method. You'll look at two common ways of instantiating a Font class: creating a font from scratch and modifying an existing font.

To create a new font from scratch, pass the constructor a font name and a size. An optional third parameter is the font style.

To create a font using an existing font, pass the constructor the Font object and a font style.

The font style is an enumerated list called FontStyle that consists of Bold, Italic, Underline, and so on. You can set multiple styles by adding the enumerated elements together.

VB .NET

Instantiate a new Font object by passing the constructor a font name and a font size. The font name is a String and the size is a Single. An optional FontStyle enumerator can be passed as the third parameter.

```
'Demonstrate creating a new font for a label
Label1.Font = New Font("Microsoft Sans Serif", 15, FontStyle.Bold)
```

Instantiate a new Font object using an existing font by passing the constructor a Font object and a FontStyle enumerator.

```
'Demonstrate modifying the existing font of a button
Button1.Font = New Font(Button1.Font, FontStyle.Bold + FontStyle.Italic)
```

C#

Instantiate a new Font object by passing the constructor a font name and a font size. The font name is a string and the size is a float. An optional FontStyle enumerator can be passed as the third parameter.

```
//Demonstrate creating a new font for a label
label1.Font = new Font("Arial", 10);
```

Instantiate a new Font object using an existing font by passing the constructor a Font object and a FontStyle enumerator.

```
//Demonstrate modifying the existing font of a button
button1.Font = new Font(button1.Font, FontStyle.Underline | FontStyle.Italic);
```

Forms

Forms are the windows that contain controls that the user works with. The basic implementation of forms has changed drastically from VB 6.0.

Table 11-2 lists the common members of the Form control.

Displaying a form in VB 6.0 consists of calling the Show() method of the form object. The .NET Framework implements forms as classes. As a result, each form must be instantiated with an object variable. Once the object variable is created, you can call the Show() method.

VB .NET

Show a new form by declaring an object variable of the Form class and calling the Show() method.

```
Dim frmMyForm As New Form1()
frmMyForm.Show()
```

C#

Show a new form by declaring an object variable of the Form class and calling the Show() method.

```
Form1 frmMyForm = new Form1();
frmMyForm.Show();
```

In VB 6.0 you can prevent a form from closing by handling the Unload event. In .NET the corresponding event is the Closing event.

VB .NET

Prevent a form from closing by setting the Cancel property of the e object to True.

```
Private Sub Form1_Closing(ByVal sender As Object, _
    ByVal e As System.ComponentModel.CancelEventArgs) Handles MyBase.Closing
    e.Cancel = True
End Sub
```

C#

Prevent a form from closing by setting the Cancel property of the e object to true.

```
private void Form1_Closing(object sender,
    System.ComponentModel.CancelEventArgs e)
{
    e.Cancel = true;
}
```

Two new properties, AcceptButton and CancelButton, have replaced properties in the VB 6.0 CommandButton control. See the "Buttons" section for more information.

Forms As Dialog Boxes

A *dialog box* is a form that locks a user out of using the other forms in your application. To create a dialog box in VB 6.0, add the vbModal parameter to the form's Show() method. If you want to create a dialog box in .NET, call the ShowDialog() method. The ShowDialog() method requires that you pass it the parent form as a parameter.

The .NET Form class adds a way for you to find out what button the user clicked. When you create a dialog box, assign the DialogResult property for each button to the appropriate value (e.g., OK, Cancel, Abort, and so on). These properties appear as a drop-down list in the Properties window. When the user clicks one of these buttons, the form automatically hides itself and control returns to the calling form. To find out what button a user clicked, you can examine the DialogResult property of the form.

This example demonstrates calling a dialog box with an OK button and a Cancel button on it. Each button had its DialogResult property set accordingly to either OK or Cancel.

VB .NET

Create an object variable of the form that will be shown. Pass the ShowDialog() method the parent form, Me. Use the DialogResult property to determine what the user clicked.

```
'Demonstrate opening a dialog box that will return either OK or Cancel.
Private Sub ShowOkDialogBox()
    Dim frmOkDialog As New OkDialog()

    frmOkDialog.ShowDialog(Me)
    Select Case frmOkDialog.DialogResult
        Case DialogResult.OK
            MessageBox.Show("OK was clicked")
        Case DialogResult.Cancel
            MessageBox.Show("You clicked on Cancel")
    End Select
End Sub
```

C#

Create an object variable of the form that will be shown. Pass the ShowDialog() method the parent form, this. Use the DialogResult property to determine what the user clicked.

```
//Demonstrate opening a dialog box that will return either OK or Cancel.
private void ShowOkDialogBox()
{
    OkDialog frmOkDialogBox = new OkDialog();
    frmOkDialogBox.ShowDialog(this);
    switch (frmOkDialogBox.DialogResult)
    {
        case DialogResult.OK:
            MessageBox.Show("OK was clicked");
            break;
        case DialogResult.Cancel:
            MessageBox.Show("You clicked Cancel");
            break;
    }
}
```

It is common for one form to want to have access to the data in another form. In VB 6.0 this is easy. From the first form, call the Show() method of the second form. After the second form closes, you can access any of the controls of the second form because it is still in memory and all of its members are declared as public. This doesn't work in .NET because it declares all the members of a form as private. If you want to make information in one form available to another form, you have to declare a public variable or property to store this information. The calling form has access to any members that you declare as public.

This example demonstrates a method that calls a dialog box to let the user log in. The dialog box has a public string variable that is set after the user enters his or her login ID. Once the form is closed, the method displays the login ID in a message box.

VB .NET

```
'Demonstrate calling a login dialog box and getting the user id after it closes
Private Sub LogUserIn()
    Dim frmLoginDialog As New LoginDialog()
    frmLoginDialog.ShowDialog(Me)
    MessageBox.Show(frmLoginDialog.UserId)
End Sub
```

C#

```
//Demonstrate calling a login dialog box and getting the user id after it closes
private void LogUserIn()
{
    LoginDialog frmLoginDialog = new LoginDialog();
    frmLoginDialog.ShowDialog(this);
    MessageBox.Show(frmLoginDialog.UserId);
}
```

MDI Forms

Multiple Document Interface (MDI) forms allow one form to serve as a parent form and open other child forms within it. Implementing MDI forms has changed from VB 6.0.

In VB 6.0, creating an MDI application requires adding an MDI form to serve as the parent form and changing the properties of the other forms to designate them as child forms.

In .NET, an MDI parent form is the standard form. You simply set the IsMdiContainer property to True. Because it is a standard form, there are no restrictions on what controls can be placed on it. Any controls placed on it will be visible at all times. Child forms will appear underneath the controls on the parent form.

A form can't be designated as a child form until runtime. When the form variable is created, set its MdiParent property to the parent form. This will make the form appear as a child form within the parent form.

VB .NET

Create an MDI parent form by setting the IsMdiContainer property to True within the View Designer. When you want to open a child form, instantiate an object variable of the Form class and set the MdiParent property to Me.

```
'Demonstrate opening a child form from an MDI parent form
Private Sub OpenMdiChild()
    Dim frmMdiChild As New MdiChildForm()
    frmMdiChild.MdiParent = Me
    frmMdiChild.Show()
End Sub
```

C#

Create an MDI parent form by setting the `IsMdiContainer` property to `true` within the View Designer. When you want to open a child form, instantiate an object variable of the `Form` class and set the `MdiParent` property to `this`.

```
//Demonstrate opening a child form from an MDI parent form
private void OpenMdiChild()
{
    MdiChildForm frmMdiChild = new MdiChildForm();
    frmMdiChild.MdiParent = this;
    frmMdiChild.Show();
}
```

Labels

Labels haven't changed much. The `Caption` property is now called `Text`. There is no longer a `WordWrap` property because the labels automatically wrap if necessary.

Table 11-3 lists the common members of the `Label` control.

TextBoxes

Text boxes in .NET are almost identical to text boxes in VB 6.0. An interesting change is that the `Locked` property in VB 6.0 signifies that a text box is read-only. In .NET the `Locked` property is used to signify that a control can't be moved in design mode. The `ReadOnly` property has been added to compensate for this.

Table 11-4 lists the common members of the `TextBox` control.

Buttons

`CommandButtons` in VB 6.0 are now referred to as just `Buttons`. In VB 6.0, having a button respond to either the Enter key or the Esc key requires setting either the `Default` or `Cancel` property to `True`. Each form is allowed to have only one button with that setting. Hence, once you set it to `True` for a button, the IDE checks if another button already has that same property set to `True`. If so, it resets it to `False`. This ensures that you don't accidentally have two buttons with that property set to `True`.

.NET takes a much more logical approach. Because there can be only one command button to have this capability per form, the property was moved to the `Form` object. The `Form` object has the properties `AcceptButton` and `CancelButton`. Each is a drop-down box listing all the buttons on the form and you select which button should be associated with the property. Not only is this more natural, but it also makes it easier for you to figure out which button is associated with each property. In VB 6.0 you have to click each button until you find the one with the property set to True.

Table 11-5 lists the common members of the Button control.

CheckBoxes and RadioButtons

One obvious change in .NET from VB 6.0 is that OptionButtons have been renamed to RadioButtons.

Both the CheckBox and RadioButton controls have a Checked property that indicates whether or not they are checked. It returns either True or False.

The CheckBox control has an additional property that the RadioButton doesn't have. It has a CheckState enumeration property that returns the state of the check box. You can get a string representation using the ToString() method. This control also has the capability to use a third state called Indeterminate. This is when the check box isn't checked or unchecked. It can be used to signify that the user hasn't set the state yet.

Table 11-6 lists the common members of the CheckBox and RadioButton controls.

There are many ways to analyze the state of the CheckBox control. Table 11-10 lists the values returned for each method.

Table 11-10. Return Values for the CheckBox Members

CHECKSTATE ENUMERATION	CHECKSTATE INDEX	CHECKSTATE.TOSTRING()	CHECKED
Unchecked	0	"Unchecked"	False
Checked	1	"Checked"	True
Indeterminate	2	"Indeterminate"	True

ListBox and ComboBox

The ListBox and ComboBox controls in .NET are very similar to their equivalent controls in VB 6.0. Each control displays a list of items that the user can choose from. The biggest change is the items in the list are now represented as a collection of objects. This means that not only can you store strings in the collection, but you can also store any type of object. This allows you to associate as much information as necessary with each item in the list. You are no longer limited to just storing one value per item as is the case in VB 6.0 with the ItemData property. .NET determines what to display for an object using the ToString() method.

Table 11-7 lists the common members of the ListBox and ComboBox controls.

In VB 6.0, the AddItem() method was used to add an item to the list. In .NET the list is a standard collection object. You add items using the Add() method. You can insert an item in the list at a specific location using the Insert() method. The first parameter is the position in the list and the second parameter is the item to add.

VB .NET

Add items to the list collection using the Add() method of the Items collection.

```
ListBox1.Items.Add(object)
```

Use the Insert() method to add an item to a certain position in the list.

```
ListBox1.Items.Insert(position, object)
```

C#

Add items to the list collection using the Add() method of the Items collection.

```
comboBox1.Items.Add(object);
```

Use the Insert() method to add an item to a certain position in the list.

```
comboBox1.Items.Insert(position, object);
```

In VB 6.0, removing an item required calling the RemoveItem() method. In .NET, removing items from the list is done using the RemoveAt() method of the Items collection. Pass it the item number as the parameter. To remove all items, call the Clear() method.

VB .NET

Remove items from the list using the RemoveAt() method of the Items collection. Call the Clear() method to remove all items.

```
ListBox1.Items.RemoveAt(number)
ListBox1.Items.Clear()
```

C#

Remove items from the list using the RemoveAt() method of the Items collection. Call the Clear() method to remove all items.

```
comboBox1.Items.RemoveAt(number);
comboBox1.Items.Clear();
```

To access specific items for the list, use the indexer of the Items collection.

VB .NET

Use the indexer of the Items collection to get a specific item.

```
ListBox1.Items(index)
```

C#

Use the indexer of the Items collection to get a specific item.

```
comboBox1.Items[index]
```

The purpose of the ListBox is to allow the user to select one or more items from the list. The SelectedIndex property indicates which item the user selected. If this is a multiselect ListBox, it will indicate the first item in the list that was selected. The GetSelected() method returns True if an item is selected. If this is a multiselect ListBox and you want to get all the items that the user selected, loop through the collection, and test each item using the GetSelected() method

Although the ComboBox can only have one item selected at a time, you can still use these properties to find out which item the user selected.

VB .NET

Use the SelectedIndex property to find the first (or only) item selected in the ListBox control. It returns –1 if no item was selected. Use the SelectedItem property to get the value of it.

```
var = ListBox1.SelectedIndex
string = ListBox1.SelectedItem.ToString()
```

Use GetSelected() to find out if an item is selected. Pass it the index number and it returns True if the item is selected.

```
If ListBox1.GetSelected(index) Then ...
```

C#

Use the SelectedIndex property to find the first (or only) item selected in the ListBox control. It returns –1 if no item was selected. Use the SelectedItem property to get the value of it.

```
var = comboBox1.SelectedIndex;
string = comboBox1.SelectedItem.ToString();
```

Use GetSelected() to find out if an item is selected. Pass it the index number and it returns true if the item is selected. This is only available for the ListBox control.

```
if (listBox1.GetSelected(index)) {...}
```

The ComboBox will either allow a user to select an item from the list or type in a new entry. Either way, the user's choice is listed in the TextBox area of the ComboBox. Use the Text property to determine what is currently shown in the ComboBox text area.

VB .NET

Use the Text property of the ComboBox to determine what the user entered.

```
string = ComboBox1.Text
```

C#

Use the Text property of the ComboBox to determine what the user entered.

```
string = comboBox1.Text;
```

PictureBox

VB 6.0 displays bitmap files using the PictureBox control (with a background bitmap) and the Image control (from which you can obtain the current contents of the control). The Image control is a less resource-intensive version of the PictureBox. The .NET PictureBox control is the equivalent of the VB 6.0 PictureBox control. .NET doesn't have an equivalent control for the VB 6.0 Image control.

Table 11-8 lists the common members of the PictureBox control.

Load a new image into the control by instantiating a new Bitmap object. The easiest way to do this is to pass a filename to the Bitmap constructor.

VB .NET

Load a new bitmap into the `PictureBox` control by instantiating a new `Bitmap` object.

```
PictureBox1.Image = New Bitmap(filename)
```

Remove a bitmap from a `PictureBox` by assigning `Nothing` to the `Image` property.

```
PictureBox1.Image = Nothing
```

C#

Load a new bitmap into the `PictureBox` control by instantiating a new `Bitmap` object.

```
pictureBox1.Image = new Bitmap(filename);
//Demonstrate loading a BMP file from the root directory
pictureBox1.Image = new Bitmap(@"C:\semicirc.bmp");
```

Remove a bitmap from a `PictureBox` by assigning `null` to the `Image` property.

```
pictureBox1.Image = null;
```

Timer

The `Timer` control in .NET works the same as the `Timer` in VB 6.0. One difference is that it doesn't appear on the form anymore. It now appears in the tray below the development environment.

Copying and Pasting with the Clipboard

The clipboard provides a means of copying data to a temporary storage area that can be accessed from any other Windows program. A program can take this data and paste it into one of its own controls. The only restriction is that the receiving control must be able to read the format of the data pasted. The `Clipboard` object can store more than a dozen different data formats.

Table 11-9 lists the common members of the `Clipboard` class.

Save information on the clipboard by calling the `SetDataObject()` method. Pass the data to save as the parameter.

VB .NET

Save data to the clipboard by calling the SetDataObject() method. Pass it the data to save.

```
'Demonstrate saving the selected text in a TextBox to the clipboard
Clipboard.SetDataObject(TextBox1.SelectedText)
```

C#

Save data to the clipboard by calling the SetDataObject() method. Pass it the data to save.

```
//Demonstrate saving the selected text in a TextBox to the clipboard
Clipboard.SetDataObject(textBox1.SelectedText);
```

Retrieving data from the clipboard requires creating an object variable from the IDataObject interface. Assign this variable to the clipboard's data object by calling the GetDataObject() method.

Once you have a reference to this object, you need to check that there is data in the clipboard and that this data can be read by the receiving control. Call the GetDataPresent() method and pass it the data type your control is expecting. It returns True if the clipboard has data in a format that you specified. The last step is to get the data from the clipboard. Use the GetData() method to do this. Once again, you have to pass it the data format to return.

VB .NET

Get a reference to the clipboard's data object with the GetDataObject() method.

```
Dim myDataObject as IDataObject
myDataObject = ClipBoard.GetDataObject()
```

Determine if the data is in a format you can use by calling the GetDataPresent() method. Retrieve the data by calling the GetData() method. Pass both methods the data format as a parameter.

```
If myDataObject.GetDataPresent(DataFormats.Text) Then
    TextBox2.Text = CType(myDataObject.GetData(DataFormats.Text), String)
End If
```

C#

Get a reference to the clipboard's data object with the GetDataObject() method.

```
IDataObject myDataObject = Clipboard.GetDataObject();
```

Determine if the data is in a format you can use by calling the GetDataPresent() method. Retrieve the data by calling the GetData() method. Pass both methods the data format as a parameter.

```
if (myDataObject.GetDataPresent(DataFormats.Text))
{
    textBox2.Text = (string)myDataObject.GetData(DataFormats.Text);
}
```

CHAPTER 12
File Access

Table 12-1. File Management Equivalent Functions

VB 6.0	.NET
ChDir	Directory.SetCurrentDirectory()
ChDrive	Directory.SetCurrentDirectory()
CurDir	Directory.GetCurrentDirectory(), Directory.GetDirectoryRoot()
Dir	File.Exists(), Directory.GetFiles()
FileCopy	File.Copy()
FileDateTime	File.GetCreationTime(), File.GetLastAccessTime(), File.GetLastWriteTime()
FileLen	FileInfo.Length
GetAttr	File.GetAttributes()
Kill	File.Delete()
MkDir	Directory.CreateDirectory()
Name	Directory.Move(), File.Move()
RmDir	Directory.Delete()
SetAttr	File.SetAttributes()

Table 12-2. Text File I/O Equivalent Functions

VB 6.0	.NET
EOF	String = Nothing/null
Close	TextReader.Close(), TextWriter.Close(), StreamReader.Close(), StreamWriter.Close()
FileOpen	StreamReader constructor, StreamWriter constructor, File.OpenText(), File.CreateText()
FreeFile	
LineInput, InputString	TextReader.Read(), TextReader.ReadLine(), TextReader.ReadToEnd(), StreamReader.Read(), StreamReader.ReadLine(), StreamReader.ReadToEnd()

Table 12-2. Text File I/O Equivalent Functions

VB 6.0	.NET
Lock	
LOF	FileInfo.Length()
Print, PrintLine, Write	TextWriter.Write(), TextWriter.WriteLine(), StreamWriter.Write(), StreamWriter.WriteLine()
Reset	

Overview

File input/output (I/O) consists of being able to manage the files and directories on a system as well as being able to read from and write to those files. Both VB 6.0 and .NET provide similar functionality for performing these actions. This chapter has two primary sections. The first section covers managing the files and directories on your system. The second section explains how to open, read, write, and close text files.

The VB 6.0 functions discussed in this chapter can also be referenced in .NET. VB .NET includes all the functions by default. If you want to use them in C#, add a reference to the library Microsoft Visual Basic .NET Runtime. Do this by selecting Project ➤ Add Reference. The functions are in the class Microsoft.VisualBasic.FileSystem.

Although you can use all the VB 6.0 file and directory management functions in .NET, the areas dealing with VB .NET and C# will only make reference to the functionality found in the .NET native classes.

Managing Files

You can manage files by viewing and changing them and the directories they are located in. Many programs have features that require you to open and create files, and this chapter shows you the steps for performing these operations. The way you work with files in VB 6.0 and .NET is almost identical.

The functionality for managing files and directories in .NET is in the System.IO namespace.

Working with Directories

It is often necessary to create and change directories before you work with files.[1] The Directory class in .NET lets you perform a variety of operations on a directory.[2] You must specify the Directory class name when calling its methods.

When you work with the directory methods in .NET, you often need to specify a directory path as a parameter. The methods will accept either a relative file path or an absolute file path.

You can find out the current directory that the user is working in by using the CurDir() function in VB 6.0. The .NET equivalent is GetCurrentDirectory(). Both functions return a string containing the full directory path. If you just want to know the drive name, .NET has the GetDirectoryRoot() method.

When the user wants to change to a new directory, VB 6.0 uses two functions: ChDrive() and ChDir(). ChDrive() enables you to change the current drive. ChDir(), as you might guess, lets you change the directory. .NET combines these two functions into one method called SetCurrentDirectory(). It switches to any drive and/or directory passed to it.

If a new directory needs to be created, use the MkDir() function in VB 6.0. It will only create one directory at a time. When you pass it a path, every directory in the path must already exist except for the last one, otherwise, an error will be raised that the path is invalid. The equivalent method in .NET is called CreateDirectory(). A nice improvement in .NET is that it will create as many directories as needed so that the entire path is valid. When you pass CreateDirectory() a path, you really only need the drive to already exist because all the other directories listed will be created if necessary.

In VB 6.0, you can use the Dir() function to find out if a directory exists as well as find out if a file exists in that directory. This is discussed in the next section, "Working with Files." To find out if a directory exists, use the Dir() function and pass the vbDirectory enumerator as the second parameter. In .NET you can find out if a directory exists using the Exists() method.

The Directory class has a method called GetFiles() that returns a list of all the files in a directory. It returns the list as a string array.

You can remove a directory in VB 6.0 with the RmDir() function. Do this in .NET by calling the Delete() method.

---

1. It's common practice for Microsoft to refer to the same thing in different ways. In this case, Windows calls a location that stores files a "Folder," but the .NET programming languages use the term "Directory." In this chapter I use the term "Directory" so that the explanations that follow are consistent with the method names.

2. The DirectoryInfo class provides almost identical functionality, but it is optimized for reusing the object many times. Consult MSDN for a full description. Go to the index and type in **System.IO.DirectoryInfo**.

The Name statement in VB 6.0 lets you rename a file or directory. The .NET equivalent is the Move() method. You can use this method to change the name of a directory as well as move a directory and its contents to a new location.

VB 6.0

The CurDir() function doesn't require any parameters. It returns the current directory as a string.

```
var = CurDir()
```

The ChDrive() statement is passed a drive letter. The ChDir() statement is passed a directory path. The drive letter is not included.

```
ChDrive driveletter
ChDir path
```

Pass the MkDir() statement a path to a new directory.

```
MkDir path
```

Pass the Dir() function a path as the first parameter and the enumerator vbDirectory as the second parameter.

```
Dir(path, vbDirectory)
```

Pass the RmDir() statement a directory path. If the directory exists, it will be deleted.

```
RmDir path
```

Pass the Name statement the name of the source file/directory and the destination file/directory. Separate the two with the As keyword.

```
Name sourceFile As destinationFile
Name sourceDirectory As DesitinationDirectory
```

VB .NET

The GetCurrentDirectory() method doesn't require any parameters. It returns a string representing the current directory.

```
var=Directory.GetCurrentDirectory()
```

The GetDirectoryRoot() method is passed a string directory path and it returns the root drive.

```
var=Directory.GetDirectoryRoot(path)
```

Pass `SetCurrentDirectory()` a path and it will switch to that directory. You can include a drive letter in the path string.

```
Directory.SetCurrentDirectory(path)
'Demonstrate moving up two directories
Directory.SetCurrentDirectory("..\..")
```

Pass `CreateDirectory()` a path and it will create that directory. It will create as many directories as necessary to make sure that the full path exists.

```
Directory.CreateDirectory(path)
```

Pass the `Exists()` method a directory path and it returns `True` if the directory exists.

```
var=Directory.Exists(path)
'Demonstrate testing for the D: drive
Console.WriteLine(Directory.Exists("D:\"))
```

Pass the `GetFiles()` method a directory path and it returns a string array of all the files in that directory. You can pass a search path as a second parameter if you want to specify certain files.

```
varArray=Directory.GetFiles(path)
'Demonstrate getting a comma-delimited list of the files in the current directory
Console.WriteLine(String.Join(",",Directory.GetFiles(".","*.*")))
```

Pass the `Delete()` method a path and it will delete the directory listed at the end of the path string. If you pass `True` as a second parameter, it will delete all files and subdirectories. Otherwise, it will only delete the directory if it is empty.

```
Directory.Delete(path)
```

Pass the `Move()` method an existing directory path as the first parameter. The second parameter is the new path. It will move the directory and its contents to the new location. This method can also be used to rename a directory by passing the second parameter an identical path string with only the directory name changed.

```
Directory.Move(originalpath, newpath)
'Demonstrate moving a subdirectory in the current directory to the root directory
Directory.Move("Directory", "c:\Directory")
```

C#

The `GetCurrentDirectory()` method doesn't take any parameters. It returns a string representing the current directory.

```
var=Directory.GetCurrentDirectory();
//Demonstrate getting the current directory
Console.WriteLine(Directory.GetCurrentDirectory());
```

The `GetDirectoryRoot()` method is passed a string directory path and it returns the root drive.

```
var=Directory.GetDirectoryRoot(path);
//Demonstrate getting the drive letter of the current folder
Console.WriteLine(Directory.GetDirectoryRoot(Directory.GetCurrentDirectory()));
```

Pass `SetCurrentDirectory()` a path and it will switch to that directory. You can include a drive letter in the path string.

```
Directory.SetCurrentDirectory(path);
```

Pass `CreateDirectory()` a path and it will create that directory. It will create as many directories as necessary to make sure that the full path exists.

```
Directory.CreateDirectory(path);
//Demonstrate creating a new directory off the root directory
Directory.CreateDirectory(@"C:\NewDirectory");
```

Pass the `Exists()` method a directory path and it returns `true` if the directory exists.

```
var=Directory.Exists();
```

Pass the `GetFiles()` method a directory path and it returns a string array of all the files in that directory. You can pass a search path as a second parameter if you want to specify certain files.

```
varArray=Directory.GetFiles(path);
var=String.Join(",",Directory.GetFiles(".","*.*"));
```

Pass the `Delete()` method a path and it will delete the directory listed at the end of the path string. If you pass `true` as a second parameter, it will delete all files and subdirectories. Otherwise, it will only delete the directory if it is empty.

```
Directory.Delete(path);
```

Pass the Move() method an existing directory path as the first parameter. The second parameter is the new path. It will move the directory and its contents to the new location. This method can also be used to rename a directory by passing the second parameter an identical path string with only the directory name changed.

```
Directory.Move(originalpath, newpath);
//Demonstrate changing the name of a directory located on a different drive
Directory.Move(@"D:\Test\OldFolder", @"D:\Test\NewFolder");
```

Working with Files

Being able to find, rename, and delete files is an important part of many applications. The File class in .NET provides you with all the functionality needed to work with files.[3] It is the same functionality that is provided in VB 6.0. The majority of these methods only have one parameter and it is the filename that you want to work with. The examples at the end of this section demonstrate the syntax for calling each method.

Before you can work with a file, you need to find out whether it exists or not. VB 6.0 uses the Dir() function to do this. When first called, the Dir() function must have a file search pattern passed to it. It then returns the first file found that matches the search pattern. Each successive call should have no parameter passed to it and it will find the next matching filename. It returns an empty string when no more files are found. .NET uses the Exists() method and it returns True if the file is found.

Not only can you find out if a file exists, but you can also get information such as the dates the file has been worked on and the size of the file. In this area, VB 6.0 and .NET are quite different. VB 6.0 only allows you to get the date and time a file was last modified. This function is called FileDateTime(). .NET will retrieve the date and time the file was created, last accessed, and last modified. These methods are called GetCreationTime(), GetLastAccessTime(), and GetLastWriteTime(). Don't let the method name mislead you into thinking that only the time is provided. They all return a date and time as a DateTime object. VB 6.0 lets you find out the file size with the FileLen() function. The equivalent function in .NET is the Length() method of the FileInfo class.

VB 6.0 lets you copy a file with the FileCopy() function. .NET uses the Copy() method to copy a file.

---

3.   The FileInfo class provides almost identical functionality, but it is optimized for reusing the object many times. Consult MSDN for a full description. Use the index and type in **System.IO.FileInfo**.

You can rename a file in VB 6.0 using the `Rename()` function. In .NET, call the `Move()` method. The `Move()` method of the `File` class is similar to the `Move()` method in the `Directory` class. Not only does the `Move()` method let you rename a file, but it also lets you move it to another location on your hard drive.

The `Kill()` function in VB 6.0 deletes a file. The equivalent method in .NET is `Delete()`.

VB 6.0

Pass the `Dir()` function a search pattern on the first call to find the first matching filename. On successive calls don't pass a parameter and it will find the next matching filename.

```
var=Dir(path)'Get the first matching filename
var=Dir()'Get the next matching filename
```

Pass the `FileDateTime()` function a filename and it returns a string with the date and time the file was last modified.

```
var=FileDateTime(filename)
```

Pass the `FileLen()` function a filename and it returns the file size.

```
var=FileLen(filename)
```

The `FileCopy()` and `Rename()` statements both expect two parameters. The first parameter is the filename of the file to copy and the second parameter is the filename of the destination file. The `FileCopy()` function makes a copy of the file and the `Rename()` function changes the name of the file.

```
FileCopy sourcefile, destinationfile
Rename oldfile, newfile
```

The `Kill` statement is passed a filename. The file is deleted.

```
Kill filename
```

VB .NET

Pass the `Exists()` method a filename and it returns `True` if the file is there.

```
var=File.Exists(filename)
'Demonstrate checking if a file exists in the parent directory
var=File.Exists("..\MyFile.txt")
```

The three methods that return a file-related date and time all have one parameter that accepts the filename. These methods are GetCreationTime(), GetLastAccessTime(), and GetLastWriteTime().

```
varDate1=File.GetCreationTime(filename)
varDate2=File.GetLastAccessTime(filename)
varDate3=File.GetLastWriteTime(filename)
```

The Copy() and Move() methods both take two parameters. The first parameter is the filename of the file to copy and the second parameter is the filename of the destination file. The Copy() function makes a copy of the file. The Move() function moves the file to another location. If the two file paths are identical and only the filename is different, the Move() function will rename the file.

```
File.Copy(sourcefile, destinationfile)
File.Move(oldfile, newfile)
'Demonstrate renaming a file in the current directory
File.Move("MyOldFile.txt", "MyNewFile.txt")
```

The Delete() method is passed the filename. The file is deleted.

```
File.Delete(filename)
```

C#
Pass the Exists() method a filename and it returns true if the file is there.

```
var=File.Exists(filename);
```

The three methods that return a file-related date and time all have one parameter that accepts the filename. These methods are GetCreationTime(), GetLastAccessTime(), and GetLastWriteTime().

```
varDate1=File.GetCreationTime(filename);
varDate2=File.GetLastAccessTime(filename);
varDate3=File.GetLastWriteTime(filename);
//Demonstrate displaying when a file in a subdirectory was last modified
Console.WriteLine(@"SubFoler\MyFile.txt");
```

The Copy() and Move() methods both take two parameters. The first parameter is the filename of the file to copy and the second parameter is the filename of the destination file. The Copy() function makes a copy of the file. The Move() function moves the file to another location. If the two file paths are identical and only the filename is different, the Move() function will rename the file.

```
File.Copy(sourcefile, destinationfile);
File.Move(oldfile, newfile);
```

The Delete() method is passed the filename. The file is deleted.

```
File.Delete(filename);
//Demonstrate deleting a file in the root directory of the current drive
File.Delete(@"F:\MyFile.txt");
```

Reading and Writing Text Files

One of the ways you can save and retrieve data is through the use of text files. This can be useful when you work with temporary data, files that need to be read by a user without special software, or when you don't want the overhead of managing a database.[4]

VB 6.0 has one primary way of working with text files. It is clean and simple. There is a lot more functionality built into the .NET classes. Consequently, the .NET classes give you more options and are more complex.

The Stream class handles reading and writing a sequence of binary data. This can be a file or any input/output device. The Stream class is the base class for many classes that specialize in reading certain types of binary data. This gives you the benefit of being able to exchange binary data between classes that store that data in different formats. For example, you can take data that is in a memory stream and save it to a file stream. You don't have to write any data conversion routines because .NET handles this for you.

There are different classes to read and write data to a variety of media. This chapter focuses on the StreamReader and StreamWriter classes because they provide equivalent functionality to the VB 6.0 text file I/O functions.

The functionality for reading and writing text files in .NET is in the System.IO namespace.

Opening a File

Before you can read or write any data to a file, you have to open the file.

VB 6.0 manages files with a file number. When you open a file, you need to get an available file number and then assign a file pointer to it. The FreeFile function retrieves the next available file number and you use it to call the Open statement. This file number is used whenever a reference to the file is needed.

---

4. If you want to manage data with databases, see Chapter 13.

.NET has a few different methods of opening a file. The easiest way to open a file is to pass the filename to the class constructor method of the StreamReader or StreamWriter class. When reading a file, the class will analyze the file to determine the character encoding. When writing to a file, it will default to Unicode. If you want to specify which encoding method to use, you can put this as the second parameter of the constructor.

You can also open a new file using the FileStream class. The benefit of using this class is that you have the option to specify any of the following properties: creation mode, read/write permission, and sharing permission. The constructor has many overloads to handle any combination of these parameters. To use the FileStream class, you have to instantiate a FileStream object and pass this object variable as a parameter to the constructor of either the StreamReader or StreamWriter class.

VB 6.0

Use the FreeFile function to get the next available file number. Pass it to the Open statement with the filename and the mode of access.

```
Dim FileNo as Integer
FileNo = FreeFile
Open FileName For Mode As #FileNo
```

VB .NET

Use the StreamReader or StreamWriter class constructor to open a file and pass it a file path. You can pass an optional second parameter specifying the encoding format.

```
Dim myFile as New StreamReader(filepath)
Dim myFile2 as New StreamWriter(filepath, encoding)
```

If you want more control over opening the file, use the FileStream class. Any of the parameters to the FileStream constructor class can be omitted. Create a new instance of this class and pass that instance to the StreamReader or StreamWriter constructor class.

```
Dim myFS As New FileStream(filepath, FileMode, FileAccess, FileShare)
Dim myFile As New StreamReader(myFS)
```

C#

Use the StreamReader or StreamWriter class constructor to open a file and pass it a file path. You can pass an optional second parameter specifying the encoding format.

```
StreamReader myFile = new StreamReader(filepath);
StreamWriter myFile = new StreamWriter(filepath, encoding);
```

If you want more control over opening the file, use the FileStream class. Any of the parameters to the FileStream constructor class can be omitted. Create a new instance of this class and pass that instance to the StreamReader or StreamWriter constructor class.

```
FileStream myFS = new FileStream(filepath, FileMode, FileAccess, FileShare);
StreamReader myFile = new StreamReader(myFS);
```

Reading from a File

Reading from a text file enables you to take the next available string and assign it to a variable. Although you will probably assign it to a string variable, you can convert the string so it can be saved to a variable of a different data type.

VB 6.0 uses two different statements to read from a file: LineInput and InputString. LineInput reads a line of text from a file and doesn't include the line feed character. InputString reads in a specified number of characters and it includes a line feed character.

To find out when you've reached the end of the file, call the EOF() function.

.NET uses the ReadLine() and ReadToEnd() methods to read text from a file. The ReadLine() method only reads one line at a time. The ReadToEnd() method reads from the current position in the file to the end. Both methods return the data as a string.

To find out when you've reached the end of the file, you have to test the return string for Nothing in VB .NET and null in C#. If the string is Nothing or null, the complete file has been read.

VB 6.0

Use either of the following functions to read a text line from a file: LineInput or Input. Use the EOF() function to find out if you've reached the end of the file.

```
If Not EOF(FileNo) Then
    Input #FileNo, myString
End If
```

VB .NET

Use the ReadLine() or ReadToEnd() method of the StringReader class to read text from a file. ReadLine() reads in the next line. ReadToEnd() reads from the current position to the end of the file. If the return string is Nothing, the end of the file has been reached.

```
myString = myFile.ReadLine()
myString = myFile.ReadToEnd()
If myString = Nothing Then ...
```

C#

Use the ReadLine() or ReadToEnd() method to read text from a file. ReadLine() reads in the next line. ReadToEnd() reads from the current position to the end of the file. If the return string is Null, the end of the file has been reached.

```
myString = myFile.ReadLine();
myString = myFile.ReadToEnd();
if (myString = null) ...
```

Writing to a File

You can save text strings by writing them to a file. You do not have to worry about putting line separators between each string because the methods do this for you.

VB 6.0 uses the Print(), PrintLine(), and Write() statements to save data to a text file. The Print() statement does not include the line feed character and the PrintLine() statement does. The Write() statement differs from the other two because it inserts commas between items and puts quotation marks around strings.

.NET uses the Write() or WriteLine() method to save data to a text file. You can pass it either a string or a character array.

VB 6.0

Use one of the following statements to write a string to a file: Print, PrintLine, or Write. Pass it the file number and the data to write.

```
Print #FileNo, myString
```

VB .NET

Use either the Write() or WriteLine() method of the StreamWriter class to save data to a text file. The Write() method does not write a line feed after the data; the WriteLine() method does.

```
myFile.Write(data)
myFile.WriteLine(data)
```

C#

Use either the `Write()` or `WriteLine()` method of the `StreamWriter` class to save data to a text file. The `Write()` method does not write a line feed after the data; the `WriteLine()` method does.

```
myFile.Write(data);
myFile.WriteLine(data);
```

Closing a File

It is important to close a file so that no data is lost. Closing a file also releases any locks that may have been on it.

   Both VB 6.0 and .NET use the `Close()` method to close a file. In .NET you have the option of calling the `Flush()` method if you don't want to close a file but you want to make sure any unwritten data gets saved.

VB 6.0

Use the `Close` statement to close a file.

```
Close #FileNo
```

VB .NET

Use the `Close()` method to close a file.

```
myFile.Close()
```

C#

Use the `Close()` method to close a file.

```
myFile.Close();
```

Example 12-1. Managing Files and Directories

This example demonstrates the different methods that enable you to create, rename, and delete files and directories. The menu options are divided between using directories or files. The first two menu options let you create a new directory or change to a different directory. The top of the menu shows the current directory. This enables you to see the results every time a change is made to the current directory. The second half of the menu lets you work with files. You can list all the files in a directory, get the modification times of a file, copy a file, or rename a file.

VB 6.0

```
'Managing files and directories in VB 6.0
'Copyright (c)2001 by Bischof Systems, Inc.

Sub Main()
    Dim menuItem As Integer
    Dim currentDirectory, input1, input2 As String
    Dim fileNames() As String, currentFile As Variant
    'FileAttributes fileAttr
    Debug.Print "File Manager"
    Do
        currentDirectory = CurDir()
        Debug.Print
        Debug.Print "Current Directory: " & currentDirectory
        Debug.Print "1. Create Directory"
        Debug.Print "2. Change Directory"
        Debug.Print "3. List File in Directory"
        Debug.Print "4. Get File Times"
        Debug.Print "5. Copy a File"
        Debug.Print "6. Rename a File"
        Debug.Print "0. Exit"
        menuItem = "0" & InputBox("Which function to perform? ")
        Select Case menuItem
            Case 1 'Create directory
                input1 = InputBox("New Directory: ")
                MkDir input1
            Case 2 'Change directory
                input1 = InputBox("Change to: ")
                ChDir input1
            Case 3 'List files in directory
                input1 = InputBox("File Search Pattern: ")
                If (input1 = "") Then
                    input1 = "*.*"
                End If
                currentFile = Dir(input1)
                While currentFile <> ""
                    Debug.Print currentFile
                    currentFile = Dir()
                Wend
            Case 4 'Get file times
                input1 = InputBox("Filename: ")
                Debug.Print "Modified: " & FileDateTime(input1)
```

```
                    Case 5 'Copy a file
                        input1 = InputBox("Filename: ")
                        input2 = InputBox("Copy to: ")
                        FileCopy input1, input2
                    Case 6 'Rename a file
                        input1 = InputBox("Filename: ")
                        input2 = InputBox("New Filename: ")
                        Name input1 As input2
                End Select
            Loop While menuItem <> 0
    End Sub
```

VB .NET

```
'Managing files and directories in VB .NET
'Copyright (c)2001 by Bischof Systems, Inc.

Imports System.IO
Imports System.Data
Module Module1

    Sub Main()
        Dim menuItem As Integer
        Dim currentDirectory, input1, input2 As String
        Dim fileNames() As String, currentFile As String
        'FileAttributes fileAttr
        Console.WriteLine("File Manager")
        Do
            currentDirectory = Directory.GetCurrentDirectory()
            Console.WriteLine()
            Console.WriteLine("Current Directory: {0}", currentDirectory)
            Console.WriteLine("1. Create Directory")
            Console.WriteLine("2. Change Directory")
            Console.WriteLine("3. List File in Directory")
            Console.WriteLine("4. Get File Times")
            Console.WriteLine("5. Copy a File")
            Console.WriteLine("6. Rename a File")
            Console.WriteLine("0. Exit")
            Console.Write("Which function to perform? ")
            menuItem = Integer.Parse("0" + Console.ReadLine())
```

```vbnet
        Select Case menuItem
            Case 1 'Create directory
                Console.Write("New Directory: ")
                input1 = Console.ReadLine()
                Directory.CreateDirectory(input1)
            Case 2 'Change directory
                Console.Write("Change to: ")
                input1 = Console.ReadLine()
                Directory.SetCurrentDirectory(input1)
            Case 3 'List files in directory
                Console.Write("File Search Pattern: ")
                input1 = Console.ReadLine()
                If (input1 = "") Then
                    input1 = "*.*"
                End If
                fileNames = Directory.GetFiles(currentDirectory, input1)
                For Each currentFile In fileNames
                    Console.WriteLine(currentFile.ToString())
                Next
            Case 4 'Get file times
                Console.Write("Filename: ")
                input1 = Console.ReadLine()
                'fileAttr=File.GetAttributes(input1)
                Console.WriteLine("Created: {0}", _
                    File.GetCreationTime(input1))
                Console.WriteLine("Modified: {0}", _
                    File.GetLastWriteTime(input1))
                Console.WriteLine("Accessed: {0}", _
                    File.GetLastAccessTime(input1).ToShortDateString())
            Case 5 'Copy a file
                Console.Write("Filename: ")
                input1 = Console.ReadLine()
                Console.Write("Copy to: ")
                input2 = Console.ReadLine()
                File.Copy(input1, input2)
            Case 6 'Rename a file
                Console.Write("Filename: ")
                input1 = Console.ReadLine()
                Console.Write("New Filename: ")
                input2 = Console.ReadLine()
                File.Move(input1, input2)
        End Select
    Loop While (menuItem <> 0)
    End Sub
End Module
```

C#

```
//Managing files and directories in C#
//Copyright (c)2001 by Bischof Systems, Inc.

using System;
using System.IO;
using System.Data;
namespace C_FileManagement
{
    class Class1
    {
        [STAThread]
        static void Main(string[] args)
        {
            int menuItem=0;
            string currentDirectory="", input1="", input2="";
            string[] files;
            //FileAttributes fileAttr;
            Console.WriteLine("File Manager");
            Console.WriteLine(File.GetCreationTime(@"testfolder3\test.txt"));
            do
            {
                currentDirectory = Directory.GetCurrentDirectory();
                Console.WriteLine("\nCurrent Directory: {0}",currentDirectory);
                Console.WriteLine("1. Create Directory");
                Console.WriteLine("2. Change Directory");
                Console.WriteLine("3. List File in Directory");
                Console.WriteLine("4. Get File Times");
                Console.WriteLine("5. Copy a File");
                Console.WriteLine("6. Rename a File");
                Console.WriteLine("0. Exit");
                menuItem=int.Parse("0" + Console.ReadLine());
                switch (menuItem)
                {
                    case 1:      //Create directory
                        Console.Write("New Directory: ");
                        input1=Console.ReadLine();
                        Directory.CreateDirectory(input1);
                        break;
                    case 2:      //Change directory
                        Console.Write("Change to: ");
                        input1=Console.ReadLine();
                        Directory.SetCurrentDirectory(input1);
                        break;
```

```
        case 3:      //List files in directory
            Console.Write("File Search Pattern: ");
            input1=Console.ReadLine();
            if (input1=="")
            {
                input1="*.*";
            }
            files = Directory.GetFiles(currentDirectory,input1);
            foreach(string file in files)
            {
                Console.WriteLine(file.ToString());
            }
            break;
        case 4:      //Get file times
            Console.Write("Filename: ");
            input1=Console.ReadLine();
            //fileAttr=File.GetAttributes(input1);
            Console.WriteLine("Created: {0}",
                File.GetCreationTime(input1));
            Console.WriteLine("Modified: {0}",
                File.GetLastWriteTime(input1));
            Console.WriteLine("Accessed: {0}",
                File.GetLastAccessTime(input1).ToShortDateString());
            break;
        case 5:      //Copy a file
            Console.Write("Filename: ");
            input1=Console.ReadLine();
            Console.Write("Copy to: ");
            input2=Console.ReadLine();
            File.Copy(input1,input2);
            break;
        case 6:      //Rename a file
            Console.Write("Filename: ");
            input1=Console.ReadLine();
            Console.Write("New Filename: ");
            input2=Console.ReadLine();
            File.Move(input1,input2);
            break;
    }
} while (menuItem!=0);
        }
    }
}
```

Example 12-1 Output

```
File Manager

Current Directory: E:\DotNet\C_FileManagement\bin\Debug
1. Create Directory
2. Change Directory
3. List File in Directory
4. Get File Times
5. Copy a File
6. Rename a File
0. Exit
Which function to perform: 2
Change to: C:\DirTest

Current Directory: C:\DirTest
1. Create Directory
2. Change Directory
3. List File in Directory
4. Get File Times
5. Copy a File
6. Rename a File
0. Exit
Which function to perform: 3
File Search Pattern: *.*
C:\DirTest\Doc2.txt
C:\DirTest\New Text Document (2).txt
C:\DirTest\New Text Document.txt

Current Directory: C:\DirTest
1. Create Directory
2. Change Directory
3. List File in Directory
4. Get File Times
5. Copy a File
6. Rename a File
0. Exit
Which function to perform: 5
Filename: Doc2.txt
Copy to: DocBak.txt

Current Directory: C:\DirTest
1. Create Directory
2. Change Directory
```

```
3. List File in Directory
4. Get File Times
5. Copy a File
6. Rename a File
0. Exit
Which function to perform: 3
File Search Pattern: Doc*
C:\DirTest\Doc2.txt
C:\DirTest\DocBak.txt

Current Directory: C:\DirTest
1. Create Directory
2. Change Directory
3. List File in Directory
4. Get File Times
5. Copy a File
6. Rename a File
0. Exit
Which function to perform: 0
```

Example 12-2. Reading and Writing Text Files

This example demonstrates the functions of writing to a text file and then reading it back. The user is presented with two options. The first is to write to a text file and the second is to read from a text file. If the user wants to write to a file, he or she simply types in as many lines as he or she wants. When the user is done, he or she enters a blank line. The file is closed and the data is saved. If the user wants to read a file, he or she enters a filename and the contents are displayed on the screen.

VB 6.0

```
'Reading and writing text files in VB 6.0
'Copyright (c)2001 by Bischof Systems, Inc.

Sub Main()
    Dim menuItem As Integer
    Dim fileName As String, fileLine As String
    Dim outFile As Integer, inFile As Integer
    Do
        menuItem = InputBox("1: Read from file" & vbCr & "2: Write to a file" & _
            vbCr & "Which function to perform? ")
```

```
          Select Case menuItem
              Case 1      'Read from a file
                  fileName = InputBox("Filename")
                  inFile = FreeFile
                  Open fileName For Input As #inFile
                  Do While Not EOF(inFile)
                      Input #inFile, fileLine
                      Debug.Print fileLine
                  Loop
                  Close #inFile
              Case 2      'Write to a file
                  fileName = InputBox("Filename")
                  outFile = FreeFile
                  Open fileName For Output As #outFile
                  Do
                      fileLine = InputBox("Text")
                      If fileLine <> "" Then
                          Print #outFile, fileLine
                      End If
                  Loop Until fileLine = ""
                  Close #outFile
          End Select
      Loop Until menuItem = 0
  End Sub
```

VB .NET

```
'Reading and writing text files in VB .NET
'Copyright (c)2001 by Bischof Systems, Inc.


Imports System.IO


Module Module1


    Sub Main()
          Dim menuItem As Integer
          Dim input, fileLine As String
          Dim outFile As StreamWriter
          Dim inFile As StreamReader
          Console.WriteLine("Text File I/O")
          Do
              Console.WriteLine()
              Console.WriteLine("1: Read from file")
              Console.WriteLine("2: Write to a file")
              Console.Write("Which function to perform? ")
```

```
            menuItem = Integer.Parse("0" + Console.ReadLine())
            Select Case menuItem
                Case 1 'Read from a file
                    Console.Write("Filename: ")
                    input = Console.ReadLine()
                    'Open the input file
                    inFile = New StreamReader(input)
                    fileLine = inFile.ReadLine()
                    'Read from the file until we reach the end
                    While (fileLine <> Nothing)
                        Console.WriteLine(fileLine)
                        'Get the next line from the file
                        fileLine = inFile.ReadLine()
                    End While
                    inFile.Close()
                Case 2 'Write to a file
                    Console.Write("Filename: ")
                    input = Console.ReadLine()
                    'Open the output file
                    outFile = New StreamWriter(input)
                    fileLine = Console.ReadLine()
                    Do While fileLine <> ""
                        'Write the user's input to the file
                        outFile.WriteLine(fileLine)
                        fileLine = Console.ReadLine()
                    Loop
                    outFile.Close()
            End Select
        Loop Until menuItem = 0
    End Sub
End Module
```

C#

```
//Reading and writing text files in C#
//Copyright (c)2001 by Bischof Systems, Inc.

using System;
using System.IO;
namespace C_FileIO
{
```

```csharp
class Class1
{
    [STAThread]
    static void Main(string[] args)
    {
        int menuItem=0;
        string input="", fileLine="";
        StreamWriter outFile;
        StreamReader inFile;
        Console.WriteLine("Text File I/O");
        do
        {
            Console.WriteLine("\n1: Read from file");
            Console.WriteLine("2: Write to a file");
            Console.Write("Which function to perform? ");
            menuItem = int.Parse("0"+Console.ReadLine());
            switch (menuItem)
            {
                case 1:     //Read from a file
                    Console.Write("Filename: ");
                    //Open the input file
                    input=Console.ReadLine();
                    inFile=new StreamReader(input);
                    //Read from the file until we reach the end
                    while ((fileLine=inFile.ReadLine())!=null)
                    {
                        Console.WriteLine(fileLine);
                    }
                    inFile.Close();
                    break;
                case 2:     //Write to a file
                    Console.Write("Filename: ");
                    input=Console.ReadLine();
                    //Open the output file
                    outFile=new StreamWriter(input);
                    fileLine=Console.ReadLine();
                    while (fileLine != "")
                    {
                        //Write the user's input to the file
                        outFile.WriteLine(fileLine);
                        fileLine=Console.ReadLine();
                    }
```

```
                outFile.Close();
                break;
            }
        } while (menuItem!=0);
    }
  }
}
```

Example 12-2 Output

```
Text File I/O

1: Read from file
2: Write to a file
Which function to perform? 2
Filename: C:\Test.txt
Line 1
Middle Line
Line 3

1: Read from file
2: Write to a file
Which function to perform? 1
Filename: C:\Test.txt
Line 1
Middle Line
Line 3

1: Read from file
2: Write to a file
Which function to perform?
0
```

CHAPTER 13

ADO.NET

Table 13-1. ADO to ADO.NET Equivalent Chart

ADO	ADO.NET
Connection	SqlConnection OleDbConnetion
Command	SqlCommand OleDbCommand
Parameters	SqlParametersCollection OleDbParametersCollection
Recordset	DataTable DataReader
Fields Collection	DataColumn
ConnectionString	ConnectionString
Open	Open()
Close	Close()
CommandText	CommandText
CommandType	CommandType
State	
CreateParameter	CreateParameter() Parameters.Add()
Execute	ExecuteQuery() ExecuteReader()
CursorLocation	
CursorType	
LockType	
RecordCount	DataTable.Rows.Count()
State	
Requery (re-executes the command)	

Table 13-1. ADO to ADO.NET Equivalent Chart (Continued)

ADO	ADO.NET
Resync (refreshes cached recordset)	
Recordset!field	
Recordset.Fields(index)	DataRow[index]
Recordset.Fields("field")	DataRow["field"]
BOF()	DataTable[0]
EOF()	DataTable[DataTable.Row.Count]
Bookmark	
AbsolutePosition	
Move	
MoveFirst	
MoveLast	
MoveNext	
MovePrevious	
Sort	DataTable.Select(Filter, Sort)
Filter	DataTable.Select(Filter, Sort)
Find	DataTable.Select(Filter, Sort)
AddNew	Add()
Delete	Delete()
Update	DataAdapter.Update()

Overview

ADO.NET is so powerful that entire books are dedicated to the different ways to use its capabilities and maximize its performance. This chapter does not attempt to replace those books because there is too much material to cover. This chapter is to be used as a quick reference for looking up various ADO.NET syntax requirements for SQL Server and OLE DB–compliant databases. This chapter covers standard, day-to-day database development.

ADO.NET is a complex topic. No matter how much I simplify it here, it still takes effort to understand all the different ways to use it. To make the learning process as simple as possible, each section in this chapter is a tutorial that is organized by task. Go to the section header that describes what you want to do, and that section will walk you through each step.[1] The tutorial sections in this chapter are as follows:

- Opening a Connection

- Calling Stored Procedures and Using SQL Statements

- Using a Table for Forward-Only Access

- Reading and Modifying Individual Records

- Viewing Data with the DataGrid Control

Introduction to ADO.NET

Microsoft has gone from "native" drivers to ODBC, DAO, RDO, ADO, and now to ADO.NET. Microsoft introduced each technology as the "ultimate" in database connectivity. So do we really need ADO.NET? Yes, we do.[2]

When Microsoft first introduced ADO in VB 6.0, it was quite a change for Windows developers. Prior to VB 6.0, most programmers relied on DAO as the primary means of data access. Unfortunately, DAO wasn't a scalable and robust solution. It also didn't take into account the number of different data sources that would become important when the Internet exploded onto the scene. DAO could access the different ODBC drivers, but it remained connected and so was not the most efficient option.

RDO was introduced as a slimmed-down version of DAO that was designed to work with SQL Server. But its life was short-lived before ADO became the new king of the hill.

ADO was a major leap forward because it introduced the concept of taking the different tasks of accessing data and separating them into individual objects.

---

1. Throughout this book, every effort is made to show how VB 6.0 compares to the .NET languages. However, there are so many differences between ADO and ADO.NET that doing direct comparisons in this chapter would unnecessarily complicate things. Instead, VB 6.0 will only be used as a reference point for helping to explain the concepts better. It won't receive as much attention as it has in the other chapters.

2. Unfortunately, the "ADO" in ADO.NET stands for "ActiveX Data Objects" and the .NET Framework doesn't use ActiveX. So why is ADO.NET named after a technology it doesn't use? I don't know. But it's my guess that Microsoft's marketing department (and not the engineering department) had the final say on this decision.

Thus, it gave data access an object-oriented overhaul. Each ADO object had a purpose and it could be linked to one or more different ADO objects. This made it a very flexible technology that could easily manage multiple types of data sources and have them seamlessly talk to each other. This was a great advancement for Windows development.

ADO also added disconnected recordsets to the arsenal of database tools. *Disconnected recordsets* give you the ability to free up client/server database connection resources. Reading and updating data is done in a batch format. Unfortunately, disconnected recordsets didn't receive as much attention as they should have and thus have not been implemented as much as they should have.

Almost every programmer that works with VB 6.0 is familiar with ADO client/server connectivity, but disconnected recordsets are a foreign concept to many. As a result of the fact that the majority of programmers use ADO connected recordsets rather than disconnected recordsets, the references to ADO in this chapter regard using connected recordsets only. This enables you to build upon your knowledge of ADO connectivity to learn the new concepts in ADO.NET.

ADO.NET reverses the focus of ADO. In standard ADO, using connected recordsets is the primary means of data access for most programmers and disconnected recordsets received less attention. ADO.NET makes working with disconnected data the primary means of data access and pushes connected recordsets into the background.

Developers discovered two major challenges with traditional connected technology: the fact that it relied on "fat" clients, and the fact that it required a connected recordset. You open a table, lock out the records, make changes, unlock the records, and close the table. When you develop for the Internet, it isn't possible to open a table and lock out records until a user is finished with it. You need to quickly pass data between the server and the browser and only update the necessary records. This is typically done using stored procedures, and you have to programmatically manage the individual changes to each record. ADO.NET has been designed to make it easier and more efficient to access any data from a browser and only pass the modified records back to the server. It takes care of the overhead of tracking which records have changed and how they have changed.

ADO.NET also passes all data as XML. This makes talking to any data source that supports XML seamless. Given the fact that XML is becoming the standard means of transferring data, it will soon be hard to find a data source that ADO.NET *won't* talk to.[3] ADO 2.6 also supports XML, but it was imple-

---

3. Although ADO.NET can talk to many data sources, this book will only make reference to the standard Microsoft data sources such as SQL Server and Microsoft Access. You can apply these concepts for use with other data sources.

mented as an "add-on" to the technology and it has a few drawbacks. ADO.NET was designed from the ground up for the purpose of using XML, making it faster and easier to use than previous versions of ADO.

It should be mentioned that because ADO.NET is the latest data access technology, it gets a lot of attention from programming magazines and .NET-related Web sites. This might give you the impression that standard ADO is an older technology that isn't useful anymore. This is not true.[4] Although ADO is not designed as a native .NET class and is slower as a result, you can still use it within .NET and it can be an excellent choice for client/server development. As an example, consider an application that involves a high volume of data entry. Each user needs access to the latest changes made by the other users. Connecting to a database and later making changes via a batch process isn't acceptable.

As with any new technology, it's tempting to get lured into believing that newer is better. Remember to consider the strengths and weaknesses of every available technology when designing your application.

Summarizing the ADO.NET Classes

Because ADO.NET is a new technology, there are new concepts to learn and there is also a repackaging of some old concepts in a new form. Table 13-2 briefly describes the classes used in ADO.NET. This chapter focuses on working with SQL Server databases using Sql-related classes and Access databases using OleDb classes. These classes are described in more detail in the sections that use them. .NET also has classes for ODBC connections, and the concepts you learn in this chapter can be applied to ODBC, but they are not discussed here. You can reference MSDN for more information on ADO.NET.

Table 13-2. ADO.NET Class Descriptions

CLASS	DESCRIPTION
SqlConnection OleDBConnection	Required for accessing data from any data source. It specifies things such as the server name, database name, user ID, and password.
SqlCommand OleDBCommand	Required for accessing data. It stores a string that tells the data source what to do: run a stored procedure, execute SQL statements, or get records from a table.

---

4. It's not really the fault of the magazine publishers. They have already written every tip and technique imaginable for ADO. They need something new to write about so you'll keep buying their magazines.

Table 13-2. ADO.NET Class Descriptions (Continued)

CLASS	DESCRIPTION
SqlParameter OleDbparameter	Used with a Command object to pass arguments to a stored procedure.
SqlDataAdapter OleDbDataAdapter	This is the link between the data source and the data objects in your program. It manages the transfer of data between the two. You must have a data adapter if you want to modify individual records.
SqlDataReader OleDbDataReader	A forward-only, read-only connected table. While it is open, you can't use the Connection object. This is the fastest method of reading data.
DataSet	This is a collection of DataTables.
DataRelation	Links two DataTables together and forms a relationship between them. Both DataTables must be in the same DataSet.
DataTable	This stores all the records in memory as a collection. Each record is called a DataRow. It also has a DataColumn collection so that it knows the schema of each column.
DataRow	A record in a table. Each field is treated as an element of a collection.
DataColumn	Defines a field's schema. Some of these properties are data type, autoincrement, default value, and so on. It can't access the field data. You must use the DataRow for this.

Within Table 13-2 are classes with a prefix of "Sql" and classes with a prefix of "OleDb." If you want to connect to a SQL Server database, use the classes prefixed with "Sql." They have been optimized to be used with SQL Server.[5] Accessing any other databases requires the use of the classes prefixed with "OleDB." This includes Microsoft Access databases.

Microsoft created the "Sql" classes so that they would have the same functionality as the "OleDb" classes but would be optimized for SQL Server. The classes are virtually identical to each other. The examples in this chapter show how each one works: The VB .NET examples use the "OleDb" classes and the C# examples use the "Sql" classes. Of course, both languages can use either set of classes. When you look at the examples, you'll see that the only difference between the two is that the C# examples have semicolons at the end of each line.

---

5. Only use with SQL Server versions 7.0 and later.

The examples in this chapter use the Northwind database. This is a sample database included with SQL Server and also included with Microsoft Access. You probably need to modify the connection string to map to your own copy of the Northwind database.

The "Sql" classes are found in the `System.Data.SqlClient` namespace. The "OleDb" classes are found in the `System.Data.OleDb` namespace. The other namespace that is used is the `System.Data` namespace (this namespace is discussed later in the chapter). It provides the classes to read and update individual records.

Looking at ADO.NET from 10,000 Feet

If you are coming from a VB 6.0 background, the new functionality in ADO.NET might seem a little strange at first. It's a good idea take a few minutes to step back and look at the general concepts of how it all works before you get into the details. This section summarizes what it takes to talk to a database.

There are two things you must always do before talking to a database. The first thing you must do is create a `Connection` object. The `Connection` object defines what database you are going to talk to, how you want to talk to it (user ID, security level, and so on), and where it is located. The second thing you must do is create a `Command` object. The `Command` object is responsible for passing the instructions to the database. This is how the database knows whether it should call a stored procedure or execute a SQL statement.

After you create the `Connection` and `Command` objects, you have some choices to make.

If you want to modify a block of records with one call to the database, pass the `Command` object the name of a stored procedure or pass it a SQL statement. It will perform the appropriate actions on the records that meet any specified criteria and return the number of records affected. Nothing else is required. This process is described in the "Calling Stored Procedures and Using SQL Statements" section.

If you want to read all of the records from the beginning of a table to the end and you don't want to make any changes, use a `DataReader` object. Set the `CommandText` property of the `Command` object to a stored procedure name or SQL statement and call the `ExecuteReader()` method. It returns a `DataReader` object. The only method you will use to move through the records is `Read()`. This method is similar to the `MoveNext()` method in ADO. You can only move forward and you can't make any changes to the data. It's important to note that the `DataReader` object has a live connection to the database that stays open as long as you are reading data. Although this is not an exclusive lock, it is a very expensive connection and you should be careful that it only remains open as long as necessary. The DataReader object is described in the "Using a Table for Forward-Only Access" section.

If you want to access individual records and be able to make changes to them, things get a little more complicated. Just like the DataReader, ADO.NET uses the Command object to return a group of records. But now you have to handle those records with different objects.

The DataAdapter object creates a DataTable to hold the all the records. It automatically inserts this new DataTable object into a DataSet object. The DataSet object holds a collection of all the DataTable objects. The DataTable now holds every record in a collection of DataRow objects. You access this collection just as you would access any other collection. It has elements (the DataRow) that are accessed by their index, and it has a lower bound and an upper bound. Any changes you make to the DataRows are not automatically saved to the database. To save changes, you have to link the DataAdapter to a CommandBuilder object. As you make changes to the DataRows, the CommandBuilder object will create the necessary SQL statements to persist those changes onto the database. Using the DataAdapter and its related objects is described in the "Reading and Modifying Individual Records" section.

Opening a Connection

The Connection object is used for identifying where the data comes from. Having a Connection object is required for accessing any data.

The Connection object in ADO.NET is similar to the Connection object in ADO. It requires a string that states the different values to pass to the data source. Each value is separated with a semicolon. The names of the required values are Provider, Server or Data Source, uid (user ID), pwd (password), and Database or Initial Catalog. Provider is not required if you are using a SqlConnection object because SQL Server is the only provider it can use. Other values that can be placed in the connection string are described in the MSDN documentation.

After you set the connection string, open the connection using the Open() method. Now you can call other methods to access the data. When you are finished using the connection, close it using the Close() method.

VB 6.0

Instantiate a Connection object by setting its properties.

```
Dim Cn As ADODB.Connection
Set Cn = New ADODB.Connection
Cn.Provider = "SQLOLEDB"
Cn.ConnectionString = "server=(local);uid=sa;database=NorthWind"
Cn.Open
```

```
'...do data access...
Cn.Close
```

VB .NET

Instantiate the OleDbConnection object by passing values in a string.

```
Imports System.Data.OleDb
...
Dim dbCn As OleDbConnection
dbCn = New OleDbConnection( _
        "Provider=Microsoft.JET.OLEDB.4.0; Data Source=C:\Northwind.Mdb")
dbCn.Open()
...do data access...
dbCn.Close()
```

C#

Instantiate the SqlConnection object by passing values in a string. The Provider value isn't used.

```
using System.Data.SqlClient;
...
SqlConnection dbCn;
dbCn = new SqlConnection("server=(local);uid=sa;database=Northwind");
dbCn.Open();
...do data access...
dbCn.Close();
```

Calling Stored Procedures and Using SQL Statements

You can perform actions on a database by calling stored procedures or by using SQL statements. The database looks at the string passed to it, and it either selects records or modifies data depending on what the string has in it. This section focuses on actions that do not return any records. Calling stored procedures and using SQL statements that return records are covered in the next two sections.

The Command object is responsible for passing instructions to the database to tell it what to do. These instructions can be as simple as the name of a stored procedure, which has its own set of instructions, or as complex as a multitable SELECT statement. Either way, the instructions have to be passed to the Command object to be executed.

Executing Commands

Instantiate the Command object with a string that has the name of a stored procedure or a SQL statement in it as the first parameter. The second parameter is the Connection object that was created in the last section.

After you instantiate the object, use the CommandType property of the Command object to tell it what type of string was passed to it. If the string is a stored procedure, set the CommandType property to "StoredProcedure." If it is a SQL statement, set it to "Text." The default is "Text," so you could omit this step for SQL statements. If it is just the name of a table, set it to "TableDirect." Only the OleDBCommand object allows you to open a table by its name only. If you want to do that with the SqlCommand object, use the SELECT * FROM table statement instead.

Execute the command by calling the ExecuteNonQuery() method. This method passes the string to the database server where the actions are carried out. The method returns an integer specifying how many records were affected.

VB 6.0

Instantiate a new Command object and set the ActiveConnection and CommandText properties before calling the Execute() method.

```
Dim Cmd As ADODB.Command
Set Cmd = New ADODB.Command
Cmd.ActiveConnection = Cn
Cmd.CommandText = "DELETE FROM TempTransactions"
Cmd.Execute
```

VB .NET

Instantiate a new Command object by passing the constructor an action string and a Connection object.

```
Dim dbCmd As OleDbCommand
Dim numRecs As Integer
dbCmd = New OleDbCommand("DELETE FROM TempTransactions", dbCn)
numRecs = dbCmd.ExecuteNonQuery()
```

C#

Instantiate a new Command object by passing the constructor an action string and a Connection object.

```
SqlCommand dbCmd;
int numRecs;
dbCmd = new SqlCommand("DELETE FROM Transactions", dbCn);
numRecs = dbCmd.ExecuteNonQuery();
```

Using Parameters

Parameters are the means of passing arguments to a stored procedure. ADO.NET gives you two ways to populate those arguments with data.

The easiest way is to create a string with the name of the stored procedure and append the parameter values to the end. Each list of values should be separated with commas. The database server will parse the values out of the string and assign them to the parameters based on their order in the string.

This example shows a VB .NET string that is used to call the stored procedure DeleteOldTransactions and pass it a company name and the month to delete:

```
sp = "DeleteOldTransactions 'Decker Compass', 'July'"
```

Although appending the values to the end of the string is easy, it may not be the most efficient way to pass parameters. If you are going to call the same stored procedure many times, asking the database server to repeatedly parse values out of a string adds a lot of overhead. You will be better off creating Parameter objects that store the individual values. The database server can access the individual Parameter objects much faster than it can parse text.

A Command object has a Parameters collection. When you first create the Command object, you have to populate the Parameters collection. Call the Add() method for each parameter that needs to be added and pass it a new Parameter instance.

When you instantiate a Parameter object, pass the constructor the parameter name, data type, and size. This creates a new parameter that can be added to the Parameters collection.

After you create the Parameter collection, assign the initial values to it. Every time you need to call the stored procedure, repopulate the parameters with new values before executing the stored procedure. If a parameter is declared for output, you can get its data by assigning it to a variable.

VB 6.0

Add a Parameter object to the Parameters collection by calling the Append() method. Create a new instance of a Parameter object by calling the CreateParameter() method.

```
Cmd.Parameters.Append Cmd.CreateParameter("UserId", adInteger, adParamterInput)
```

After you create all the parameters, set their values via the Parameters collection.

```
Cmd.Parameters("UserId").Value = 230
```

The Parameter object can have data passed back from the stored procedure.

```
Salary = Cmd.Parameters("Salary").Value
```

VB .NET

Add a `Parameter` object to the `Parameters` collection by calling the `Add()` method. Instantiate a new `Parameter` object and use its constructor to define it.

```
dbCmd.Parameters.Add(New OleDbParameter("@UserId", OleDbType.Integer))
```

After you create all the parameters, set their values via the `Parameters` collection. The values can be set using their index number or their name.

```
dbCmd.Parameters(0).Value = 230
```

The `Parameter` object can have data passed back from the stored procedure.

```
Console.WriteLine(dbCmd.Parameters(2).Value)
```

C#

Add a `Parameter` object to the `Parameters` collection by calling the `Add()` method. Instantiate a new `Parameter` object and use its constructor to define it.

```
dbCmd.Parameters.Add(new SqlParameter("@Name", SqlDbType.NChar, 50));
```

After you create all the parameters, set their value via the `Parameters` collection. The values can be set using their index number or their name.

```
dbCmd.Parameters["@Name"].Value = "Luis Orea";
```

The `Parameter` object can have data passed back from the stored procedure.

```
double newSalary;
newSalary = (double)dbCmd.Parameters["Salary"].Value * 1.1;
```

Using a Table for Forward-Only Access

If you only need to read data without making any changes to it, use a `DataReader` object. It is a table with forward-only, read-only access. Because it doesn't have to track previously viewed records or data changes, it uses fewer resources than other data objects. This results in significant performance increases. In VB 6.0, the equivalent is to create a recordset object with the `CursorType` property set to `ForwardOnly` and the `LockType` property set to `ReadOnly`.

The `DataReader` object is returned by the `ExecuteReader()` method of the `Command` object. The `CommandText` property should be assigned a string that returns one or more records.

The `DataReader` works by referencing a single record at a time. It always points to the current record. Accessing the fields of that record is done via the object indexer. You can pass it either an integer representing the field number or the field name as a string. The indexer returns an object that references the value. Because this is not type-safe, there are numerous methods that return the value cast as a particular data type. Each of these method names starts with "Get" followed by the data type it returns.

When the `DataReader` object is first instantiated, it automatically references the first record available. The `Read()` method lets you navigate to the next record. There is no method to go to a prior record. The `Read()` method returns `True` if it retrieved a record. If it reaches the end of the file, it returns `False`. VB 6.0 uses the `EOF()` method to determine when the end of the file is reached.

When you are finished reading records from the `DataReader` object, call the `Close()` method. This closes the database connection.

The `DataReader` class is in the `System.Data` namespace.

The following examples build on the `Command` object shown in prior examples.

VB 6.0

Create a `Recordset` object that is forward-only and read-only.

```
Dim Rs As ADODB.Recordset
Set Rs.CursorType = adForwardOnly
Set Rs.LockType = adLockReadOnly
Set Rs = Cmd.Execute
```

Use the `EOF()` method to determine when the end of the file is reached.

```
Do While (Not Rs.EOF())
    var=Rs!Name
Loop
```

Call the `Close()` method when you are finished reading the records.

```
Rs.Close
```

VB .NET

Create a `DataReader` object by calling the `ExecuteReader()` method of the `Command` object.

```
Imports System.Data
...
Dim dbDr As OleDbDataReader
dbDr = dbCmd.ExecuteReader()
```

Use the Read() method to get the next record. It returns False when the end of the file is reached.

```
Do While (dbDr.Read())
    Console.WriteLine("Field {0} is {1}", dbDr.GetName(0), dbDr.GetInt32(1))
Loop
```

Call the Close() method when you are finished reading the records.

```
dbDr.Close()
```

C#

Create a DataReader object by calling the ExecuteReader() method of the Command object.

```
using Sytem.Data;
...
SqlDataReader dbDr;
dbDr = dbCmd.ExecuteReader();
```

Use the Read() method to get the next record. It returns False when the end of the file is reached.

```
while (dbDr.Read())
{
    Console.WriteLine("Field Last Name is {0}", dbDr["Name"].ToString());
}
```

Call the Close() method when you are finished reading the records.

```
dbDr.Close();
```

Reading and Modifying Individual Records

Just like ADO, ADO.NET gives you the ability to access individual records and modify the values in each field. This is useful when a user is making a variety of changes to individual records and there is no way to perform a block update using a SQL statement.

ADO.NET is optimized for Internet development because it is designed to keep connections open for only a short time while data is being transferred from the server to the client or back to the server. All records are stored in memory on the client side as a collection, and any changes made to the records are made on the client side. Updating the data requires passing the changes back to the server so that they can be persisted.

Before you go any further, consider the impact on your application of having the entire table in memory. Depending on the size of a record, if you are accessing thousands of records, you are going to be pushing a lot of data over the network. While this data is being transferred, it can have a negative impact on your database server's performance as well as on other network traffic. Once the data gets to the client, the memory requirements to store every record in a collection can adversely affect the client machine's performance.

These problems don't exist with ADO-connected recordsets. It allows you to open a million record table and it will keep the connection open while it manages which records have been read into the cache and which ones have been modified. The drawback with ADO is that it keeps the connection open the entire time the user is making changes to the table (which could be hours). Keeping the connection open consumes an expensive resource. With ADO.NET, the connection is only open a short time, but managing which records should be read and when they should be read becomes your responsibility. These issues require you to plan and performance-test the different methods of accessing your data.[6]

In addition to using the `SqlClient` or `OleDb` namespace mentioned earlier, using all the classes discussed in this section requires adding the `System.Data` namespace to your application.

Creating a DataTable Object

Just like the other methods of accessing a database, accessing and modifying individual records requires a `Connection` object and a `Command` object. The `Command` object is used to specify which records to retrieve.

After you instantiate a `Connection` object and a `Command` object, instantiate a `DataAdapter` object. The `DataAdapter` object is used as the means of moving data from the database to the `DataSet` object.

Link the `Command` object to the `DataAdapter` object by passing the `Command` object to the `SelectCommand()` method of the `DataAdapter`. Next, call the `Fill()` method of the `DataAdapter` object and pass it the `DataSet` object and a name for the new table. This name is how you will reference the table in the `DataSet` collection. The `Fill()` method retrieves all the records from the database, instantiates and populates a `DataTable`, and inserts the `DataTable` into the `DataSet` collection.

---

6. Once you start having to work through these issues, it's time to get a book solely dedicated to ADO.NET and evaluate the different options.

VB 6.0

Create a `Recordset` object by calling the `Execute` method of the `Command` object.

```
Dim Rs As New ADODB.Recordset
Rs.CursorType = adOpenForwardOnly
Rs.LockType = adLockReadOnly
Set Rs = Cmd.Execute
```

VB .NET

Instantiate a `DataSet` object and then instantiate a `DataAdapter` object. Pass the `SelectCommand()` method the `Command` object. Call the `Fill()` method by passing it the `DataSet` object and the name of the table to create.

```
Dim ds As New DataSet()
Dim dbDa As New OleDbDataAdapter()
dbDa.SelectCommand = dbCmd
dbDa.Fill(ds, "TableName")
```

C#

Instantiate a `DataSet` object and then instantiate a `DataAdapter` object. Pass the `SelectCommand()` method the `Command` object. Call the `Fill()` method by passing it the `DataSet` object and the name of the table to create.

```
DataSet ds = new DataSet();
SqlDataAdapter dbDa = new SqlDataAdapter();
dbDa.SelectCommand = dbCmd;
dbDa.Fill(ds, "TableName");
```

Reading Records

When the `Fill()` method of the `DataAdapter` object is called, it automatically instantiates a `DataTable` object and populates it. Get a reference to the `DataTable` object by passing the table name to the `DataSet` indexer.

The `DataTable` object has a `DataColumn` collection and a `DataRow` collection. A `DataColumn` defines the schema of each column, but it doesn't store any data—this is the responsibility of the `DataRow`. A `DataRow` stores the values for each field in the record. Unless you need to examine the schema of a `DataColumn`, you probably won't need to access any of its members.

The `Rows` collection of the `DataTable` gets the collection where all the records are stored. Pass it the row number as an integer and it returns a `DataRow` object. Use it to get the field values.

The `Count` property of the `Rows` collection returns the number of records in a table. In VB 6.0, you have to call the `MoveLast()` method before the `RecordCount` property can be accurate. This is not necessary in .NET because the `Fill()` method of the `DataAdapter` always reads every record when it is called. Thus, it knows how many records are in the table without requiring you to move to the last one.

A `DataRow` is an object that stores the values of each field in the record. You access the fields by using the indexer of the `DataRow` object. The indexer is overloaded so you can pass it either the column number or the column name.

You can navigate through then entire `DataRow` collection in the `DataTable` by using a `For Next` loop or a `For Each` loop. VB 6.0 uses the `MovePrevious()` and `MoveNext()` methods to navigate through a recordset. These methods are not available in .NET because there is no concept of having a pointer that must move from the current record to a different record. Each record is readily accessible by its row number.

The VB 6.0 `BOF()` and `EOF()` functions are not a part of .NET either. You know that the first record has an index of 0 and the last record has an index of the `Count()` property minus 1.

Where Are My Move Methods?

When you look at Table 13-1, you might notice that there is a large group of ADO methods that doesn't have any equivalent ADO.NET methods. The `Move` methods have disappeared from ADO.NET.

The `Move` methods aren't necessary in ADO.NET because the concept of having a cursor that points to the current record is gone. When using a disconnected recordset, you have all the records in memory from the very beginning. You don't need to move to the next record and read it from the table. Therefore, the methods `MoveNext()`, `MovePrevious()`, `MoveFirst()`, and `MoveLast()` are no longer necessary.

The `BOF()` and `EOF()` methods are gone as well. When working with connected recordsets, you need a way to determine when the cursor has reached the beginning or the end of a table. With disconnected recordsets, you know how many records are in the table immediately after it is loaded into memory.

ADO.NET treats every record in a table as an object in a collection. You navigate through the elements of the collection to access the different records. This eliminates the need for `Move` methods and `BOF()`/`EOF()` methods.

VB 6.0

Access the columns in a recordset by passing the indexer a column number or a column name.

```
var = Rs(ColumnNumber)
```

Navigate through the recordset by using the MoveNext() method and checking for the end of the file.

```
Do While (Not Rs.Eof())
    Debug.Print Rs(columnNumber)
    Rs.MoveNext
Loop
```

VB .NET

Set a reference to the DataTable object by passing the table name or number as an index to the DataSet.Tables property. Access a record by passing a row number to the Rows() property of the DataTable object.

```
Dim dt As DataTable
Dim rowNumber As Integer
dt = ds.Tables("TableName")
Dim dr As DataRow
dr = dt.Rows(rowNumber)
```

Access the columns in the DataRow object by passing the indexer a column number or a column name.

```
Dim var As Integer
Dim columnNumber As Integer
var = CType(dr(columnNumber), Integer)
```

Navigate through all the rows in the table by using a For Next loop or a For Each loop.

```
Dim rowNumber As Integer
Dim dr As DataRow
For rowNumber = 0 To dt.Rows.Count-1
    dr = dt.Rows(rowNumber)
    Console.WriteLine(dr(columnNumber))
Next
```

C#

Set a reference to the DataTable object by passing the table name or number as an index to the DataSet.Tables property. Access a record by passing a row number to the Rows() property of the DataTable object.

```
DataTable dt;
dt = ds.Tabels["TableName"];
DataRow dr;
dr = dt.Rows[rowNumber];
```

Access the columns in the DataRow object by passing the indexer a column number or a column name.

```
var = dr["columnName"];
```

Navigate through all the rows in the table by using a for next loop or a foreach loop.

```
foreach (DataRow dr in ds.Tables["tableName"].Rows)
{
    Console.WriteLine(dr["columnName"]);
}
```

Modifying Records

The DataRow object has methods to make modifications to the table data. You can use these methods to add, edit, and delete records.

To edit a record in a DataRow, simply assign a new value to the appropriate column. In VB 6.0 you also edit a record by assigning a new value to the appropriate column. To persist the changes, you have to either call the Update() method or move to a different row.

To add a new row to a table, call the NewRow() method of the DataTable object and assign the result to a DataRow object variable. The NewRow() method instantiates a new DataRow object and defines the columns within it using the column schemas in the DataColumn collection. Once the DataRow object has been instantiated, assign values to each column. Add the DataRow object to the Rows collection by passing it to the Rows.Add() method. In VB 6.0, use the AddNew() method to create a new record. Set the column values and then call the Update() method to persist it to the database.

Delete a row by calling the Delete() method of the Rows collection. If you want to delete every row, call the Clear() method. In VB 6.0 call the Delete() method to delete a record.

When you make changes to a record, you are only making changes to the in-memory copy of the table. None of the changes have been persisted to the database server yet. To persist the changes, you need to create a `CommandBuilder` object and associate it with the `DataAdapter` object. The `CommandBuilder` object will automatically generate a list of all the SQL statements needed to persist the changes to the database. To make the `CommandBuilder` object execute these SQL statements on the database, call the `Update()` method of `DataAdapter` object.

After you call the `Update()` method, the changes to the tables have been persisted to the database, but the in-memory copy of the table is still tracking a history of the old changes that have just been saved. It is necessary to clean up the `DataTable` object so that the changes are saved to memory and their history is cleared. You do this by calling the `AcceptChanges()` method of the `DataAdapter`.

VB 6.0

Edit a record by assigning values to the columns. Persist the changes by calling the `Update()` method.

```
rs("ColumnName") = value
```

Add a new record by calling the `AddNew()` method. Set the column values and then call `Update()`.

```
rs.AddNew
rs(column) = value
rs.Update
```

Delete a record by calling the `Delete` method.

```
rs.Delete
```

VB .NET

Edit a record by assigning values to the columns.

```
dr(columnNumber) = value
```

Add a new row by first creating a new `DataRow` object using the `NewRow()` method of the `DataTable`. Assign values to the columns. Add the new `DataRow` to the `Rows` collection by calling the `Add()` method and passing it the new `DataRow`.

```
dr = dt.NewRow()
dr(column) = value
dt.Rows.Add(dr)
```

Delete a row by calling the Delete() method of the DataRow object.

```
dt.Rows(rowNumber).Delete()
```

To persist the changes made to all the DataRows, create a CommandBuilder object and pass the constructor the DataAdapter object. After all changes have been made to the rows in a table, call the Update() method of the DataAdapter. Pass it the DataSet and table name that had the changes made to it. After you call the Update() method, call the AcceptChanges() method to clean up the DataTable.

```
Dim dbBldr As New OleDbCommandBuilder(dbDa)
dbDa.Update(dbDs, "tableName")
dt.AcceptChanges()
```

C#

Edit a record by assigning values to the columns.

```
dr[columnNumber] = value;
```

Add a new row by first creating a new DataRow object using the NewRow() method of the DataTable. Assign values to the columns. Add the new DataRow to the Rows collection by calling the Add() method and passing it the new DataRow.

```
dr = dt.NewRow();
dr[column] = value;
dt.Rows.Add(dr);
```

Delete a row by calling the Delete() method of the DataRow object.

```
dt.Rows[rowNumber].Delete();
```

To persist the changes made to all the DataRows, create a CommandBuilder object and pass the constructor the DataAdapter object. After all changes have been made to the rows in a table, call the Update() method of the DataAdapter. Pass it the DataSet and table name that had the changes made to it. After you call the Update() method, call the AcceptChanges() method to clean up the DataTable.

```
SqlCommandBuilder dbBldr = new SqlCommandBuilder(dbDa);
dbDa.Update(dbDs, "tableName");
dt.AcceptChanges();
```

Filtering and Sorting Records

Once you create a table, there are times when you may want to temporarily filter out some records or sort the table in a different way. If you send a new SQL statement to the database, you're asking the database server to reprocess your request and use resources that may be needed for other processing. It is more efficient to apply a filter or a sort to the table that is already in memory.

The Select() method of the DataTable lets you pass it a filter string and a sort string. It reorganizes the rows according to what is in the strings and returns a new DataRow array.

The filter string is similar to the Where clause in a SQL statement. It uses a field name, a relational operator, and a constant. It will filter out any records that don't meet the string criteria. You can filter on more than one field by using the appropriate SQL syntax.[7] VB 6.0 uses the Filter property to set the filter.

```
filter = "Name = 'Joe' Or Name = 'Joanne'"
```

The sort string specifies a field name and a sort order. By default, the field is sorted in ascending order. If you want to specify a descending sort, list "DESC" after the field name. You can sort on more than one field by separating the fields with commas. VB 6.0 uses the Sort property to sort on a column.

```
sort = "Salary DESC, Age"
```

Pass the DataTable's Select() method the filter string as the first parameter and the sort string as the second parameter. Assign it to a DataRow array object.

VB 6.0

Use the Filter property to set the filter. Use the Sort property to set the sort order.

```
Rs.Filter = "Age > 65"
Rs.Sort = "LastName"
```

VB .NET

The Select() method of the DataTable object returns an array of DataRows. Pass it a filter string as the first parameter and a sort string as the second parameter.

---

7. If you want to learn SQL programming, there are numerous books on the market that teach you how.

```
Dim newDr() As DataRow
Dim filter As String, sort As String
filter = "Month = 2"
sort = "Day"
newDr = dt.Select(filter, sort)
```

C#

The Select() method of the DataTable object returns an array of DataRows. Pass it a filter string as the first parameter and a sort string as the second parameter.

```
DataRow[] newDr;
string filter, sort;
filter = "Month = 2";
sort = "Day";
newDr = dt.Select(filter, sort);
```

Viewing Data with the DataGrid Control

The DataGrid control is a simple way to view tables in an easy to read format. With the exception of Chapter 11, this book focuses primarily on language syntax. However, the DataGrid control is so commonly used that I will show you the basics of using it in this section.

The DataGrid displays data in the standard spreadsheet format. You have to set its properties so that it knows which table to connect to. It analyzes the table and automatically populates the rows and columns for you.

Use the SetDataBindings() method of the DataGrid control to link a DataGrid to a table and display its data. The SetDataBindings() method takes two parameters. The first parameter is the DataSet object. The second parameter is the name of the table to display.

This example assumes that you have a Windows Form application with a DataGrid and that you have included the necessary libraries, as discussed earlier in the chapter.

VB .NET

```
'Demonstrate binding the Northwind Shippers table to a DataGrid
'Use the SetDataBindings() method to connect the table to the grid.
Sub AttachTableToGrid()
        Dim ds As New DataSet()
        Dim dbCmd As OleDbCommand
        Dim dbDa As OleDbDataAdapter = New OleDbDataAdapter()
        'Open the database connection
```

```
                    Dim dbCn As OleDbConnection = New OleDbConnection _
                    ("Provider=Microsoft.JET.OLEDB.4.0;Data Source=C:\Northwind.Mdb")
                    dbCn.Open()
                    'Prepare the SQL statement
                    dbCmd = New OleDbCommand("Shippers", dbCn)
                    dbCmd.CommandType = CommandType.TableDirect
                    'Read the table into the DataSet using the DataAdapter
                    dbDa.SelectCommand = dbCmd
                    dbDa.Fill(ds, "Shippers")

                    'Bind the table to the DataGrid
                    DataGrid1.SetDataBinding(ds, "Shippers")
                    'Clean up resources
                    dbCn.Close()
                    ds = Nothing
                    dbDa = Nothing
                    dbCmd = Nothing
                    dbCn = Nothing
            End Sub
```

C#

```
//Demonstrate binding the Northwind Shippers table to a DataGrid
//Use the SetDataBindings() method to connect the table to the grid.
void AttachTableToGrid()
{
    //Declare the Sql objects
    SqlConnection dbCn = new SqlConnection("Server=(local);Uid=sa;" +
        "Database=NorthWind");
    SqlCommand dbCmd;
    SqlDataAdapter dbDa = new SqlDataAdapter();
    DataSet ds = new DataSet();
    //Open the database connection
    dbCn.Open();
    //Prepare the SQL statement
    dbCmd = new SqlCommand("Select * From Shippers", dbCn);
    dbCmd.CommandType = CommandType.Text;
    //Read the table into the DataSet using the DataAdapter
    dbDa.SelectCommand = dbCmd;
    dbDa.Fill(ds,"Shippers");
```

```
    //Bind the table to the DataGrid
    this.dataGrid1.SetDataBinding(ds, "Shippers");
    //Clean up resources
    dbCn.Close();
    ds = null;
    dbDa = null;
    dbCmd = null;
    dbCn = null;
}
```

Example 13-1. Viewing and Updating the Northwind Database

In this example, you view and modify records in the Shippers table of the Northwind database.

The example lets you print the Shippers table, add a new row, edit a row, and delete a row. When printing the table, you can print either the in-memory table or the physical table. Each of the menu options works with the database in a different way. This example demonstrates many of the data access techniques discussed in this chapter.

Options 1 and 2 enable you to print the table contents. The reason you have two ways to print the table is so that you can see that changes you make to the table only affect the in-memory table. The physical table doesn't change until you commit the changes (option 6).

Editing a record, option 3, shows you how to get a single row using a filter and then modify the columns in that row. Adding a record, option 4, shows you how to create a new `DataRow` and add it to the `Rows` collection. Deleting a record, option 5, shows you how to select a record by passing the row number to the `Rows` collection via the indexer. The first part of the output shows that after editing a record, the contents of the in-memory table are different than the contents of the physical table. After you choose option 6, the physical table is printed and you can see that all the changes were made.

VB .NET

```
'Viewing and updating the Northwind database using VB .NET
'Copyright (c)2001 by Bischof Systems, Inc.

Imports System.Data
Imports System.Data.OleDb

Module Module1

    Sub Main()
        'Declare the OleDb objects
        Dim dbCn As OleDbConnection
        Dim dbCmd As OleDbCommand
        Dim dbDa As OleDbDataAdapter
        Dim dbBldr As OleDbCommandBuilder
        Dim dbDr As OleDbDataReader
        'Declare the Data objects
        Dim ds As DataSet
        Dim dt As DataTable
        Dim dr As DataRow
        'Declare the user input variables
        Dim selection As Integer, rowCount As Integer
        Dim input As String
        'Open the database connection
        dbCn = New OleDbConnection("Provider=Microsoft.JET.OLEDB.4.0;" & _
            "Data Source=C:\Northwind.Mdb")
        dbCn.Open()
        'Prepare the SQL statement
        dbCmd = New OleDbCommand("Shippers", dbCn)
        dbCmd.CommandType = CommandType.TableDirect
        'Read the table into the DataSet using the DataAdapter
        ds = New DataSet()
        dbDa = New OleDbDataAdapter()
        dbDa.SelectCommand = dbCmd
        dbDa.Fill(ds, "Shippers")
        dbBldr = New OleDbCommandBuilder(dbDa)
        'Set a reference to the table
        dt = ds.Tables("Shippers")
        'Don't keep the connection open longer than necessary
        dbCn.Close()
        Console.WriteLine("ADO.NET")
```

```
Do
    Console.WriteLine()
    Console.WriteLine("1. Print In-Memory Table")
    Console.WriteLine("2. Print Physical Table")
    Console.WriteLine("3. Edit a record")
    Console.WriteLine("4. Add a record")
    Console.WriteLine("5. Delete a record")
    Console.WriteLine("6. Commit Changes to Database")
    Console.Write("Your selection: ")
    selection = Integer.Parse("0" & Console.ReadLine())
    Select Case selection
    Case 1 'Print the in-memory table
        Console.WriteLine()
        For rowCount = 0 To dt.Rows.Count - 1
            dr = dt.Rows(rowCount)
            If dr.RowState() <> DataRowState.Deleted Then
                Console.WriteLine("Row #{0}: {1} {2} {3}", _
                rowCount + 1, dr(0), dr(1).ToString.PadRight(30), _
                dr(2))
            End If
        Next
    Case 2       'Print the table in the physical database
        Console.WriteLine()
        rowCount = 1
        dbCn.Open()
        dbDr = dbCmd.ExecuteReader()
        While (dbDr.Read())
            Console.WriteLine("Row #{0}: {1} {2} {3}", rowCount, _
            dbDr.GetInt32(0), dbDr.GetString(1).PadRight(30), _
            dbDr.GetString(2))
            rowCount += 1
        End While
        dbDr.Close()
        dbCn.Close()
    Case 3       'Edit a row based on the primary key
        Console.Write("Which Id?")
        input = Console.ReadLine()
        'Set the filter to get the selected row
        dr = dt.Select("ShipperId = " & input)(0)
        'Get user changes
        Console.Write("Current : {0} New: ", dr("CompanyName"))
        input = Console.ReadLine()
```

```vb
                If (input <> "") Then
                    dr("CompanyName") = input
                End If
                Console.Write("Current : {0} New: ", dr("Phone"))
                input = Console.ReadLine()
                If (input <> "") Then
                    dr("Phone") = input
                End If
            Case 4 'Add a new row
                'Create the row object and populate it
                dr = dt.NewRow()
                Console.Write("Company Name: ")
                input = Console.ReadLine()
                dr("CompanyName") = input
                Console.Write("Phone: ")
                input = Console.ReadLine()
                dr("Phone") = input
                'Add the row object to the data table row collection
                dt.Rows.Add(dr)
            Case 5      'Delete a row using the row index
                Console.Write("Row Number: ")
                input = Console.ReadLine()
                'Delete the record
                dt.Rows(Integer.Parse(input) - 1).Delete()
            Case 6       'Commit the changes to the database
                'The SQLCommandBuilder will commit the changes for you
                dbDa.Update(ds, "Shippers")
                dt.AcceptChanges()
                'Clear the current table and refresh it
                dt.Reset()
                dbDa.Fill(ds, "Shippers")
            End Select
        Loop While (selection <> 0)
    End Sub
End Module
```

C#

```
//Viewing and updating the Northwind database using C#
//Copyright (c)2001 by Bischof Systems, Inc.

using System;
using System.Data;   //needed for the DataSet class
using System.Data.SqlClient;

namespace C_ADO
{
    class Class1
    {
        [STAThread]
        static void Main(string[] args)
        {
            //Declare the Sql objects
            SqlConnection dbCn = new SqlConnection();
            SqlCommand dbCmd = null;
            SqlDataAdapter dbDa = null;
            SqlCommandBuilder dbBldr = null;
            SqlDataReader dbDr = null;
            //Declare the Data objects
            DataSet ds = null;
            DataTable dt = null;
            DataRow dr = null;
            //Declare the user input variables
            int selection = 0; int rowCount = 0;
            string input = "";
            //Open the database connection
            dbCn.ConnectionString = "Server=(local);Uid=sa;Database=NorthWind";
            dbCn.Open();
            //Prepare the SQL statement
            dbCmd = new SqlCommand("Select * From Shippers", dbCn);
            dbCmd.CommandType = CommandType.Text;
            //Read the table into the DataSet using the DataAdapter
            ds = new DataSet();
            dbDa = new SqlDataAdapter();
            dbDa.SelectCommand = dbCmd;
            dbDa.Fill(ds,"Shippers");
            dbBldr = new SqlCommandBuilder(dbDa);
            //Set a reference to the table
            dt = ds.Tables["Shippers"];
```

```
                    //Don't keep the connection open longer than necessary
                    dbCn.Close();
                    Console.WriteLine("ADO.NET");
                    do
                    {
                        Console.WriteLine("\n1. Print In-Memory Table");
                        Console.WriteLine("2. Print Physical Table");
                        Console.WriteLine("3. Edit a record");
                        Console.WriteLine("4. Add a record");
                        Console.WriteLine("5. Delete a record");
                        Console.WriteLine("6. Commit Changes to Database");
                        Console.Write("Your selection: ");
                        selection = int.Parse('0'+Console.ReadLine());
                        switch (selection)
                        {
                            case 1:      //Print the in-memory table
                            Console.WriteLine();
                            for (rowCount=0;rowCount < dt.Rows.Count; rowCount++)
                            {
                                dr = dt.Rows[rowCount];
                                if (dr.RowState != DataRowState.Deleted)
                                {
                                    Console.WriteLine("Row #{0}: {1} {2} {3}",
                                        rowCount + 1, dr[0],
                                        dr[1].ToString().PadRight(30), dr[2]);
                                }
                            }
                            break;
                            case 2:      //Print the table in the physical database
                                Console.WriteLine();
                                rowCount=1;
                                dbCn.Open();
                                dbDr = dbCmd.ExecuteReader();
                                while (dbDr.Read())
                                {
                                    Console.WriteLine("Row #{0}: {1} {2} {3}",rowCount,
                                        dbDr.GetInt32(0), dbDr.GetString(1).PadRight(30),
                                        dbDr.GetString(2));
                                }
                                dbDr.Close();
                                dbCn.Close();
                                break;
```

```csharp
case 3:      //Edit a row based on the primary key
    Console.Write("Which Id?");
    input = Console.ReadLine();
    //Set the filter to get the selected row
    dr = dt.Select("ShipperId = "+input)[0];
    //Get user changes
    Console.Write("Current : {0} New: ",
        dr["CompanyName"]);
    input = Console.ReadLine();
    if (input!= "")
    {
        dr["CompanyName"] = input;
    }
    Console.Write("Current : {0} New: ", dr["Phone"]);
    input = Console.ReadLine();
    if (input!= "")
    {
        dr["Phone"] = input;
    }
    break;
case 4:      //Add a new row
    //Create the row object and populate it
    dr = dt.NewRow();
    Console.Write("Company Name: ");
    input = Console.ReadLine();
    dr["CompanyName"] = input;
    Console.Write("Phone: ");
    input = Console.ReadLine();
    dr["Phone"] = input;
    //Add the row object to the data table row collection
    dt.Rows.Add(dr);
    break;
case 5:      //Delete a row using the row index
    Console.Write("Row Number: ");
    input = Console.ReadLine();
    //Delete the record
    dt.Rows[int.Parse(input)-1].Delete();
    break;
```

```
                                 case 6:       //Commit the changes to the database
                                     //The SQLCommandBuilder will commit the changes for you
                                     dbDa.Update(ds, "Shippers");
                                     dt.AcceptChanges();
                                     //Clear the current table and refresh it
                                     dt.Reset();
                                     dbDa.Fill(ds, "Shippers");
                                     break;
                            }
                        } while (selection!=0);
                    }
                }
            }
```

Example 13-1 Output

```
ADO.NET

1. Print In-Memory Table
2. Print Physical Table
3. Edit a record
4. Add a record
5. Delete a record
6. Commit Changes to Database
Your selection: 1

Row #1: 1 Slow Shippers                    (818) 999-1212
Row #2: 2 United Printers                  (593) 828-8999
Row #3: 3 Parcel Post                      (198) 123-4192
Row #4: 44 Paul Revere Delivery            (456) 787-1234

1. Print In-Memory Table
2. Print Physical Table
3. Edit a record
4. Add a record
5. Delete a record
6. Commit Changes to Database
Your selection: 3
Which Id?2
Current : United Printers New: Divided Writers
Current : (593) 828-8999 New: (789) 788-9876
```

1. Print In-Memory Table
2. Print Physical Table
3. Edit a record
4. Add a record
5. Delete a record
6. Commit Changes to Database
Your selection: 1

Row #1: 1 Slow Shippers	(818) 999-1212
Row #2: 2 Divided Writers	(789) 788-9876
Row #3: 3 Parcel Post	(198) 123-4192
Row #4: 44 Paul Revere Delivery	(456) 787-1234

1. Print In-Memory Table
2. Print Physical Table
3. Edit a record
4. Add a record
5. Delete a record
6. Commit Changes to Database
Your selection: 2

Row #1: 1 Slow Shippers	(818) 999-1212
Row #2: 2 United Printers	(593) 828-8999
Row #3: 3 Parcel Post	(198) 123-4192
Row #4: 44 Paul Revere Delivery	(456) 787-1234

1. Print In-Memory Table
2. Print Physical Table
3. Edit a record
4. Add a record
5. Delete a record
6. Commit Changes to Database
Your selection: 4
Company Name: On Time - All the Time
Phone: (123) 323-5343

1. Print In-Memory Table
2. Print Physical Table
3. Edit a record
4. Add a record
5. Delete a record
6. Commit Changes to Database
Your selection: 5
Row Number: 4

1. Print In-Memory Table
2. Print Physical Table
3. Edit a record
4. Add a record
5. Delete a record
6. Commit Changes to Database
Your selection: 6

1. Print In-Memory Table
2. Print Physical Table
3. Edit a record
4. Add a record
5. Delete a record
6. Commit Changes to Database
Your selection: 2

Row #1: 1 Slow Shippers   (818) 999-1212
Row #2: 2 United Printers   (593) 828-8999
Row #3: 3 Parcel Post   (198) 123-4192
Row #4: 45 On Time - All the Time (123) 323-5343

1. Print In-Memory Table
2. Print Physical Table
3. Edit a record
4. Add a record
5. Delete a record
6. Commit Changes to Database
Your selection: 0

CHAPTER 14

Date and Time Functions

Table 14-1. Date and Time Equivalent Functions

VB 6.0	SYSTEM.DATETIME
DateAdd(), DateDiff()	AddYears(), AddDays(), AddHours(), AddMinutes(), AddSeconds(), AddMilliseconds(), Add(), Subtract(), AddTicks()
DatePart()	
	FromFileTime()
	FromOADate()
DateSerial()	(DateTime Constructor)
DateValue()	Parse(), ToString(), ToShortDateString(), ToLongDateString()
Day()	Day
Hour()	Hour
Minute()	Minute
Month()	Month
MonthName()	MonthName() (VB .NET only)
	DaysInMonth()
Now()	Now
Second()	Second
TimeOfDay()	TimeOfDay
Timer()	TimeOfDay
TimeSerial()	(DateTime Constructor)
TimeString()	ToShortTimeString(), ToLongTimeString()
	ToFileTime()
	ToOADate()
TimeValue()	Parse()
Today()	Today

Table 14-1. Date and Time Equivalent Functions (Continued)

VB 6.0	SYSTEM.DATETIME
WeekDay()	DayOfWeek (VB .NET), (int)DayOfWeek (C#)
	DayOfYear
WeekDayName()	DayOfWeek.ToString() (VB .NET), DayOfWeek (C#)
Year()	Year
	IsLeapYear()
	Ticks

Overview

The date and time functions in VB 6.0 have been duplicated in the System.DateTime class. When working with this class in .NET, it's important to keep in mind that some of the methods are used with an instance of the DateTime object and other methods are static. The static methods are called using the DateTime class, not an instance of the class. This is identified within this chapter.

VB .NET can define a variable using either the Date data type or using the DateTime data type of the .NET Framework. They are equivalent to each other. For consistency purposes, VB .NET code in this chapter will use the DateTime data type.

Storing Date and Time Values

VB 6.0 stores the date and time as a Double data type where the whole part of the number represents the number of days that has elapsed since 12/30/1899 and the fractional part represents the time of day. It was common practice to truncate the decimals from the date field to eliminate the time part and isolate the date part. This is no longer possible in .NET because a different storage method is used for the DateTime class. It stores the date and time as a long number that represents the number of ticks (a 100-nanosecond unit) since 1/1/0001 12:00:00 AM through 12/31/9999 11:59:59 PM.

Getting the Current Date and Time

There are many times when a program will need to use the current date and time. .NET provides you with this functionality using the Now and Today properties. Both of these are static properties of the DateTime class.

VB .NET

The Now property returns the current date and time. The Today property only returns the current date. These are both static properties of the DateTime class.

```
Dim myDate As DateTime

myDate = DateTime.Now
myDate = DateTime.Today
```

C#

The Now property returns the current date and time. The Today property only returns the current date. These are both static properties of the DateTime class.

```
DateTime myDate;

myDate = DateTime.Now;
myDate = DateTime.Today;
```

Inputting Dates

Given that the date is now stored as a large number of ticks, there are a variety of ways to convert the human form of a date into the computer form.

Using the DateTime Constructor

You can use the DateTime constructor method to create a date by passing the year, month, and day as Integers. This method requires that you specify the year as a four-digit number.

VB .NET

Instantiate DateTime variables using the constructor for the DateTime class.

```
Dim myDate As Date = New DateTime(1930 ,11, 8)
```

C#

Instantiate DateTime variables using the constructor for the DateTime class.

```
DateTime myDate = new DateTime(1929, 6, 14);
```

Converting a String to DateTime

To convert a String to DateTime, you can either use the Convert.ToDateTime() method or the DateTime.Parse() method. Both accept a string representing a date and time (in a variety of formats) and convert it to the system DateTime date type. Both of these methods can also be used when declaring a variable.

VB .NET

Pass a string to the Convert.ToDateTime() method.

```
Dim myDate As DateTime
myDate = Convert.ToDateTime("Jun 8, 1995 4:48 PM")
```

Pass a string to the DateTime.Parse() method.

```
Dim myDate As DateTime = DateTime.Parse("3/18/94 10:26 PM")
```

C#

Pass a string to the Convert.ToDateTime() method.

```
DateTime myDate;
myDate = Convert.ToDateTime("January 26, 1990 5:58 PM");
```

Pass a string to the DateTime.Parse() method.

```
DateTime myDate = DateTime.Parse("9/7/85 5:59 AM");
```

Displaying the Date and Time

You have many options for printing the date and time. Not only can you display the full date and time in a variety of formats, but you can also break out the individual parts. Table 14-2 shows the output of using these properties and methods. The examples demonstrate a few of them.

Table 14-2. Properties/Methods to Display the Date and Time

PROPERTY/METHOD	SAMPLE OUTPUT
ToString()	7/5/1958 11:11:00 AM
ToLongDateString()	Saturday, July 05, 1958
ToShortDateString()	7/5/1958
ToLongTimeString()	11:11:00 AM
ToShortTimeString()	11:11 AM
Day	5
Month	7
Year	1958
Hour	11
Minute	11
Second	0
DayOfWeek	6 (VB .NET) Saturday (C#)
DayOfYear	186
MonthName() (VB .NET built-in function[1])	July

The properties and methods in Table 14-2 are self-explanatory. But there are a few that deserve mentioning.

The .NET Framework uses a DayOfWeek property, which is an enumerated class ranging from 0 (Sunday) to 6 (Saturday). This DayOfWeek property behaves differently depending on whether it is used from VB .NET or C#. In VB .NET, it returns the day of the week as an integer. In C#, it returns a string representing the name of the day.

In VB .NET, get the text representation of the day of the week using the ToString() method.

```
Console.WriteLine(myDate.DayOfWeek.ToString())
```

---

1. Because this is a VB .NET built-in function, it is not part of the System.DateTime class. Call it as you would a normal function. I put it in this chart so that it wouldn't be forgotten.

In C#, get the integer representation of the day of the week by casting the property as an int.

```
Console.WriteLine((int)myDate.DayOfWeek);
```

The `MonthName()` function is unusual because it isn't part of the `DateTime` class. It is a built-in function in VB .NET. There is no C# equivalent.

```
Console.WriteLine(MonthName(myDate.Month))
```

VB .NET

Use members of the `DateTime` object to display the date in different formats.

```
Dim myDate As DateTime = DateTime.Now
Console.WriteLine(myDate.ToLongDateString())
Console.WriteLine(myDate.Month)
```

C#

Use members of the `DateTime` object to display the date in different formats.

```
DateTime myDate = DateTime.Now;
Console.WriteLine(myDate.ToLongDateString());
Console.WriteLine(myDate.Month);
```

Performing Date and Time Calculations

The `DateTime` class has many methods for performing calculations with dates. There are methods for adding a year, adding a day, adding an hour, and so on. If you want to subtract a unit, use a negative value. These are not static methods. They must be called with an existing `DateTime` object.

The `Add()`, `Subtract()`, and `AddTicks()` methods use a `TimeSpan` object to perform calculations on the date. This is discussed in the section "Using the TimeSpan Class."

VB .NET

Use one of the `Add___` methods to modify a date. The parameter it expects is the amount to modify it by.

```
myDate = DateTime.Now
myDate = myDate.AddYears(value)
myDate = myDate.AddHours(-value)
```

C#

Use one of the `Add___` methods to modify a date. The parameter it expects is the amount to modify it by.

```
myDate = DateTime.Now;
myDate = myDate.AddYears(value);
myDate = myDate.AddHours(-value);
```

Using the TimeSpan Class

The `TimeSpan` class takes a value in `Ticks` (100-nanosecond intervals) and uses it for a variety of functions. Use it when you need to store a length of time in a single variable. There are numerous `TimeSpan` methods and properties available. See the MSDN documentation for a complete listing.[2]

The arithmetic methods of the `DateTime` class return a `TimeSpan` object. You need to use the properties of the `TimeSpan` object to interpret the method's results. Some of these properties are `Days`, `Months`, `Years`, `Hours`, and so on.

Use an object instance of the `TimeSpan` class to modify a date. The methods of the `TimeSpan` object that return a `DateTime` object are `Add()`, `Subtract()`, and `AddTicks()`. Be careful when using the `Add()` and `Subtract()` methods. If you want to see the results as a number of days, do not use the `TimeSpan` object. Depending on the time that is stored in the object variable, the difference between the two dates may not have enough ticks to qualify as a full day. Thus, a date for tomorrow may be marked as being 0 days from today. You have to force it to do the calculation using only the date value. Do this by using the `Date` property.

VB .NET

Use the `TimeSpan` class to display the number of days between two dates.

```
Dim myTime As TimeSpan
Dim myDate1 As DateTime = DateTime.Parse("9/14/1964")
Dim myDate2 As DateTime = DateTime.Parse("8/30/1960")
myTime = myDate1.Subtract(myDate2.Date)
Console.WriteLine("Number of days is {0}", myTime.Days)
```

---

2. In the MSDN Help file, use the index and type in **System.TimeSpan**.

C#

Use the `TimeSpan` class to display the number of days between two dates.

```
DateTime myDate1 = new DateTime(1998,5,26);
DateTime myDate2 = DateTime.Parse("1/19/1991");
TimeSpan myTime;
myTime = myDate1.Subtract(myDate2.Date);
Console.WriteLine(myTime.Days);
```

Example 14-1. Working with Your Birthday

This example enables you to enter your birthday and performs a variety of date manipulations on it. This example shows you many different ways to use the date class in your program. Notice that there are two print statements at the end of the program that calculate the number of days before your next birthday. The second calculation shows how using the `TimeSpan` data type can give an incorrect result.

VB .NET

```
'Working with your birthday in VB .NET
'Copyright (c)2001 by Bischof Systems, Inc.

Module Module1

    Sub Main()
        Dim birthday, nextBirthday As DateTime
        Dim Today As DateTime = DateTime.Now
        Dim ts As TimeSpan
        Dim value As Integer
        'Get the user's birthday
        Console.WriteLine("What day were you born?")
        birthday = DateTime.Parse(Console.ReadLine())
        'Is it a leap year?
        If (DateTime.IsLeapYear(birthday.Year)) Then
            Console.WriteLine("You were born on a leap year!")
        Else
            Console.WriteLine("This is not a leap year")
        End If
```

```vbnet
        'Calculate the next birthday
        nextBirthday = New DateTime(Today.Year, birthday.Month, _
            birthday.Day)
        If (Today.Month > birthday.Month) Then
            nextBirthday = nextBirthday.AddYears(1)
        End If
        Console.WriteLine("Your next birthday is {0}", _
            nextBirthday.ToShortDateString())
        'Use the Date property for subtraction.
        ts = nextBirthday.Subtract(Today.Date)
        Console.WriteLine("It is {0} days from now", ts.Days)
        'What happens if we use the TimeSpan for the calculation?
        ts = nextBirthday.Subtract(Today)
    Console.WriteLine("Using TimeSpan(not right)- It is {0} days from now", _
            ts.Days)
        Console.ReadLine()
    End Sub
End Module
```

C#

```csharp
//Working with your birthday in C#
//Copyright (c)2001 by Bischof Systems, Inc.

using System;

namespace C_Birthday
{
    class Class1
    {
        [STAThread]
        static void Main(string[] args)
          {
            DateTime birthday, nextBirthday;
            DateTime today = DateTime.Now;
            TimeSpan ts;
            int value;
            //Get the user's birthday
            Console.WriteLine("What day were you born?");
            birthday = DateTime.Parse(Console.ReadLine());
```

```
                //Is it a leap year?
                if (DateTime.IsLeapYear(birthday.Year))
                {
                    Console.WriteLine("You were born on a leap year!");
                }
                else
                {
                    Console.WriteLine("This is not a leap year");
                }
                //Calculate the next birthday
                nextBirthday = new DateTime(today.Year, birthday.Month,
                    birthday.Day);
                if (today.Month > birthday.Month)
                {
                    nextBirthday = nextBirthday.AddYears(1);
                }
                Console.WriteLine("Your next birthday is {0}",
                    nextBirthday.ToShortDateString());
                //Use the Date property for subtraction.
                ts = nextBirthday.Subtract(today.Date);
                Console.WriteLine("It is {0} days from now", ts.Days);
                //What happens if we use the TimeSpan for the calculation?
                ts = nextBirthday.Subtract(today);
                Console.WriteLine("Using TimeSpan (not right) - It is {0} days"
                    + "from now", ts.Days);
                Console.ReadLine();
            }
        }
}
```

Example 14-1 Output

```
What day were you born?
5/23/1968
You were born on a leap year!
Your next birthday is 5/23/2002
It is 257 days from now
Using TimeSpan (not right)- It is 256 days from now
```

CHAPTER 15
Math and Financial Functions

Table 15-1. Intrinsic Math Function Equivalents

VB 6.0	SYSTEM.MATH
Abs()	Abs()
	ACos()
	ASin()
Atn()	Atan()
	Atan2()
	Ceiling()
Cos()	Cos()
	Cosh()
	E
Exp()	Exp()
Fix()	
	Floor()
	IEEERemainder()
	Log()
	Log10()
	Max()
	Min()
	PI
	Pow()
Randomize	
Rnd()	System.Random

Table 15-1. Intrinsic Math Function Equivalents (Continued)

VB 6.0	SYSTEM.MATH
	Round()
Sgn()	Sign()
Sin()	Sin()
	Sinh()
Sqr()	Sqrt()
Tan()	Tan()
	Tanh()

Overview

VB 6.0 has an extensive number of intrinsic math and financial functions. .NET gives you these same functions and more. They are now part of the System libraries. Calling these functions requires knowing the proper libraries to reference in your program.

Math Functions

The .NET System.Math library has replaced the VB 6.0 built-in math functions. This library is referenced by default in VB .NET and C#. Table 15-1 shows that there are twice as many functions in the System.Math library than there are in VB 6.0. Although most are self-explanatory, there are a few new functions that are interesting and deserve special mention (see Table 15-2).

Table 15-2. Interesting Math Functions in .NET

MATH FUNCTION	DESCRIPTION
E	Natural logarithmic base
PI	PI
Floor(Double)	Returns the largest whole number less than or equal to the specified number
Ceiling(Double)	Returns the smallest whole number greater than or equal to the specified number

Table 15-2. Interesting Math Functions in .NET (Continued)

MATH FUNCTION	DESCRIPTION
Round(Decimal, Integer)	Rounds a number to the nearest precision specified
Min(number, number)	Returns the smaller of two numbers
Max(number, number)	Returns the larger of two numbers

New Constants

Two new constants are available. The first is E, the natural logarithmic base. This value is 2.71828(...). The second is the ever-popular PI, commonly known as 3.14159(...).[1]

Truncating Decimals

There are three new functions for working with decimals: Floor(), Ceiling(), and Round().

Two new functions will convert a Double to the nearest whole number. They are slightly different than simply truncating the decimal portion of a number. The Floor() function returns the next lowest whole number. The Ceiling() function returns the next highest whole number.

If you want to round the number either up or down to a certain precision, then use the Round() function. When passed a decimal and the precision, it will round up or down to the nearest number using the precision specified.

Table 15-3 shows the results of using the three different functions on a number. The Precision column only applies to the Round() function.

Table 15-3. Sample Function Results for Truncating Digits

NUMBER	PRECISION	CEILING()	FLOOR()	ROUND()
15.2	0	16	15	15
15.5	0	16	15	16
0.555	2	1	0	0.56
-4.999	2	-4	-5	-5

---

1. It seems that every programming book I've ever read always uses PI as the example of how to declare a constant. I wonder what all those authors are going to use now....

Comparing Two Numbers

Two new functions, Min() and Max(), have been added. These functions compare two numbers. Each function takes two numbers and returns either the minimum or maximum number accordingly. Each function is overloaded to compare numbers of all data types. Hence, you can compare Integer with Integer or Decimal with Decimal. However, each comparison must consist of numbers of the same data type. You can't compare an Integer to a Float or a Decimal to a Long.

Generating Random Numbers

VB 6.0 uses the Rnd() function with the Randomize statement to generate random numbers. For backward compatibility, VB .NET also provides you with this capability. The .NET Framework has a System.Random class, which is a more robust random number generator.

When you instantiate an object variable from the Random class, it will automatically provide you with a seed value based upon the system time. Thus, there is no need to call a Randomize statement. Calling the method Next() returns a random number as an Integer. You can set the range of random numbers by passing it a minimum value and a ceiling. You can also pass it only the ceiling value. The ceiling states that any numbers below it can be returned. In other words, if you use 10 as the ceiling value, the largest number it will return is 9. Calling the method NextDouble() returns a random number between 0.0 and 1.0, but doesn't include 1.0.

VB .NET

Instantiate an object variable from the Random class and call the method Next() or NextDouble().

```
Dim var As Random = New Random()
Console.WriteLine(var.Next())
Console.WriteLine(var.NextDouble())
'Demonstrate getting a random number with a range of 1000 to 1099
Dim myRandom As Random = New Random()
Dim newValue As Integer
newValue = myRandom.Next(1000, 1100)
```

C#

Instantiate an object variable from the Random class and call the method Next() or NextDouble().

```
Random var = new Random();
Console.WriteLine(var.Next());
Console.WriteLine(var.NextDouble());
//Demonstrate getting a random number with a range of 0 to 9
Random myRandom = new Random();
int newValue;
newValue = myRandom.Next(10);
```

Financial Functions

The financial functions are replaced by the `Microsoft.VisualBasic.Financial` library. This library was added for the purpose of keeping compatibility with older VB 6.0 programs and it is included in VB .NET by default. It isn't included in C# by default, but that doesn't mean you can't use these functions in your program. Just add a reference to `Microsoft Visual Basic .NET Runtime` library in your project. The functions in the .NET library are identical to those in VB 6.0. They are listed in Table 15-4. All functions return a `Double` data type.

Table 15-4. Financial Functions

FINANCIAL FUNCTION	DESCRIPTION
DDB(Cost, Salvage, Life, Period, Factor)	Double declining balance
FV(Rate, NPer, Pmt, PV, Due)	Future value
IPmt(Rate, Per, NPer, PV, FV, Due)	Interest payment
IRR(ValueArray(), Guess)	Internal rate of return
MIRR(ValueArray(), FinanceRate, ReinvestRate)	Modified internal rate of return
NPer(Rate, Pmt, PV, FV, Due)	Number of periods for an annuity
NPV(Rate, ValueArray())	Net present value
Pmt(Rate, NPer, PV, FV, Due)	Payment for an annuity
PPmt(Rate, Per, NPer, PV, FV, Due)	Principal payment for an annuity
PV(Rate, NPer, Pmt, FV, Due)	Present value
Rate(NPer, Pmt, PV, FV, Due, Guess)	Interest rate per period for an annuity
SLN(Cost, Salvage, Life)	Straight line depreciation
SYD(Cast, Salvage, Life, Period)	Sum of years digits depreciation

Example 15-1. Minimum and Maximum Numbers

This example demonstrates the `Min()` and `Max()` functions. The user is prompted to enter how many numbers he or she wants to test. A loop lets the user enter these numbers into an array. This array is passed to a procedure that calls the `Min()` and `Max()` functions repeatedly until every array element has been tested. The program then displays the results.

VB .NET

```
'Minimum and maximum numbers in VB .NET
'Copyright (c)2001 by Bischof Systems, Inc.

Module Module1

    Sub Main()
        Dim qtyToEnter As Integer
        Dim minimum, maximum As Integer
        Dim values(), valueIndex As Integer
        Console.Write("How many numbers to compare? ")
        qtyToEnter = Integer.Parse(Console.ReadLine())
        'Instantiate an array with the number of elements to enter
        ReDim values(qtyToEnter - 1)
        'Enter the numbers into an integer array
        For valueIndex = 0 To qtyToEnter - 1
            Console.Write("Enter a number: ")
            values(valueIndex) = Integer.Parse(Console.ReadLine())
        Next
        GetMinMax(minimum, maximum, values)
        Console.WriteLine("The minimum is {0}", minimum)
        Console.WriteLine("The maximum is {0}", maximum)
        Console.ReadLine()
    End Sub

    'Calculate the smallest and largest numbers
    Sub GetMinMax(ByRef Minimum As Integer, ByRef Maximum As Integer, _
        ByVal Values() As Integer)
        Dim valueIndex As Integer
```

```
        'Initialize the default values
        Minimum = Values(0)
        Maximum = Values(0)
        If (Values.Length > 1) Then
            'Loop through each number to test for the min and max
            For valueIndex = 1 To Values.Length - 1
                Minimum = Math.Min(Minimum, Values(valueIndex))
                Maximum = Math.Max(Maximum, Values(valueIndex))
            Next
        End If
    End Sub
End Module
```

C#

```csharp
//Minimum and maximum numbers in C#
//Copyright (c)2001 by Bischof Systems, Inc.

using System;

namespace C_Math
{
    class Class1
    {
        [STAThread]
        static void Main(string[] args)
        {
            int qtyToEnter;
            int minimum, maximum;
            int[] values;
            Console.WriteLine("How many numbers to compare?");
            qtyToEnter = int.Parse(Console.ReadLine());
            //Instantiate an array with the number of elements to enter
            values = new int[qtyToEnter];
            //Enter the numbers into an integer array
            for (int valueIndex=0; valueIndex<qtyToEnter; valueIndex++)
            {
                Console.WriteLine("Enter a number");
                values[valueIndex] = int.Parse(Console.ReadLine());
            }
            GetMinMax(out minimum, out maximum, values);
            Console.WriteLine("The minimum is {0}", minimum);
            Console.WriteLine("The maximum is {0}", maximum);
            Console.ReadLine();
        }
```

```
                    //Calculate the smallest and largest number
                    static void GetMinMax(out int Minimum, out int Maximum, int[] Values)
                    {
                        //Initialize the default values
                        Minimum = Values[0];
                        Maximum = Values[0];
                        if (Values.Length > 1)
                        {   //Loop through each number to test for the min and max
                            for (int valueIndex=1; valueIndex<Values.Length; valueIndex++)
                            {
                                Minimum = Math.Min(Minimum, Values[valueIndex]);
                                Maximum = Math.Max(Maximum, Values[valueIndex]);
                            }
                        }
                    }
                }
            }
```

Example 15-1 Output

```
How many numbers to compare?
5
Enter a number
10
Enter a number
22
Enter a number
33
Enter a number
101
Enter a number
3
The minimum is 3
The maximum is 101
```

Example 15-2. Common Financial Functions

This example demonstrates how to use some common financial functions: present value, future value, amount of loan applied to interest, and monthly loan payment. The user is prompted for the function to perform. The user is then prompted for the common values needed to call these functions. Any value that is not needed for the calculation can be entered as 0. It's left to the user to know which values are required. The program will calculate the result and display it.

The C# program needs to add a reference to the Microsoft Visual Basic.NET Runtime library and include the statement using Microsoft.VisualBasic.

VB .NET

```
'Common financial funcions in VB .NET
'Copyright (c)2001 by Bischof Systems, Inc.


Module Module1

    Sub Main()
        Dim rate, per, nper, pmt, pv, fv As Double
        Dim selection As Integer
        Dim result As Double = 0
        Console.WriteLine("Common Financial Functions")
        Console.WriteLine()
        Console.WriteLine("Function Menu")
        Console.WriteLine("1. Present Value (Rate,Years,PMT,FV) ")
        Console.WriteLine("2. Future Value (Rate,Years,PMT,PV)")
        Console.WriteLine("3. Interst Paid (Rate,Per,Years,PV,FV)")
        Console.WriteLine("4. Monthly Payment (Rate,Years,PV,FV)")
        Console.Write("Which function to perform? ")
        selection = Integer.Parse(Console.ReadLine())
        Console.WriteLine("Enter the appropriate value, or zero to skip")
        Console.Write("Interest Rate - whole number: ")
        'The interest rate must be converted to a percentage
        'and then converted to a per month value
        rate = (Double.Parse(Console.ReadLine()) / 100) / 12
        Console.Write("Period: ")
        per = Double.Parse(Console.ReadLine())
        Console.Write("Number of Years: ")
        'Convert number of years to the number of monthly payments
        nper = Double.Parse(Console.ReadLine()) * 12
        Console.Write("Payment: ")
        pmt = Double.Parse(Console.ReadLine())
        Console.Write("Present Value: ")
        'Present value has to be a negative number
        pv = Double.Parse(Console.ReadLine()) * -1
        Console.Write("Future Value: ")
        fv = Double.Parse(Console.ReadLine())
```

```
            Select Case selection
                Case 1 'Present Value
                    result = Financial.PV(rate, nper, pmt, fv, _
                        DueDate.EndOfPeriod)
                Case 2 'Future Value
                    result = Financial.FV(rate, nper, pmt, pv, _
                        DueDate.EndOfPeriod)
                Case 3 'Interest Paid
                    result = Financial.IPmt(rate, per, nper, pv, fv, _
                        DueDate.EndOfPeriod)
                Case 4 'Monthly Payment
                    result = Financial.Pmt(rate, nper, pv, fv, _
                        DueDate.EndOfPeriod)
            End Select
            Console.WriteLine("The result is {0}", _
                String.Format(result.ToString("n")))
            Console.ReadLine()
        End Sub
End Module
```

C#

```
//Common financial funcions in C#
//Copyright (c)2001 by Bischof Systems, Inc.

using System;
//The next line requires adding a reference to the
//Microsoft Visual Basic.NET Runtime
using Microsoft.VisualBasic;

namespace C_Financial
{
    class Class1
    {
        [STAThread]
        static void Main(string[] args)
        {
            double rate, per, nper, pmt, pv, fv;
            int selection;
            double result=0;
            Console.WriteLine("Common Financial Functions\n");
```

```
Console.WriteLine("Function Menu");
Console.WriteLine("1. Present Value (Rate,Years,PMT,FV) ");
Console.WriteLine("2. Future Value (Rate,Years,PMT,PV)");
Console.WriteLine("3. Interst Paid (Rate,Per,Years,PV,FV)");
Console.WriteLine("4. Monthly Payment (Rate,Years,PV,FV)");
Console.Write("Which function to perform? ");
selection = int.Parse(Console.ReadLine());
Console.WriteLine("Enter the appropriate value, or zero to skip");
Console.Write("Interest Rate - whole number: ");
//The interest rate must be converted to a percentage
//and then converted to a per month value
rate = (double.Parse(Console.ReadLine())/100)/12;
Console.Write("Period: ");
per = double.Parse(Console.ReadLine());
Console.Write("Number of Years: ");
//Convert number of years to the number of monthly payments
nper= double.Parse(Console.ReadLine())*12;
Console.Write("Payment: ");
pmt = double.Parse(Console.ReadLine());
Console.Write("Present Value: ");
//Present value has to be a negative number
pv = double.Parse(Console.ReadLine())*-1;
Console.Write("Future Value: ");
fv = double.Parse(Console.ReadLine());
switch(selection)
{
    case 1: //Present Value
        result = Financial.PV(rate, nper, pmt, fv,
            DueDate.EndOfPeriod);
        break;
    case 2: //Future Value
        result = Financial.FV(rate, nper, pmt, pv,
            DueDate.EndOfPeriod);
        break;
    case 3: //Interest Paid
        result = Financial.IPmt(rate, per, nper, pv, fv,
            DueDate.EndOfPeriod);
        break;
    case 4: //Monthly Payment
        result = Financial.Pmt(rate, nper, pv, fv,
            DueDate.EndOfPeriod);
        break;
}
```

```
        Console.WriteLine("The result is {0}", String.Format
            (result.ToString("n")));
        Console.ReadLine();
        }
    }
}
```

Example 15-2 Output

A sample output for calculating the monthly payment for a 30-year, $100,000 loan at 6 percent interest is as follows:

```
Common Financial Functions

Function Menu
1. Present Value (Rate,Years,PMT,FV)
2. Future Value (Rate,Years,PMT,PV)
3. Interst Paid (Rate,Per,Years,PV,FV)
4. Monthly Payment (Rate,Years,PV,FV)
Which function to perform? 4
Enter the appropriate value, or zero to skip
Interest Rate - whole number: 6
Period: 0
Number of Years: 30
Payment: 0
Present Value: 100000
Future Value: 0
The result is 599.55
```

CHAPTER 16

Collections

Table 16-1. Collection Class Equivalent Chart

VB 6.0	COLLECTION METHODS
Add	Add()
Count	Count
Item	Item()
Remove	Remove()
	Clear()
	ContainsKey()

Overview

Collections are a way of managing a group of similar data, such as a list of objects. Visual Studio uses collections to manage such things as the forms in your program, the fields in a table, and the printers available to the system.

Collections are an advanced form of arrays. Arrays are very simplistic because they are filled upon initialization, they have to be manually resized, an element's index is fixed, and the items are indexed with integers. Collections are an improvement because the elements aren't automatically created when the array is initialized, they automatically resize themselves, the elements within the collection are dynamic, and they can be referenced with keys.

.NET has a `System.Collections` namespace containing interfaces and classes that define various collections of objects. These collections consist of lists, queues, arrays, hash tables, and dictionaries. This chapter focuses on the `Hashtable` class because it is a general-purpose collection that serves most needs and it is very similar to the VB 6.0 `Collection` class.

VB .NET also uses a special class called `Collection` that has identical syntax to the VB 6.0 `Collection` class. We can assume it was added to make migrating VB 6.0 programs easier. C# doesn't have access to it, but this isn't necessary because C# can use the more sophisticated namespaces in .NET.

This chapter examines declaring a collection and manipulating its elements. At the end of the chapter, Table 16-2 summarizes the different .NET collection classes that you can explore with MSDN.

Declaring a Collection

The `Collection` class is declared the same as any other class. You can either declare an empty object variable as a `Collection`, or you can instantiate a new `Collection` object. When you only declare an object variable, you are creating a pointer that can reference an existing collection class. It isn't capable of storing or manipulating any data. Instantiating a collection object creates a collection object in memory with no elements. You can then add and modify elements of it.

The VB 6.0 collection class is called `Collection`. The `Hashtable` collection in .NET is in the `System.Collections` namespace. The `Hashtable` class, as well as any class derived from a `Dictionary` class, can be created with an initial number of elements. This is passed to the constructor as an integer. The algorithm that the `Hashtable` uses to manage elements is optimized if you instantiate it with a prime number (not evenly divisible by an integer other than itself). The following prime numbers give you a good start: 11, 53, 101, 503, 1,009, 5,003, and 10,007.

Collections manage their elements by using the hash code of an object. The .NET Framework automatically generates a hash code for every object created. This hash code is used for quickly sorting and accessing an object from a collection. You can view the hash code for any object by calling its `GetHashCode()` method.

VB 6.0
Declare and instantiate an object variable of type `Collection`.

```
Dim myCollection As Collection
Set myCollection = New Collection
```

VB .NET
Include the `System.Collections` namespace to access the `Hashtable` class. Pass the `Hashtable` constructor an initial number of elements. This should be a prime number.

```
Imports System.Collections
...
Dim myCollection As New Hashtable(101)
```

C#

Include the `System.Collections` namespace to access the `Hashtable` class. Pass the `Hashtable` constructor an initial number of elements. This should be a prime number.

```
using System.Collections;
...
Hashtable myCollection = new Hashtable(503);
```

Adding Elements

When you first start using a class, you must add elements to it because a collection is empty when it is instantiated. Adding elements simply consists of calling the `Add()` method of the object. The VB 6.0 `Add()` method needs the object and its key passed to it as the parameters. If you don't specify a key, the system will automatically use the next available index number. The `Hashtable.Add()` method needs the key and the object data passed as the parameters. It is helpful to specify a key that describes the element. An example of a key is a social security number or a product code.

    Notice that the order of the parameters for a VB 6.0 collection and a `Hashtable` are reversed. This is because a VB 6.0 key is optional and therefore must come last. The `Hashtable` requires the key to be passed, so there is no restriction on its placement.

VB 6.0

Pass the `Add()` method a variable or value that you want to store. The key is optional.

```
myCollection.Add data, key
```

VB .NET

Pass the `Add()` method the key and the object that you want to store.

```
myCollection.Add(key, object)
```

C#

Pass the `Add()` method the key and the object that you want to store.

```
myCollection.Add(key, object);
```

Accessing and Modifying Elements

Elements in a collection are accessed and modified by using either the element key or its index. They can be modified by either editing the data or deleting them altogether. Each of the three languages implements these methods differently.

VB 6.0 collection elements can be accessed with either the `Item()` method or the indexer. Both the `Item()` method and indexer can be passed either the key or index number. VB 6.0 collections don't allow you to change the data once it has been added. Once a key or index has been used, it is constant. To change it you must first remove the element by calling the `Remove()` method. After the element has been removed, call the `Add()` method again with the new data you want to insert.

.NET collection elements are accessed two different ways depending on which language you are using. VB .NET accesses an element by using the `Item()` method and using the indexer. Both ways of accessing the element require that you pass it the element key. Using an index number is not allowed with the `Hashtable`.[1] C# only uses the indexer. If you look under the IntelliSense in C#, the `Item()` method will not be listed. Remember that C# uses square brackets to designate the indexer. Although each language uses a different method for accessing the element, they both allow you to modify the data that is associated with a key. Thus, you don't have to remove an element first like you do in VB 6.0.

Of course, .NET has a `Remove()` method where you can delete one of the elements by passing it the element key. A new method is the `Clear()` method, which will remove all elements from the list at one time.

VB 6.0

An element's value can be accessed by using the indexer or the `Item()` method. You can pass either the index number or key.

```
Debug.Print myCollection(1)
Debug.Print myCollection(key)
Debug.Print myCollection.Item(key)
```

Modifying the data associated with a key requires removing the key first and then adding a new key.

```
myCollection.Remove key
myCollection.Add data, key
```

---

1. The `Sort` collection does allow you to access an element with the index number. See Table 16-2 for a summary of the different collections available.

VB .NET

An element's value is accessed using the indexer or the `Item()` method. You can only pass it the key.

```
Console.WriteLine(myCollection(key))
Console.WriteLine(myCollection.Item(key))
```

Modify an element by assigning the new data to it.

```
myCollection(key) = newObject
myCollection.Item(key) = newObject
```

Remove an element by calling the `Remove()` method. Pass it the key of the element to remove.

```
myCollection.Remove(key)
```

Remove all elements from the list by calling the `Clear()` method.

```
myCollection.Clear()
```

C#

An element's value can be accessed only using the indexer and passing it the key.

```
Console.WriteLine(myCollection[key]);
```

Modify an element by assigning the new data to it.

```
myCollection[key] = newObject;
```

Remove an element by calling the `Remove()` method. Pass it the key of the element to remove.

```
myCollection.Remove(key);
```

Remove all elements from the list by calling the `Clear()` method.

```
myCollection.Clear();
```

Examining the Elements

Once you have finished populating the collection with data, you will often want to examine the data in the collection. Each language has a few different ways of doing this.

VB 6.0 and .NET both provide the Count() property. This property tells you how many elements are in the collection.

.NET has a method called ContainsKey(). You pass it a key and it indicates if the key is already in the collection or not.

Both VB 6.0 and .NET use the For Each structure to traverse the elements in a collection. This is explained in detail in Chapter 4. The Hashtable requires you to use an element data type of DictionaryElement.

Other Collections in .NET

The .NET namespace provides an assortment of other collections you can use in your program. Table 16-2 provides a listing of these collections. You can look them up in MSDN for more information.[2]

Table 16-2. Collections Provided in the .NET System.Collections Namespace

COLLECTION NAME	DESCRIPTION
ArrayList	An array that is resized as needed
DictionaryBase	Used when you want to create your own collection class
Queue	A first-in, first-out storage mechanism
SortedList	Similar to a Hashtable, but you get to access members by their index number
Stack	A last-in, first-out storage mechanism

Example 16-1. Managing a Collection

This example demonstrates the functionality of collections by letting the user add, edit, and remove elements from the collection. As you can see from the sample output, the user can enter a new element by typing in the key and a string as the data. An existing element can be modified by entering the key and new data. If the key doesn't exist, a new element will be created. An element can

---

2. In the MSDN Help file, go to the index and type in **System.Collections namespace**. Select the .NET Framework Class Library location.

also be removed. As elements are added and deleted, a running total is printed at the top of the menu. The last option prints out all the elements. Within the programming code, the key is always checked to see if it exists or not. This is useful because if you are adding a new element, you don't want to get an error by attempting to duplicate keys. If you are removing an element, you want to make sure the key really does exist in the collection.

VB 6.0

```
'Managing a collection in VB 6.0
'Copyright (c)2001 by Bischof Systems, Inc.

Sub Main()
    Dim myCollection As New Collection
    Dim menuItem As Integer
    Dim key, data As String
    Dim myEntry As Variant
    Do
        Debug.Print
        Debug.Print "Collection Menu"
        Debug.Print "Total Elements: " & myCollection.Count
        Debug.Print "1. Add string"
        Debug.Print "2. Modify string"
        Debug.Print "3. Remove string"
        Debug.Print "4. List collection"
        Debug.Print "0. Exit"
        Debug.Print "Selection: "
        menuItem = "0" & InputBox("item")
        Select Case menuItem
        Case 1 'Add an element
            key = InputBox("Key:")
            data = InputBox("String: ")
            myCollection.Add data, key
        Case 2 'Modify data
            key = InputBox("Key: ")
            data = InputBox("String: ")
            myCollection.Remove key
            myCollection.Add data, key
        Case 3 'Remove an element
            key = InputBox("Key: ")
            myCollection.Remove key
```

```
        Case 4 'List the elements
            For Each myEntry In myCollection
                Debug.Print myEntry
            Next
        End Select
    Loop While menuItem <> 0
End Sub
```

VB .NET

```
'Managing a collection in VB .NET
'Copyright (c)2001 by Bischof Systems, Inc.

Module Module1

    Sub Main()
        Dim myCollection As Hashtable = New Hashtable(101)
        Dim menuItem As Integer
        Dim key, data As String
        Dim myEntry As DictionaryEntry
        Do
            Console.WriteLine()
            Console.WriteLine("Collection Menu")
            Console.WriteLine("Total Elements: {0}", myCollection.Count)
            Console.WriteLine("1. Add string")
            Console.WriteLine("2. Modify string")
            Console.WriteLine("3. Remove string")
            Console.WriteLine("4. List collection")
            Console.WriteLine("0. Exit")
            Console.Write("Selection: ")
            menuItem = Integer.Parse("0" & Console.ReadLine())
            Select Case menuItem
            Case 1 'Add an element
                Console.Write("Key: ")
                key = Console.ReadLine()
                Console.Write("String: ")
                data = Console.ReadLine()
                'Make sure it doesn't exist yet
                If (myCollection.ContainsKey(key)) Then
                    Console.WriteLine("Key already exists")
                Else
                    myCollection.Add(key, data)
                End If
```

```vb
        Case 2 'Modify data
            Console.Write("Key: ")
            key = Console.ReadLine()
            Console.Write("String: ")
            data = Console.ReadLine()
            'Check if it already exists
            If (myCollection.ContainsKey(key)) Then
                'It does exist, so modify it
                myCollection(key) = data
            Else
                'It doesn't exist, let's add it
                myCollection.Add(key, data)
            End If
        Case 3 'Remove an element
            Console.Write("Key: ")
            key = Console.ReadLine()
            'Make sure it exists before we delete it
            If (myCollection.ContainsKey(key)) Then
                myCollection.Remove(key)
            Else
                Console.WriteLine("Key doesn't exist")
            End If
        Case 4 'List the elements
            For Each myEntry In myCollection
                Console.WriteLine("{0}: {1}", myEntry.Key, _
                    myEntry.Value)
            Next
            End Select
    Loop While menuItem <> 0
    End Sub
End Module
```

C#

```csharp
//Managing a collection in C#
//Copyright (c)2001 by Bischof Systems, Inc.

using System;
using System.Collections;
```

```
namespace C_Collections
{
    class Class1
    {
        [STAThread]
        static void Main(string[] args)
        {
            Hashtable myCollection = new Hashtable(101);
            int menuItem = 0;
            string key="", data="";
            do
            {
                Console.WriteLine("\nCollection Menu");
                Console.WriteLine("Total Elements: {0}", myCollection.Count);
                Console.WriteLine("1. Add string");
                Console.WriteLine("2. Modify string");
                Console.WriteLine("3. Remove string");
                Console.WriteLine("4. List collection");
                Console.WriteLine("0. Exit");
                Console.Write("Selection: ");
                menuItem = int.Parse(Console.ReadLine());
                switch (menuItem)
                {
                    case 1:      //Add an element
                        Console.Write("Key: ");
                        key = Console.ReadLine();
                        Console.Write("String: ");
                        data = Console.ReadLine();
                        //Make sure it doesn't exist yet
                        if (myCollection.ContainsKey(key))
                        {
                            Console.WriteLine("Key already exists");
                        }
                        else
                        {
                            myCollection.Add(key, data);
                        }
                        break;
```

```
            case 2:      //Modify data
                Console.Write("Key: ");
                key = Console.ReadLine();
                Console.Write("String: ");
                data = Console.ReadLine();
                //Check if it already exists
                if (myCollection.ContainsKey(key))
                {   //It does exist, so modify it
                    myCollection[key] = data;
                }
                else
                {   //It doesn't exist, let's add it
                    myCollection.Add(key, data);
                }
                break;
            case 3:      //Remove an element
                Console.Write("Key: ");
                key = Console.ReadLine();
                //Make sure it exists before we delete it
                if (myCollection.ContainsKey(key))
                {
                    myCollection.Remove(key);
                }
                else
                {
                    Console.WriteLine("Key doesn't exist");
                }
                break;
            case 4:      //List the elements
                foreach (DictionaryEntry myEntry in myCollection)
                {
                    Console.WriteLine("{0}: {1}", myEntry.Key,
                        myEntry.Value);
                }
                break;
        }
    }while (menuItem!=0);
  }
}
```

Example 16-1 Output

```
Collection Menu
Total Elements: 0
1. Add string
2. Modify string
3. Remove string
4. List collection
0. Exit
Selection: 1
Key: a
String: hello

Collection Menu
Total Elements: 1
1. Add string
2. Modify string
3. Remove string
4. List collection
0. Exit
Selection: 3
Key: b
Key doesn't exist

Collection Menu
Total Elements: 1
1. Add string
2. Modify string
3. Remove string
4. List collection
0. Exit
Selection: 1
Key: b
String: goodbye

Collection Menu
Total Elements: 2
1. Add string
2. Modify string
3. Remove string
4. List collection
0. Exit
```

```
Selection: 4
b: goodbye
a: hello

Collection Menu
Total Elements: 2
1. Add string
2. Modify string
3. Remove string
4. List collection
0. Exit
Selection: 2
Key: a
String: good morning

Collection Menu
Total Elements: 2
1. Add string
2. Modify string
3. Remove string
4. List collection
0. Exit
Selection: 3
Key: b

Collection Menu
Total Elements: 1
1. Add string
2. Modify string
3. Remove string
4. List collection
0. Exit
Selection: 4
a: good morning

Collection Menu
Total Elements: 1
1. Add string
2. Modify string
3. Remove string
4. List collection
0. Exit
Selection: 0
```

CHAPTER 17

Program Interaction

Overview

Your program can interact with outside applications and data in a variety of ways. Two primary types of interaction consist of using COM objects and editing the system registry. .NET has specific classes just for doing these tasks.

Working with COM Objects

COM objects have been the primary means for developing reusable programming code within Windows. There are literally thousands of programs in use today that use COM as their primary architecture. .NET is not designed to write COM objects. It is designed to write managed code. However, that doesn't mean that it can't use COM objects. COM objects will be around for many years to come and .NET has been designed to seamlessly work with them. So if you know how to click the mouse a few times, you know how to use COM objects.

Early Binding to COM Objects

Early binding with COM objects in .NET is as simple as using any library file. Just set a reference to it and include it in your file using the Imports statement in VB .NET or the using statement in C#. This is a three-step process: Add a reference to the object, include the new library file, and instantiate the object.

Adding a Reference to the COM Object

When you include a library in your project, you have to add a reference to it. You do this by selecting Project ➤ Add Reference from the Visual Studio menu. The Add Reference dialog box has three tabs: .NET, COM, and Project. You will find most of the libraries you need listed on the .NET tab. However, if you want to reference a COM object, choose the COM tab and look for the appropriate DLL in the list. After you click OK to close the dialog box, you can look at the Solution

Explorer window and see that the class name for the DLL has been added to your project.

The internal workings of linking a .NET program to a COM object are a complex topic.[1] Here is a quick and dirty explanation without getting into all those details. The way COM objects talk to each other is totally different from the way .NET assemblies talk to each other. So .NET has a mechanism to analyze a COM object and write a wrapper around it. This is called the *Runtime Callable Wrapper* (RCW). When your .NET application makes a request of a COM object, this request is passed to the RCW, which converts it to a COM-compatible request. Any response from the COM object goes back through the RCW in reverse before it gets to your .NET application. The RCW is created and stored in the same folder that your project is located in. You can distribute this file with your application to ensure that nothing crashes. Actually, you can't prevent crashing because COM is unprotected code and you still have to worry about DLL Hell. But those are separate issues that you are probably already familiar with.

Another approach for creating the RCW file is to use the type library importer. It is called `tlbimp.exe` and it is usually in the path `C:\Program Files\Microsoft.Net\FrameworkSDK\Bin`. This program will also analyze the COM object and save it to a file. But you get the option of specifying the name of the RCW. To run this program, go to the command line and change the folder to the one where you want to store the file. Enter this command:

```
tlbimp ComLibrary.DLL /out:ComLibraryRCW.DLL
```

The "out:" option is what makes it save to a different filename. Of course, you need to replace "ComLibrary.DLL" with the name of the actual DLL. Notice that the suffix RCW was added to the end of the filename. This makes it easy to know which file it is a wrapper for, and it keeps the names unique. After you create the RCW file manually, you still need to go to the Add Reference dialog box. This time click the Browse button, find the file in the proper folder, and select it.

In summary, making the RCW file is very simple. Either make it with the Add Reference dialog box or use the type library importer.

Including the Library File

Adding a reference to the COM object is all you need to do to start using it. However, if you want to save yourself some typing, you can include the library

---

1. Lucky for me, this is a reference book so I don't have worry about explaining all those details here. Of course, Apress publishes books that go into enough detail to make any C++ hacker happy.

in your program with the `Imports` statement in VB .NET or with the `using` statement in C#.

The COM object you referenced will be listed in the Solutions window under References. If you had the IDE create the RCW for you, it will be listed using its type library. If you created the RCW file manually with the type library importer, the library name is the name of the RCW file—it won't be the name of the type library. In other words, the way you would normally reference this COM object from another COM-compatible program (using the ProgID stored in the registry) doesn't work here. The library name has been replace with the RCW filename. Fortunately, the classes and class members haven't changed and you call them as you always did before. Once again, this only applies if you used the type library importer to create the RCW.

VB .NET
Include the library file using the name listed under References in the Solutions window.

```
Imports library
```

C#
Include the library file using the name listed under References in the Solutions window.

```
using library;
```

Instantiating the Class

A .NET application instantiates the COM classes the same way it instantiates a .NET library. Simply declare an object variable of that class.

VB .NET
Declare and instantiate the class.

```
Dim myObject As libraryClass = New libraryClass()
```

C#
Declare and instantiate the class.

```
libraryClass myObject = new libraryClass();
```

Steps to Early Bind to a COM Object

The following list is a summary of the steps to perform early binding to a COM object.

1. Add a reference to the COM object file. Go to the Add Reference dialog box and select it from the COM list. Or you can run the `tlbimp.exe` program from the command line and manually add the file by selecting Browse from the Add Reference dialog box.

2. Include the library file. Find out the library name within the References list of the Solutions folder. Include it in your application.

3. Declare and instantiate the class the same as you would instantiate any .NET class.

Late Binding to COM Objects

When your program uses late binding to make calls to a COM object, it doesn't have any information about the COM object until the moment that the call is made. In fact, your program won't know anything about the object until it loads it into memory. This is different from early binding because you create a RCW file that maps out everything about the object. Early binding makes COM class information available to your program while you are writing it (which makes it easy to fix typos). The steps for late binding are getting a reference to the type library, instantiating the COM object, creating an array of parameters, and invoking the method call on the COM object.

Getting a Reference to the Type Library

To use the COM object, you need to use the ProgID to create instantiate a `Type` object. The `Activator` class in the next step uses this object. Declare a `Type` object variable. Call the method `GetTypeFromProgID()` and pass it the ProgID. Assign the return object of this method call to the `Type` object.

The `System` library is required for using the `Type` class. It is included in VB .NET by default.

VB .NET

Declare an object variable of the `Type` class.

```
Dim typeObject As Type
typeObject = Type.GetTypeFromProgID("library.class")
```

C#

Declare an object variable of the Type class. The Type class is in the System namespace.

```
using System;
...
Type typeObject;
typeObject = Type.GetTypeFromProgID("library.class");
```

Instantiating the COM Object

The Activator class is responsible for taking the Type object that was instantiated in the previous step and creating an instance of the COM object in memory. Do this by first declaring an Object variable and then call the CreateInstance() method of the Activator class. Assign the return object to the Object variable. You now have an instance of the COM object in memory.

The System.Reflection library is required for using the Activator class.

VB .NET

Declare an object variable of the Object class. Instantiate it using the Activator.CreateInstance() method. The Activator class is in the System.Reflection namespace.

```
Imports System.Reflection
...
Dim activatorObject As Object
activatorObject = Activator.CreateInstance(typeObject)
```

C#

Declare an object variable of the Object class. Instantiate it using the Activator.CreateInstance() method. The Activator class is in the System.Reflection namespace.

```
using System.Reflection;
...
object activatorObject;
activatorObject = Activator.CreateInstance(typeObject);
```

Creating an Array of Parameters

Now that there is an instance of the COM object in memory, you need to call one of its methods. But before you do that, you need to create an object array to store all the parameters that will be passed to the method. Once you create this array, populate it with the proper parameter values.

VB .NET

Declare an array of the objects to be passed as parameters to the COM object. Use as many parameters as necessary for the method call.

```
Dim parameters(n) As Object;
parameters(0) = object0
...
```

C#

Declare an array of the objects to be passed as parameters to the COM object. Use as many parameters as necessary for the method call.

```
object[] parameters = new object[n];
parameters[0] = object0;
...
```

Invoking the Method Call

Everything is now ready to call one of the methods of the COM object. Using the Type object created in the first step, call InvokeMember() and pass it the method name, a bindings flag, Nothing/null, the object instance created with the Activator class, and the array of objects that hold the parameters. If this method returns a value, assign it to an object variable or cast it with the proper data type.

VB .NET

Call InvokeMember() and pass it the method name, a bindings flag, Nothing, the object instance created with the Activator class, and the array of objects that hold the parameters.

```
typeObject.InvokeMember("GetFileVersion", BindingFlags.InvokeMethod, _
    Nothing, activatorObject, parameters)
```

C#

Call `InvokeMember()` and pass it the method name, a bindings flag, `null`, the object instance created with the `Activator` class, and the array of objects that hold the parameters.

```
var = typeObject.InvokeMember("GetFileVersion", BindingFlags.InvokeMethod,
    null, activatorObject, parameters);
```

Steps to Late Bind to a COM Object

The following list is a summary of the steps to perform late binding to a COM object.

1. Get a reference to the type library using the `Type.GetFromProgID()` method and passing it a ProgID string.

2. Instantiate the COM object by calling `Activator.CreateInstance()`.

3. Create an array of the parameters.

4. Invoke the method call using `Type.InvokeMember()`.

Working with the System Registry

The system registry is the central repository of data storage for almost every Windows program. It was originally meant to be a replacement for the multitude of INI files that were used by programs prior to the release of Windows 95. It is now a huge file that tracks everything from user IDs and program default settings to hidden registration keys.

Reading and writing to the registry in VB 6.0 is very simple. It consists of calling either `GetSetting()` or `SaveSetting()` for every value. You pass each function an application name, section name, and the key name. Unfortunately, this simplicity results in making VB 6.0 useful only for setting application settings. You are not able to do general registry work. .NET keeps the same simple calls as VB 6.0 (e.g., `GetValue` and `SetValue`) and adds more. Because .NET adds more functionality, it also adds a little more complexity. This chapter focuses on traversing to a single key and then getting, setting, and deleting its values. The `RegistryKey` class also enables you to do things such as delete a key, delete *all* the child keys (use with caution), and find out how many keys there are. These topics can be explored using MSDN.[2]

Working with the system registry consists of selecting a root key, traversing the registry hierarchy, modifying the key, and closing the registry.

Selecting a Root Key

The registry is accessed using the `Registry` and `RegistryKey` classes from the `Microsoft.Win32` namespace. To navigate the registry hierarchy, you first have to get one of the root nodes by calling a member of the `Registry` class. The root nodes are listed in Table 17-1.

Table 17-1. Registry Base Key Mapping to Registry Class Member

REGISTRY BASE KEY	REGISTRY CLASS MEMBER
HKEY_CLASSES_ROOT	ClassesRoot
HKEY_CURRENT_CONFIG	CurrentConfig
HKEY_CURRENT_USER	CurrentUser
HKEY_DYN_DATA	DynData
HKEY_LOCAL_MACHINE	LocalMachine
HKEY_PERFORMANCE_DATA	PerformanceData
HKEY_USERS	Users

Calling the proper member of the `Registry` class gives you a `RegistryKey` object. This object gives you access to one of the base key nodes. From this point forward, you call methods of the `RegistryKey` object to obtain a child node of the current key.

VB .NET

Get a reference to the registry base node using members of the `Registry` class. The `Registry` and `RegistryKey` classes are in the `Microsoft.Win32` namespace.

```
Imports Microsoft.Win32
...
Dim rk As RegistryKey
rk = Registry.member        'member is from
```

2. Using the MSDN Help file, go to the index and type in **RegistryKey class**.

C#

Get a reference to the registry base node using members of the Registry class. The Registry and RegistryKey classes are in the Microsoft.Win32 namespace.

```
using Microsoft.Win32;
...
RegistryKey rk;
rk = Registry.member;      //member is from Table 17-2
```

Traversing the Registry Tree

The RegistryKey class gives you full access to create and modify the key that it is currently referencing. You get the first reference to this key from the Registry class in the previous step. Thus, it is currently pointing to one of the base keys in the registry. More than likely, the key you want to modify is somewhere many levels deeper. You need to navigate down the registry to get to this key. Traversing down the tree consists of repeatedly getting the proper child record of the current key. Do this until you reach your destination.

Get the child key from the current key with one of two methods, OpenSubKey() or CreateSubKey(), and pass it the name of the child key.

OpenSubKey() defaults to giving you read-only access to the key. If you want write access, pass it a Boolean True value as the second parameter. If the key you requested doesn't exist, it will return a Null reference.

CreateSubKey() gives you read/write access to the key by default. If the key you requested doesn't exist, it will create it for you.

There is one alternative to traversing the tree that should be mentioned. You can short-circuit this looping process by passing one of the previous methods the full key path. It's much easier to get a registry key by writing a single line of code rather than using this looping method I discuss. But there is one big problem: Working with the registry is very dangerous. At its worst, taking a shortcut could result in a computer that won't boot. The benefit of traversing the tree key by key is that if anything goes wrong, the system will immediately throw an exception. You will be able to catch the error and handle it properly. You will also know which key caused the error. Passing the entire path in one method call may raise an error, but you won't know which key caused the error. It's better to be safe than sorry.

VB .NET

Access the child key by repeatedly calling the OpenSubKey() method. Pass True as the second parameter if you want to get write access.

```
rk = rk.OpenSubKey("keyname1")
rk = rk.OpenSubKey("keyname2", True)
```

Access the child key by calling the CreateSubKey() method.

```
rk = rk.CreateSubKey("keyname1")
rk = rk.CreateSubKey("keyname2")
```

Access the child key by passing the full key path.

```
rk = rk.CreateSubKey("keyname1\keyname2")
```

C#

Access the child key by repeatedly calling the OpenSubKey() method. Pass true as the second parameter if you want to get write access.

```
rk = rk.OpenSubKey("keyname1");
rk = rk.OpenSubKey("keyname2", true);
```

Access the child key by calling the CreateSubKey() method.

```
rk = rk.OpenSubKey("keyname1");
rk = rk.CreateSubKey("keyname2");
```

Access the child key by passing the full key path.

```
rk = rk.CreateSubKey(@"keyname1\keyname2");
```

Modifying the Key

If you managed to get this far, you have a RegistryKey object that references the key you want to modify in the registry. Now let's do something with it. You can read, write, and delete the key values using the methods GetValue(), SetValue(), and DeleteValue(). These are very straightforward methods.

Passing the GetValue() method a value name will return the value data as an Object. Cast it to the proper type. The data is returned as the cast type. Passing the SetValue() method a value name and the data will save the data in the registry. And, as you might expect, passing the `DeleteValue()` method a value name will delete the value.

VB .NET

Pass the `GetValue()` method a value name. Use `CType()` if you want to cast it as a specific data type.

```
var = CType(rk.GetValue("valuename"), type)
```

Pass the `SetValue()` method a value name and the value data.

```
rk.SetValue("valuename", valuedata)
```

Pass the `DeleteValue()` method a value name.

```
rk.DeleteValue("valuename")
```

C#

Pass the `GetValue()` method a value name. Cast it as a specific data type.

```
variable = (type)rk.GetValue("valuename");
```

Pass the `SetValue()` method a value name and the value data.

```
rk.SetValue("valuename", valuedata);
```

Pass the `DeleteValue()` method a value name.

```
rk.DeleteValue("valuename");
```

Closing the Registry Key

You should close the key when you are finished working with it.

VB .NET

Close the key by calling the `Close()` method.

```
rk.Close()
```

C#

Close the key by calling the `Close()` method.

```
rk.Close();
```

Example 17-1. Getting a Program's Version Number Using Early Binding

This example performs early binding to call the GetFileVersion() method of the FileSystemObject class. It determines the version number of the Windows Explorer program that has been installed in your WinNT folder. The program displays a single line indicating the version number.

Prior to typing in this code, go to Visual Studio's IDE and select Project ➤ Add Reference. Under the COM tab you will find the entry "Microsoft Scripting Runtime." Select this item and close the dialog box.

The example instantiates an instance of the FileSystemObject class just as it would instantiate a .NET class. This is because using early binding makes COM access seamless.

VB .NET

```
'Getting a program's version number using early binding in VB.Net
'Copyright (c)2001 by Bischof Systems, Inc.

'Add a COM reference to Microsoft Scripting Runtime
Imports Scripting

Module Module1

    Sub Main()
        'Add an early bound reference to the FileSystemObject from
        'the Scripting library (SCCRRUN.DLL)
        Dim fs As FileSystemObject = New FileSystemObject()
        'Display a file version number
        Dim version As String
        'You may need to change the path for this file
        version = fs.GetFileVersion("C:\WinNT\explorer.exe")
        Console.WriteLine("Windows Explorer - Version {0}", version)
        Console.ReadLine()
    End Sub
End Module
```

C#

```
//Getting a program's version number using early binding in C#
//Copyright (c)2001 by Bischof Systems, Inc.

using System;
//Add a COM reference to Microsoft Scripting Runtime
using Scripting;

namespace C_EarlyBinding
{
    class Class1
    {
        [STAThread]
        static void Main(string[] args)
        {
            //Add an early bound reference to the FileSystemObject from
            //the Scripting library (SCCRRUN.DLL)
            FileSystemObject fs = new FileSystemObject();
            //Display a file version number
            string version;
            //You may need to change the path for this file
            version = fs.GetFileVersion(@"C:\WinNT\explorer.exe");
            Console.WriteLine("Windows Explorer - Version {0}", version);
            Console.ReadLine();
        }
    }
}
```

Example 17-1 Output

```
Windows Explorer - Version 5.0.3315.2846
```

Example 17-2. Getting a Program's Version Number Using Late Binding

This example is the same as the first example, except that this uses late binding. Thus, the output is still the version number of Windows Explorer.

As you would expect, it is more complicated than the first example because it uses reflection to access the COM object's interface. It uses the methods `Type.GetTypeFromProgID()` and `Reflection.Activator.CreateInstance()` to load an instance of the COM object into memory. Then it calls `Type.InvokeMember()` to call a method of the COM object and return the version number.

VB .NET

```
'Getting a program's version number using late binding in VB .NET
'Copyright (c)2001 by Bischof Systems, Inc.

Imports System.Reflection

Module Module1

    Sub Main()
        'Declare the variables needed for late binding
        Dim fsType As Type
        Dim fs As Object
        Dim parameters(0) As String
        'Instantiate the COM file system Type object
        fsType = Type.GetTypeFromProgID("Scripting.FileSystemObject")
        'Instantiate the file system object
        fs = Activator.CreateInstance(fsType)
        'Populate the parameter array for passing parameters to object
        'You may need to change the path for this file
        parameters(0) = "C:\WinNT\Explorer.Exe"
        'Call the method of the COM object
        Dim version As String
        'Cast the return value from an object to a string
        version = fsType.InvokeMember("GetFileVersion", _
            BindingFlags.InvokeMethod, Nothing, fs, parameters)
        Console.WriteLine("Windows Explorer - Version {0}", version)
        Console.ReadLine()
    End Sub
End Module
```

C#

```
//Getting a program's version number using early binding in C#
//Copyright (c)2001 by Bischof Systems, Inc.

using System;
using System.Reflection;
```

```
namespace C_LateBinding
{
    class Class1
    {
        [STAThread]
        static void Main(string[] args)
        {
            //Declare the variables needed for late binding
            Type fsType;
            object fs;
            string[] parameters;
            //Instantiate the COM file system Type object
            fsType = Type.GetTypeFromProgID("Scripting.FileSystemObject");
            //Instantiate the file system object
            fs = Activator.CreateInstance(fsType);
            //Populate the parameter array for passing parameters to object
            // You may need to change the path for this file
            parameters = new string[] {@"C:\WinNT\Explorer.Exe"};
            //Call the method of the COM object
            string version;
            //Cast the return value from an object to a string
            version = (string)fsType.InvokeMember("GetFileVersion",
                BindingFlags.InvokeMethod,null,fs,parameters);
            Console.WriteLine("Windows Explorer - Version {0}", version);
            Console.ReadLine();
        }
    }
}
```

Example 17-2 Output

```
Windows Explorer - Version 5.0.3315.2846
```

Example 17-3. A Generic COM Interface Class

This example was written to make it easy to access a COM object using late binding. It is a class you can use in your program to instantiate any COM object and call its methods. The class is called CreateObject and you instantiate it by passing it the ProgID of a COM object. Then you can use any method in the COM object by calling the CreateObject.Execute() method and passing it the method name and any parameters that the method needs. The method's return value is returned as an object data type.

VB .NET

```
'A generic COM interface class in VB .NET
'Copyright (c)2001 by Bischof Systems, Inc.

Imports System.Reflection

Module Module1

    Sub Main()
        Dim version As String
        Dim fileSystem As CreateObject
        fileSystem = New CreateObject("Scripting.FileSystemObject")
        'You may need to change the path for this file
        version = fileSystem.Execute("GetFileVersion", _
            "C:\WinNT\Explorer.exe").ToString
        Console.WriteLine("Windows Explorer - Version {0}", version)
        Console.ReadLine()
    End Sub


    'Generic class to use late binding for accessing a COM object
    Public Class CreateObject
        'Declare the variables needed for late binding
        Private comType As Type
        Private comObject As Object
        'Constructor takes the ProgID of the COM object
        Public Sub New(ByVal ProgId As String)
            'Reference COM object interface using the ProgID
            comType = Type.GetTypeFromProgID(ProgID)
            'Instantiate the COM object
            comObject = Activator.CreateInstance(comType)
        End Sub
        'Generic call to a late-bound COM method and return a value
        Public Function Execute(ByVal Method As String, _
            ByVal ParamArray Parameters() As Object) As Object
            'Call the method of the COM object
            Return comType.InvokeMember(Method, BindingFlags.InvokeMethod, _
                Nothing, comObject, Parameters)
        End Function
    End Class
End Module
```

C#

```csharp
//A generic COM interface class in C#
//Copyright (c)2001 by Bischof Systems, Inc.

using System;
using System.Reflection;

namespace C_LateBindingGeneric
{
    class Class1
    {
        [STAThread]
        static void Main(string[] args)
        {
            string version;
            CreateObject fileSystem;
            fileSystem = new CreateObject("Scripting.FileSystemObject");
          //You may need to change the path for this file
            version = (string)fileSystem.Execute("GetFileVersion",
                @"C:\WinNT\Explorer.exe");
            Console.WriteLine("Windows Explorer - Version {0}", version);
            Console.ReadLine();
        }
    }
    //Generic class to use late binding for accessing a COM object
    public class CreateObject
    {
        //Declare the variables needed for late binding
        private Type comType;
        private object comObject;
        //Constructor takes the ProgID of the COM object
        public CreateObject(string ProgID)
        {
            //Reference COM object interface using the ProgID
            comType = Type.GetTypeFromProgID(ProgID);
            //Instantiate the COM object
            comObject = Activator.CreateInstance(comType);
        }
```

```
        //Generic call to a late-bound COM method and return a value
        public object Execute(string Method, params object[] Parameters)
        {
            //Call the method of the COM object
            return comType.InvokeMember(Method,BindingFlags.InvokeMethod,
                null,comObject,Parameters);
        }
    }
}
```

Example 17-3 Output

```
Windows Explorer - Version 5.0.3315.2846
```

Example 17-4. A RegEditor Class

This example was written to make it easy for you to work with the registry. It is a class you can use in your program to get a registry key and edit or delete its values. The class is called RegEditor and you instantiate it by passing it the key path. Use the methods GetValue(), SetValue(), and DeleteValue() to modify the key.

To demonstrate how the class works, this example creates a key in the registry called "Apress" and creates a value name called "BestSellers." The data stored with that value name is "The .NET Languages: A Quick Translation Guide." After the key value has been written and read back, it is deleted. To show the user what is happening, output is sent to the console as each step is performed.

The custom RegEditor class works by first accessing the LocalMachine root key. Then it parses the key path using "\" as the delimiter and traverses to the proper key. I use a CreateSubKey() method to ensure that every key exists. This key is kept open by the class so that the various methods can work with it.

It is left as an exercise for the reader to make the class more robust. You can pass another parameter to the constructor to specify which root key to use. You can add more method calls to make it more fully match the RegistryKey class and you can also add error handling. A nice challenge would be to have it inherit from the RegistryKey class.

VB .NET

```
'A RegEditor class in VB .NET
'Copyright (c)2001 by Bischof Systems, Inc.


Imports Microsoft.Win32

Module Module1

    Sub Main()
        Dim regEdit As RegEditor
        Dim keyName As String = "Best Sellers"
        Dim keyData As String = "The .NET Languages: " & _
            "A Quick Translation Guide"
        Dim newData As String
        'Tell the user the what key we are going to write
        Console.WriteLine("Writing to Registry")
        Console.WriteLine("Key Name :{0}", keyName)
        Console.WriteLine("Key Value:{0}", keyData)
        'Instantiate the custom registry editor
        regEdit = New RegEditor("SOFTWARE/Apress")
        'Write the string to the registry key
        regEdit.SetValue(keyName, keyData)
        'Read it back to a new variable to check if it worked
        newData = regEdit.GetValue(keyName)
        Console.WriteLine("Reading from the Registry")
        Console.WriteLine("Key Value:{0}", newData)
        'We're done, so delete it
        Console.WriteLine("Deleting it...")
        regEdit.DeleteValue(keyName)
        newData = regEdit.GetValue(keyName)
        Console.WriteLine("Key Value:{0}", newData)
        Console.WriteLine("Done")
        Console.ReadLine()
    End Sub

    'This class will write keys to a specified path in the registry tree.
    'It is designed to work with the HKey_Local_Machine
    Public Class RegEditor
        Private regKey As RegistryKey
        'Constructor needs the registry path
        Public Sub New(ByVal RegPath As String)
            regKey = GetRegistryKey(RegPath)
        End Sub
```

```vb
            'Write a value to the registry
            Public Sub SetValue(ByVal KeyName As String, ByVal KeyValue As Object)
                regKey.SetValue(KeyName, KeyValue)
            End Sub
            'Get a value from the registry - return strings for simplicity's sake
            Public Function GetValue(ByVal KeyName As String) As String
                Return regKey.GetValue(KeyName)
            End Function
            'Delete the value key
            Public Sub DeleteValue(ByVal KeyName As String)
                regKey.DeleteValue(KeyName)
            End Sub
            'Take a registry key path and get the key associated with it
            Private Function GetRegistryKey(ByVal RegPath As String) As RegistryKey
                Dim regKey As RegistryKey
                Dim pathMembers() As String = RegPath.Split("/"c)
                Dim currentMember As Integer
                'The root path is HKEY_LOCAL_MACHINE. A good modification
                'here would be to use a parameter that specifies the root path.
                regKey = Registry.LocalMachine
                'Traverse through the registry till we get the proper key
                For currentMember = 0 To pathMembers.Length - 1
                    'Use CreateSubKey to make sure the key exists
                    regKey = regKey.CreateSubKey(pathMembers(currentMember))
                Next
                Return regKey
            End Function
        End Class
End Module
```

C#

```csharp
//A RegEditor class in C#
//Copyright (c)2001 by Bischof Systems, Inc.

using System;
using Microsoft.Win32;

namespace C_Registry
{
```

```
class Class1
{
    static void Main(string[] args)
    {
        RegEditor regEdit;
        string keyName = "Best Sellers";
        string keyData = "The .NET Languages: " +
            "A Quick Translation Guide";
        string newData;
        //Tell the user the what key we are going to write
        Console.WriteLine("Writing to Registry");
        Console.WriteLine("Key Name :{0}", keyName);
        Console.WriteLine("Key Value:{0}", keyData);
        //Instantiate the custom registry editor
        regEdit = new RegEditor(@"SOFTWARE/Apress");
        //Write the string to the registry key
        regEdit.SetValue(keyName, keyData);
        //Read it back to a new variable to check if it worked
        newData = regEdit.GetValue(keyName);
        Console.WriteLine("Reading from the Registry");
        Console.WriteLine("Key Value:{0}", newData);
        //We're done, so delete it
        Console.WriteLine("Deleting it...");
        regEdit.DeleteValue(keyName);
        newData = regEdit.GetValue(keyName);
        Console.WriteLine("Key Value:{0}", newData);
        Console.WriteLine("Done");
        Console.ReadLine();
    }
}

//This class will write keys to a specified path in the registry tree.
//It is designed to work with the HKey_Local_Machine
class RegEditor
{
    private RegistryKey regKey;
    //Constructor needs the registry path
    public RegEditor(string RegPath)
    {
        regKey = GetRegistryKey(RegPath);
    }
```

```
            //Write a value to the registry
            public void SetValue(string KeyName, object KeyValue)
            {
                regKey.SetValue(KeyName, KeyValue);
            }
            //Get a value from the registry - return strings for simplicity's sake
            public string GetValue(string KeyName)
            {
                return (string)regKey.GetValue(KeyName);
            }
            //Delete the value key
            public void DeleteValue(string KeyName)
            {
                regKey.DeleteValue(KeyName);
            }
            //Take a registry key path and get the key associated with it
            private RegistryKey GetRegistryKey(string RegPath)
            {
                RegistryKey regKey;
                string[] pathMembers = RegPath.Split('/');
                //The root path is HKEY_LOCAL_MACHINE. A good modification
                //here would be to use a parameter that specifies the root path.
                regKey = Registry.LocalMachine;
                //Traverse through the registry till we get the proper key
                for (int currentMember=0; currentMember<pathMembers.Length;
                    currentMember++)
                {
                    //Use CreateSubKey to make sure the key exists
                    regKey = regKey.CreateSubKey(pathMembers[currentMember]);
                }
                return regKey;
            }
        }
    }
}
```

Example 17-4 Output

```
Writing to Registry
Key Name :Best Sellers
Key Value:The .NET Languages: A Quick Translation Guide
Reading from the Registry
Key Value:The .NET Languages: A Quick Translation Guide
Deleting it...
Key Value:
Done
```

CHAPTER 18
The App Object

Table 18-1. App Object Equivalent Properties in the FileVersionInfo Class

APP OBJECT	PROPERTY	DESCRIPTION
EXEName	OriginalFileName	The application's filename
FileDescription	FileDescription	The application description
	FileVersion	A version string in the format of "major.minor.build.private"
Major	FileMajorPart	The major part of the version number
Minor	FileMinorPart	The minor part of the version number
Revision	FileBuildPart	The build part of the version number
	FilePrivatePart	The private part of the version number
ProductName	ProductName	Name of the product this file is distributed with
Comments	Comments	Application comments
CompanyName	CompanyName	Company name
LegalCopyright	LegalCopyright	Copyright information
LegalTrademark	LegalTrademark	Trademark information

Table 18-2. Members of the EventLog Class for Logging Events

EVENTLOG MEMBER	DESCRIPTION
Log	Sets which log file to use. Typically you will use "Application."
Source	The source name to register.
WriteEntry(message)	The message to write to the Event Log.
Close()	Closes the Event Log. Messages are written immediately without waiting for the log to be closed.

Overview

The Application object (App object) in VB 6.0 is used for getting a variety of information about your application. It is also helpful for writing to the NT Event Log. The App object is not used in .NET and there is no direct equivalent for it. Instead, you need to use an assortment of different functions scattered throughout .NET. The means of doing this is detailed in this chapter.

Getting Application-Specific Details

The App object in VB 6.0 gives application details such as the application name, application path, version number, comments, and company name. .NET gives this information as well, but you have to work a little harder for it. Fortunately, this chapter makes it easy.

Getting application information within a .NET application requires two libraries: System.Reflection and System.Diagnostics. Add them to VB .NET with the Imports statement or add them to C# with the using statement.

The Reflection library is used for finding out about the application assembly. There are dozens of members in this class and it is recommended that you refer to MSDN for a full description.[1] The property you are concerned with is Assembly.GetExecutingAssembly().Location. This property is a string with the full file path for the executable. Use this location string with the System.Diagnostics library to find out more details about your application.

The Diagnostics library is used for finding out the small details of an application assembly. The class that you need from this library is FileVersionInfo. Calling the GetVersionInfo() method of this class and passing it the Location string (from the Reflection library) returns a FileVersionInfo object. This object has properties for retrieving information about your class.

To make it easier, here are the steps to take to get application information.

1. Include the System.Reflection and System.Diagnostics libraries.

2. Save the AssemblyLocation to a string.

3. Get an instantiation of the FileVersionInfo class.

4. Reference properties of the FileVersionInfo object. These properties are listed in Table 18-1.

---

1. In MSDN, use the index and type in **System.Reflection.Assembly class**.

MSDN lists even more properties you may be interested in. The following examples demonstrate the steps for writing to the Event Log in each language.

VB .NET

Include the `System.Reflection` and `System.Diagnostics` libraries.

```
Imports System.Reflection
Imports System.Diagnostics
```

Save the `AssemblyLocation` to a string.

```
Dim fileLocation as String
fileLocation = Reflection.Assembly.GetExecutingAssembly().Location
```

Get an instantiation of the `FileVersionInfo` class.

```
Dim fileInfo as FileVersionInfo
fileInfo = FileVersionInfo.GetVersionInfo(fileLocation)
```

Reference properties of the `FileVersionInfo` object.

```
Console.WriteLine(fileInfo.OriginalFilename)
```

C#

Include the `System.Reflection` and `System.Diagnostics` libraries.

```
using System.Reflection;
using System.Diagnostics;
```

Save the `AssemblyLocation` to a string.

```
string fileLocation;
fileLocation = Assembly.GetExecutingAssembly().Location;
```

Get an instantiation of the `FileVersionInfo` class.

```
FileVersionInfo fileInfo;
fileInfo = FileVersionInfo.GetVersionInfo(fileLocation);
```

Reference properties of the `FileVersionInfo` object.

```
Console.WriteLine(fileInfo.OriginalFilename);
```

Writing to the Event Log

The Event Log is a Windows-based tool to manage the messages from applications on a computer. Frequently, the Event Log is used as a centralized error repository for applications. Rather than creating a custom error-logging tool, it's much easier to write to the Event Log. Not only that, but every system administrator knows how to use the Event Viewer.

The App object in VB 6.0 makes writing to the Event Log easy. Just call the LogEvent() method and everything is done for you. .NET is just about as easy. .NET uses the EventLog class to log messages. This class requires your application to include the System.Diagnostics library. Using the EventLog class consists of four simple steps:

1. Create an instance of the EventLog class.

2. Set the log entry properties (Log and Source).

3. Write the entry to the log.

4. Close the log file when you are done.

The members of the EventLog class are listed in Table 18-2.

The following examples demonstrate the steps for writing to the Event Log in each language.

VB .NET

Create an instance of the EventLog class.

```
Dim myLog As EventLog = New EventLog()
```

Set the log entry properties.

```
myLog.Log = "Application"
myLog.Source = "source text"
```

Write the entry to the log.

```
myLog.WriteEntry("log entry")
```

Close the log file.

```
myLog.Close()
```

C#

Create an instance of the EventLog class.

```csharp
EventLog myLog = new EventLog();
```

Set the log entry properties.

```csharp
myLog.Log = "Application";
myLog.Source = "source text";
```

Write the entry to the log.

```csharp
myLog.WriteEntry("log entry");
```

Close the log file.

```csharp
myLog.Close();
```

Example 18-1. Displaying Application Information

This example displays the following information about the application: name, file path, version number, major number, minor number, build number, and private number. Simply run the application to see the results. This example can be copied directly to your program for easy retrieval of application information.

VB .NET

```vbnet
//Displaying application information in VB .NET
//Copyright (c)2001 by Bischof Systems, Inc.


Imports System.Reflection
Imports System.Diagnostics

Module Module1
    Sub Main()
        'Define the class that gets application info
        Dim fileInfo As FileVersionInfo
        'Define the misc info variables
        Dim fileLocation, fileName, verFull As String
        Dim verMajor, verMinor, verBuild, verPrivate As Integer
```

```
'Get the file location string
'Note: Assembly is enclosed in brackets b/c it is a reserved word
fileLocation = [Assembly].GetExecutingAssembly().Location
'Get the file information object
fileInfo = FileVersionInfo.GetVersionInfo(fileLocation)
'Get the various file details
fileName = fileInfo.OriginalFilename
verFull = fileInfo.FileVersion
verMajor = fileInfo.FileMajorPart
verMinor = fileInfo.FileMinorPart
verBuild = fileInfo.FileBuildPart
verPrivate = fileInfo.FilePrivatePart
'Display all the details
Console.WriteLine("File name      : {0}", fileName)
Console.WriteLine("Full filepath  : {0}", fileLocation)
Console.WriteLine("Version number : {0}", verFull)
Console.WriteLine("Major part     : {0}", verMajor)
Console.WriteLine("Minor part     : {0}", verMinor)
Console.WriteLine("Build part     : {0}", verBuild)
Console.WriteLine("Private part   : {0}", verPrivate)
Console.ReadLine()
End Sub
End Module
```

C#

```
//Displaying application information in C#
//Copyright (c)2001 by Bischof Systems, Inc.

using System;
using System.Reflection;
using System.Diagnostics;

namespace C_AppObject
{
    class Class1
    {
        [STAThread]
        static void Main(string[] args)
```

```
        {
            //Define the class that gets application info
            FileVersionInfo fileInfo;
            //Define the misc info variables
            string fileLocation, fileName;
            string verFull;
            int verMajor, verMinor, verBuild, verPrivate;
            //Get the file location string
            fileLocation = Assembly.GetExecutingAssembly().Location;
            //Get the file information object
            fileInfo = FileVersionInfo.GetVersionInfo(fileLocation);
            //Get the various file details
            fileName = fileInfo.OriginalFilename;
            verFull = fileInfo.FileVersion;
            verMajor = fileInfo.FileMajorPart;
            verMinor = fileInfo.FileMinorPart;
            verBuild = fileInfo.FileBuildPart;
            verPrivate = fileInfo.FilePrivatePart;
            //Display all the details
            Console.WriteLine("File name        : {0}", fileName);
            Console.WriteLine("Full filepath    : {0}", fileLocation);
            Console.WriteLine("Version number   : {0}", verFull);
            Console.WriteLine("Major part       : {0}", verMajor);
            Console.WriteLine("Minor part       : {0}", verMinor);
            Console.WriteLine("Build part       : {0}", verBuild);
            Console.WriteLine("Private part     : {0}", verPrivate);
            Console.ReadLine();
        }
    }
}
```

Example 18-1 Output

```
File name       : AppObject.exe
Full filepath   : E:/DotNet/AppObject/bin/Debug/AppObject.exe
Version number  : 1.0.616.38003
Major part      : 1
Minor part      : 0
Build part      : 616
Private part    : 38003
```

Example 18-2. Logging Errors Using the Event Log

This example uses the EventLog class to write a generic error handler procedure. You pass it an instance of the Exception class, any additional error tracking information, and a Boolean stating if you want to save the stack trace. It goes through the four steps of writing to the Event Log to save the error message. You can view the log entry by opening the Windows built-in Event Viewer application. The System.Diagnostics library must be included.

VB .NET

```
'Logging errors using the event log in VB .NET
'Copyright (c)2001 by Bischof Systems, Inc.

Imports System.Diagnostics

Module Module1

    Sub Main()
        Dim x, y As Integer
        Try
            x /= y
        Catch e As Exception
            LogError(e, "I knew this wouldn't work!", True)
        End Try
    End Sub

    'Standard error logging procedure
    Sub LogError(ByVal e As Exception, ByVal MoreInfo As String, _
        ByVal Trace As Boolean)
        Dim errMessage As String
        'Create the EventLog object
        Dim log As EventLog = New EventLog()
        'Create the error message
        errMessage = e.Message
        If MoreInfo <> "" Then
            errMessage += ", More Info: " + MoreInfo
        End If
        If Trace Then
            errMessage += ", StackTrace:" + e.StackTrace
        End If
        'Set the EventLog properties
        log.Log = "Application"
        log.Source = e.Source
```

```
            'Write the entry
            log.WriteEntry(errMessage)
            'Close the log file
            log.Close()
        End Sub
End Module
```

C#

```csharp
//Logging errors using the event log in C#
//Copyright (c)2001 by Bischof Systems, Inc.

using System;
using System.Diagnostics;

namespace Event_Log
{
    class Class1
    {
        [STAThread]
        static void Main(string[] args)
        {
            int x=0, y=0;
            try
            {
                x /= y;
            }
            catch (Exception e)
            {
                LogError(e, "I knew this wouldn't work!", true);
            }
        }

        //Standard error logging procedure
        static void LogError(Exception e, string MoreInfo, bool Trace)
        {
            string errMessage;
            //Create the EventLog object
            EventLog log = new EventLog();
            //Create the error message
            errMessage = e.Message;
```

```
            if (MoreInfo != "")
            {
                errMessage += ", More Info: " + MoreInfo;
            }
            if (Trace)
            {
                errMessage += ", StackTrace:" + e.StackTrace;
            }
            //Set the EventLog properties
            log.Log = "Application";
            log.Source = e.Source;
            //Write the entry
            log.WriteEntry(errMessage);
            //Close the log file
            log.Close();
        }
    }
}
```

CHAPTER 19

Drawing with Forms and Printers

Overview

The drawing-related classes in .NET give you the ability to draw images on forms and printed documents. Rather than adding controls and graphics to the form in design mode or using a report writer, you can write programming code to create dynamic graphics for both formats.

The .NET Framework implements drawing and printing using classes derived from the `System.Drawing` class. This benefits you because once you learn how to draw to a form, you can use the same techniques to send output to a printer.

All the graphics-related classes in this chapter are in the `System.Drawing` namespace. This namespace is automatically included in the VB .NET and C# Windows Form applications. It is not necessary to use this namespace qualifier when you reference the classes in a Windows Form application.

Drawing and printing with Windows is made possible with the Graphical Device Interface (GDI). The GDI originated with the first version of Windows as a way for programmers to send output to different devices without having to worry about the complexity of device compatibility issues. This made it Windows' responsibility to manage the low-level calls to the video and printer drivers. Because GDI was developed in Windows' infancy, it was created for C developers and thus had functional implementation similar to the C language.

The .NET Framework has revamped GDI and given it an object-oriented face-lift. You now have GDI+, which is an object-oriented implementation of GDI. GDI+ uses a multitude of classes that implement graphics functionality. These classes are derived from the `System.Drawing` class and are shared amongst each other through the different parameter lists.

The VB 6.0 graphics objects are now gone. This is a huge benefit to programmers. The graphic primitives, such as `Line` and `Circle`, are a thing of the past. You no longer have to use Win32 API calls for graphics operations. The VB 6.0 graphics objects have all been replaced by the powerful classes in the `System.Drawing` namespace.

The core object that you work with is the Graphics object. It is the canvas that you paint your graphics onto. You use this object when drawing to a form or printing a page. Many objects are used to display graphics on the Graphics object, including Pen, Brush, and Image. There are too many of these objects to cover in this chapter, but you learn how to use the basic ones here. Learning the basic tools makes researching the other ones in MSDN much easier.

To learn how to draw and print, you need to learn how to work with the Graphics object. Ideally, that would be the first topic this chapter covers. However, it is a little hard to learn how to use the object if you don't know how to see the results of what it does. As a result, this chapter first shows how to print an object to a form. Next, it shows how to send information to the printer. After demonstrating how to output to both of these devices, the chapter goes into the details of using the Graphics object. Because the same Graphics object is used for outputting to both forms and printing, the examples in the first two sections only demonstrate printing a simple bitmap. The "Drawing Graphics" section of this chapter has examples to create more complex output. These examples can be used with either method. In fact, you can even make a generic class for handling graphics and it can be called for either a form or a print document.

Efficient Memory Management for Graphics Objects

When you create the different graphics objects described in this section, you have two options of how to declare them. One way is to declare a variable for each object and pass this variable to the method parameter of a graphics object. After calling the method, dispose of the graphics object so that the resources are freed. Another way is to instantiate a new object within the method call. Each option has its pros and cons.

The first option, declaring a variable for each object and then disposing of it, is the most efficient. You are in control of when the object is destroyed and this gives you more efficient memory utilization. The drawback to this method is that declaring and destroying objects requires more coding on your part.

The second option, instantiating an object within the method call, is a faster way of coding. But just like many aspects of programming, getting one benefit usually means giving up another benefit. In this case, the benefit of faster coding results in poor memory management. Objects will not be destroyed until they are garbage collected. The short-term benefit of faster coding is not worth the long-term drawback of poor memory management. There is one instance where might find yourself doing this: when you are writing code to test out new concepts and you will not use the code in a final application.

Although instantiating objects within the method call should only be done on rare occasions, it's inevitable that you'll see many programmers doing this and you'll read about it in magazine articles. So that you are familiar with both methods, the examples in this chapter show both of them. But let me stress that applications you anticipate using regularly should create and dispose of the objects.

Drawing on a Form

When you draw graphics on a form, the entire form is the region that you work with. To place a shape or image object on the form, you need a reference to an object that can display these items. As you may have guessed, this is the Graphics object.

Drawing on a form requires creating a variable that references the form's Graphics object. Getting a reference to this object is done in two different ways. The first is by calling the Form.CreateGraphics() method. This method returns a Graphics object and you assign it to a variable.

A problem with using the CreateGraphics() method is that the image drawn on the form isn't permanent. Once a user minimizes the form or places another form on top of it, Windows erases your image to show the new form. Once the form is restored, your image is not redrawn by Windows. You have to do that yourself. To avoid this problem, you can use the Paint event, which is the second way of getting a reference to the Graphics object.

The Paint event is triggered whenever Windows needs to display your form. This can happen when the form is first opened or when another form is placed on top of it (as discussed in the previous paragraph). The argument of the event handler is the variable e, which is an instance of the Windows.Forms.PaintEventArgs class. The e argument has a Graphics property that you can assign to your variable.

Once you have a reference to the Graphics object of the form, call the methods of the object to draw on the form.

VB .NET

Use the form's CreateGraphics() method to get a reference to the Graphics object.

```
'Demonstrate displaying a bitmap
Private Sub ShowImage()
    Dim myCanvas As Graphics
    Dim background As Bitmap
    myCanvas = Me.CreateGraphics()
    background = New Bitmap("C:\WinNt\Soap Bubbles.bmp")
    'Add images to the Graphics object here
    myCanvas.DrawImage(background, 0, 0)
    ...
```

```
    myCanvas.Dispose()
    background.Dispose()
End Sub
```

Write an event handler for the form's `Paint` method to have your image auto-matically refreshed by Windows. Get a reference to the `e.Graphics` property.

```
'Demonstrate displaying a bitmap
Private Sub Form1_Paint(ByVal sender As Object, ByVal e As _
    System.Windows.Forms.PaintEventArgs) Handles MyBase.Paint
    Dim myCanvas As Graphics
    Dim background As Bitmap
    myCanvas = e.Graphics
    'Add images to the Graphics object here
    background = New Bitmap("C:\WinNt\Soap Bubbles.bmp")
    myCanvas.DrawImage(background, 0, 0)
    ...
    background.Dispose()
End Sub
```

C#

Use the `CreateGraphics()` method of the form to get a reference to the `Graphics` object.

```
//Demonstrate displaying a bitmap
private void ShowImage()
{
    Graphics myCanvas;
    Bitmap background;
    myCanvas = this.CreateGraphics();
    //Add images to the Graphics object here
    background = new Bitmap(@"C:\WinNt\Soap Bubbles.bmp");
    myCanvas.DrawImage(background, 0, 0);
    ...
    background.Dispose();
    myCanvas.Dispose();
}
```

Write an event handler for the form's `Paint` method to have your image auto-matically refreshed by Windows. Get a reference to the `e.Graphics` property.

```
this.Paint += new System.Windows.Forms.PaintEventHandler(this.Form1_Paint);
...
//Demonstrate displaying a bitmap
private void Form1_Paint(object sender, System.Windows.Forms.PaintEventArgs e)
{
    Graphics myCanvas;
    Bitmap background;
    myCanvas = e.Graphics;
    //Add images to the Graphics object here
    background = new Bitmap(@"C:\WinNt\Soap Bubbles.bmp");
    myCanvas.DrawImage(background, 0, 0);

    ...
    background.Dispose();
}
```

Printing Documents

Compared to VB 6.0, the process of printing documents has changed drastically in .NET. In VB 6.0, printing consists of printing a page, calling the NewPage() method, and then printing another page. It is similar to running a script. The .NET Framework changes this process by making it event driven.

Sending a Document to the Printer

Printing a page in .NET consists of a few simple steps. First, instantiate a PrintDocument object. Then create a new instance of the PrintDialog object and set a reference to the PrintDocument object. Show the dialog box so that the user can select the printer and its properties. When the user closes the dialog box, call the PrintDocument.Print() method. This causes the PrintPage event to be triggered for every new page. Create a procedure to handle the PrintPage event so that it fills the Graphics object with the information you want to display. This procedure is called repeatedly as long as you set the HasMorePages property to True. By default, HasMorePages is False and does not need to be set if you don't want to print any more pages.

Using the PrintDocument object is pretty straightforward. You create a new instance of it and assign it to the PrintDialog object.

The PrintDialog object is used to let the user select which printer he or she wants to print to and set the printer settings. Create a new instance of it, assign the PrintDocument object to its Document property, and call ShowDialog().

After the ShowDialog() method returns, call the Print() method of the PrintDocument object.

VB .NET

Instantiate a `PrintDocument` object and a `PrintDialog` object. Assign the `PrintDocument` object to the `Document` property of `PrintDialog`. Call the `PrintDialog()` method to let the user choose the printer and its settings. Then call the `Print()` method of the `PrintDocument` object.

```
Private Sub PrintIt()
    Dim myDoc As New Printing.PrintDocument()
    Dim myPrinter As New PrintDialog()
    myPrinter.Document = myDoc
    myPrinter.ShowDialog()
    'This triggers the PrintPage event and handles it
    'The event PrintPageHandler is shown in the next code example
    AddHandler myDoc.PrintPage, AddressOf Me.PrintPageHandler
    myDoc.Print()
End Sub
```

C#

```
private void PrintIt()
{
    System.Drawing.Printing.PrintDocument myDoc =
        new System.Drawing.Printing.PrintDocument();
    PrintDialog myPrinter = new PrintDialog();
    myPrinter.Document = myDoc;
    //This triggers the PrintPage event and handles it
    //The event PrintPageHandler is shown in the next code example
    myDoc.PrintPage += new System.Drawing.Printing.PrintPageEventHandler
        (this.PrintPageHandler);
    myPrinter.ShowDialog();
    myDoc.Print();
}
```

Calling the `PrintDocument.Print` method triggers the `PrintPage` event. You have to add code to handle this event. This code is responsible for sending information to the `Graphics` object and telling the printer how many pages to print. This is done using the properties of the `PrintPageEventArgs` object.

VB .NET

With the `PrintPage` event handler, add images to the `e.Graphics` object. If you want the printer to print another page, set the `e.HasMorePages` property to `True` (it is `False` by default). You can reference the `e.Graphics` object directly or assign it to a variable.

```
Private Sub PrintPageHandler(ByVal sender As Object, _
    ByVal e As Printing.PrintPageEventArgs)
    Dim myCanvas as Graphics = e.Graphics
    Dim background As Bitmap
    myCanvas = e.Graphics
    'Add images to the Graphics object here
    background = New Bitmap("C:\WinNt\Soap Bubbles.bmp")
    myCanvas.DrawImage(background, 0, 0)
    ...
    background.Dispose()
End Sub
```

C#

With the `PrintPage` event handler, add images to the `e.Graphics` object. If you want the printer to print another page, set the `e.HasMorePages` property to `true` (it is `false` by default). You can reference the `e.Graphics` object directly or assign it to a variable.

```
private void PrintPageHandler(object sender,
    System.Drawing.Printing.PrintPageEventArgs e)
{
    Bitmap background;
    //Add images to the Graphics object here
    background = new Bitmap(@"C:\WinNt\Soap Bubbles.bmp");
    e.Graphics.DrawImage(background, 0, 0);
    ...
    background.Dispose();
}
```

Another way to print documents is to add the printer controls to your form in Design View. The benefit of adding these objects to your form is that you can use the Properties window to visually link them together. You can also double-click the `PrintDocument` object to have the IDE create an empty event handler for the `PrintPage` event. Adding these controls to your form and setting their properties is fairly simple and is the same as adding any other control to your form. These details are not covered in this chapter.

Displaying a Print Preview

Providing a print preview feature for your application lets users view a document before they print it. Adding this feature couldn't be easier. Simply take the code that prints a standard document and replace the `PrintDialog` object with a `PrintPreview` object. You also need to remove the line of code that calls the PrintDocument.Print() method because this is now controlled from the Print Preview window.

VB .NET

```
Private Sub PreviewIt()
    Dim myDoc As New Printing.PrintDocument()
    Dim myPreview As New PrintPreviewDialog()
    myPreview.Document = myDoc
    'This triggers the PrintPage event and handles it
    'The event handler is shown in the PrintPageHandler procedure
    AddHandler myDoc.PrintPage, AddressOf Me.PrintPageHandler
    myPreview.ShowDialog()
End Sub
```

C#

```
private void PreviewIt()
{
    System.Drawing.Printing.PrintDocument myDoc =
        new System.Drawing.Printing.PrintDocument();
    PrintPreviewDialog myPreview = new PrintPreviewDialog();
    myPreview.Document = myDoc;
    //This triggers the PrintPage event and handles it
    //The event handler is shown in the PrintPageHandler method
    myDoc.PrintPage += new System.Drawing.Printing.PrintPageEventHandler
        (this.PrintPageHandler);
    myPreview.ShowDialog();
}
```

Drawing Graphics

All the examples in the chapter thus far have been based off using the Graphics object to display a bitmap image. The Graphics object, as well as all the other related drawing objects, is located in the System.Drawing namespace. Within this namespace, there are also classes for creating fonts and icons, displaying cursors and text, and performing a host of other tasks.[1]

---

1. In the MSDN Help file, go to the index and type in **System.Drawing**.

Fundamental Drawing Classes

The majority of the methods that you call to create images use four classes: the Point class, the Pen class, the Brush class, and the Font class.

The Point class is used to specify a coordinate on the screen. When you instantiate a new Point object, pass the constructor two integers that represent the X and Y coordinates. You can later access those two points using the X and Y properties of the class. The drawing methods that require a Pen object sometimes allow you to enter the X and Y coordinates directly without instantiating a Pen object. Consult the MSDN Help file for the object you are using to see when this is available.

The Pen class is used to draw a line. It can be a solid line or a broken line. Instantiating a Pen object requires passing it a Color. There are dozens of colors to choose from.[2] You can also create a custom RGB color using the FromARGB() method of the Color class. For quicker coding, you can also use a member of the Pens class. The members are all pens of width 1 with a different color. By default, a pen has a width of 1, but you can make it thicker by passing the constructor a width. If you make the width thicker, you have the option of making it the same color throughout, or you can fill it with a pattern using the Brush object.

The Brush class is used to fill in an area of an object. An area can consist of the space within the edges of a line or the space within the boundary of an object, such as a triangle. You can create brushes that are a solid color or brushes that are filled with a pattern. There are a variety of brushes to choose from.[3] Just like the Pens class, there is a Brushes class whose members consist of solid brushes of a single color.

The Font class is really only used for drawing text strings, not for generic shapes. But that doesn't mean it isn't important. Creating a new font consists of passing the constructor a font name string and a font size. You can also pass a font style as an optional parameter. The font style is an enumerated list called FontStyle and it consists of Bold, Italic, Underline, and so on. In VB .NET you can set multiple styles by adding the enumerated elements together. In C#, use the logical OR (|) to do this. Chapter 11 discusses how to create a new font object using an existing font object.

---

2. To see all the available colors listed in the MSDN Help file, go to the index and type in **System.Drawing.Color structure**.

3. For a list of the different brushes in the MSDN Help file, go to the index and type in **System.Drawing.Brush class**. The classes derived from the Brush object are listed within the text.

VB .NET

Create a `Point` object by passing the constructor two integers representing the X and Y coordinates.

```
Dim myPoint As Point = New Point(5, 20)
```

Create a `Pen` object by passing the constructor a color and/or a width. You can use a predefined member of the `Pens` class as a shortcut, but it doesn't use the `New` constructor.

```
Dim myPen1 As Pen = New Pen(Color.Green)
Dim myPen2 As Pen = New Pen(Color.WhiteSmoke, 5)
Dim myPen3 As Pen = Pens.BurlyWood 'Many interesting colors are available
'Use a custom RGB color - this one is white
Dim myPen4 As Pen = New Pen(Color.FromArgb(255, 255, 255))
```

Create a `Brush` object of a solid color using the `SolidBrush` object and pass it a color. To create a brush that uses hatching, use a `HatchBrush` object. `HatchBrush` objects are found in the `System.Drawing.Drawing2D` class. Instantiate a `HatchBrush` object by passing it a style and a color. If you use a predefined member of the `Brushes` class as a shortcut, don't use the `New` constructor.

```
Dim myBrush1 as SolidBrush = New SolidBrush(Color.BlanchedAlmond)
Imports System.Drawing.Drawing2D
Dim myBrush2 as Drawing2D.HatchBrush = New _
    Drawing2D.HatchBrush(Drawing2D.HatchStyle.DiagonalBrick, _
    Color.ForestGreen)
Dim myBrush3 as Brush = Brushes.Beige
```

Create a `Font` object by passing the constructor a font name and a font size. An optional third parameter is the font style.

```
Dim myFont as Font = New Font("Arial", 15, FontStyle.Bold)
```

C#

Create a `Point` object by passing the constructor two integers representing the X and Y coordinates.

```
Point myPoint = new Point(5, 20);
```

Create a `Pen` object by passing the constructor a color and/or a width. You can use a predefined member of the `Pens` class as a shortcut, but it doesn't use the new constructor.

```
Pen myPen1 = new Pen(Color.Blue);
Pen myPen2 = new Pen(Color.DarkGoldenrod, 5);
Pen myPen3 = Pens.MediumSlateBlue;
//Use a custom RGB color - this one is black
Pen myPen4 = new Pen(Color.FromArgb(0,0,0));
```

Create a Brush object of a solid color using the SolidBrush object and pass it a color. To create a brush that uses hatching, use a HatchBrush object. HatchBrush objects are found in the System.Drawing.Drawing2D class. Instantiate a HatchBrush object by passing it a style and a color. If you use a predefined member of the Brushes class as a shortcut, don't use the new constructor.

```
SolidBrush myBrush1 = new SolidBrush(Color.SteelBlue);
using System.Drawing.Drawing2D;
HatchBrush myBrush2 = new HatchBrush(HatchStyle.DiagonalBrick,
    Color.Turquoise);
Brush myBrush3 = Brushes.Magenta;
```

Create a Font object by passing the constructor a font name and a font size. An optional third parameter is the font style. Combine font styles using the logical OR (|).

```
Font myFont = new Font("Arial", 15, FontStyle.Bold | FontStyle.Italic);
```

Using the Drawing Methods

You can draw many different types of shapes and images—for instance, triangles, arcs, polygons, bitmaps, and text strings. Covering all of these shapes and images in this chapter isn't necessary because they are so similar. Once you understand how to do a few of them, it is easy to reference the MSDN Help file for the rest.

Drawing shapes and objects requires calling different methods of the Graphics class. As discussed earlier in this chapter, forms and print documents have a Graphics object as one of their properties. When you get a reference to this object and call its drawing methods, the images appear on either the form or the printed page. All of the methods described in this section and their related methods can be used for either type of output.

Each of the drawing methods uses a parameter list that requires some combination of objects described in the "Fundamental Drawing Classes" section. As mentioned at the beginning of this chapter, you can pass the methods these parameters in two different ways. The first way is to create and instantiate separate variables for each type of object needed, pass these variables to the method, and then dispose of them. The other approach is to instantiate the objects within the method call. You don't have to create a new object instance if you are using structures such as Point and Color or if you are using collections such as Pens and Brushes. When you create instances of new objects, you should do so outside of the method call and then call the Dispose() method. This isn't mandatory if you are writing temporary code that won't be used in an application. This section shows both methods of instantiating the objects.

Some of the methods for drawing standard shapes are DrawLine(), DrawRectangle(), and DrawPolygon(). The parameters needed by these methods consist of a Pen or Brush object and a Point object (or an array of Point objects).

You can draw bitmaps, icons, and metafile images by calling the DrawImage() method. Pass it an Image object and a Point object (or the X and Y coordinates).

Displaying text on the screen is done by calling the DrawString() method. The parameters consist of the text to print, a Font object, a Brush object, and a Point object (or the X and Y coordinates).

The following examples use two different ways of referencing the Graphics object. The VB .NET examples use the myCanvas object that was created for the examples in the "Drawing on a Form" section. The C# examples act as if they are being used in an event handler of a print document. They use the e.Graphics object of the PrintPageEventArgs parameter. Of course, all methods can be applied in either instance. The examples are done this way to be thorough.

VB .NET

The DrawLine() method is passed a Pen object and two Point objects representing the start and end of the line.

```
myCanvas.DrawLine(Pens.Coral,New Point(0,0), New Point(20,100))
```

The DrawRectangle() method is passed a Pen object and four numbers representing the X and Y positions as well as the width and height of the rectangle. Only the outline is drawn.

```
myCanvas.DrawRectangle(Pens.BurlyWood,5,20,100,70)
```

The FillPolygon() method is passed a Brush object and an array of Point objects. Each element in the array represents a corner of the polygon.

```
'This example fills a polygon using a TextureBrush derived from a bitmap file
Dim myBrush As TextureBrush
Dim background As Bitmap
background = New Bitmap("C:\WinNt\Soap Bubbles.bmp")
myBrush = New TextureBrush(background)
Dim myPolygon() As Point = {New Point(10, 10), New Point(500, 100), _
    New Point(300, 300), New Point(50, 390)}
myCanvas.FillPolygon(myBrush, myPolygon)
background.Dispose()
myBrush.Dispose()
```

The DrawImage() method is passed an Image object and a Point object (or the X and Y coordinates).

```
myCanvas.DrawImage(Image.FromFile("C:\WinNt\Soap Bubbles.bmp"), 0, 0)
```

The DrawString() method is passed the string to display, a Font object, a Brush object, and a Point object (or the X and Y coordinates).

```
Dim myFont As Font = New Font("Arial",50)
myCanvas.DrawString("Sample Text", myFont, Brushes.Green,10,10)
myFont.Dispose()
```

C#

The DrawLine() method is passed a Pen object and two Point objects representing the start and end of the line.

```
e.Graphics.DrawLine(new Pen(Color.Red,5),new Point(0,0), new Point(20,100));
```

The FillRectangle() method is passed a Brush object and four numbers representing the X and Y positions as well as the width and height of the rectangle. The entire shape is filled in with the Brush object properties.

```
e.Graphics.FillRectangle(Brushes.Blue,5,20,100,70);
```

The DrawPolygon() method is passed a Pen object and an array of Point objects. Each element in the array represents a corner of the polygon. Only the outline is drawn.

```
Point[] myPolygon = {new Point(10,10), new Point(500,100), new Point(300,300),
    new Point(50, 390)};
Pen myPen = new Pen(Color.Gold, 10);
e.Graphics.DrawPolygon(myPen, myPolygon);
myPen.Dispose();
```

The DrawImage() method is passed an Image object and a Point object (or the X and Y coordinates).

```
Bitmap background = new Bitmap(@"C:\WinNt\Soap Bubbles.bmp");
e.Graphics.DrawImage(background, 0, 0);
background.Dispose();
```

The DrawString() method is passed the string to display, a Font object, a Brush object, and a Point object (or the X and Y coordinates).

```
e.Graphics.DrawString("Sample Text", new Font("Arial",50), Brushes.Red,
    new Point(20,20));
```

Index

Symbols

@, adding before strings, 30

\ (escape sequence), using in a string, 30

' (apostrophe), 7

( ) (parentheses)

    declaring static sized arrays in, 31

    designating dynamic arrays with empty, 32

    in subroutines, 17–18

*/, 7

// (forward slashes), adding before C# single-line comments, 7

/// (forward slashes), adding before XML comments, 8

/*, 7

: (colon), 128, 130

:=, 18

; (semicolon), 6

[ ] (square brackets), 31

_ (underscore), 6

A

about this book, 1–2

access modifiers, 16–17

ActiveX Data Objects. *See* ADO

adding

    elements to collection, 301

    records, 261, 262, 263

ADO (ActiveX Data Objects)

    ADO to ADO.NET equivalent chart, 243–244

    ADO.NET vs., 246

    Move methods in, 259

    origins of, 245–246

    viability of, 247

ADO.NET, 243–276

    about, 244–247

    ADO methods unavailable in, 259

    chart of equivalent ADO features, 243–244

    classes for, 247–249

    opening connection in, 250–251

    origins and viability of ADO, 245–246, 247

    reading and modifying individual records, 256–265

    stored procedures and SQL statements, 251–254

        executing commands, 252

        passing arguments to stored procedure, 253–254

    tables for forward-only access, 254–256

    talking to database from, 249–250

    viewing

        data with DataGrid control, 265–267

        and updating Northwind database, 267–276

analyzing strings, 182–185

apostrophe (') before VB comments, 7

App object, 335–344

    displaying application information, 339–341

    equivalent properties in FileVersionInfo class, 335

    getting application-specific details, 336–337

    logging errors using Event Log, 342–344

    members of EventLog class for logging events, 335

    overview, 336

    writing to Event Log, 338–339

applications. *See* interacting with applications

arguments

    ADO.NET parameters for passing to stored procedures, 253–254

    passing to procedures, 13–14

arithmetic operators, 25–26, 42–44

arrays, 31–34

    collections as, 299

    creating array of parameters to be passed to COM object, 318

    declaring

        dimensions and upper bound element of, 32–33

        dynamic, 32

        static sized, 31–32

    initializing elements of, 33–34

As keyword, 10

B

base classes

    extending with new methods, 141–142

    overriding existing methods in, 142–143

    writing for class inheritance, 139–140

birthdate example, 284–286

Boolean operators

    comparing, 54–60

    conversion chart of, 26

Boolean values in enumerated data types, 37

Boolean variables, 28

Brush class, 353

button members, 196

buttons

    about, 208–209

    finding out what button user clicked, 205–206

    RadioButtons, 196, 209

ByRef keyword, 14

ByVal keyword, 14

C

C#

    access modifiers in, 16–17

    accessing and modifying elements, 302–304

    arithmetic operators, 42–44

    arrays, 31–34

    Boolean variables, 28

    calculating days to birthday, 284, 285–286

    calling procedures, 17–23

    Capacity property, 171–172

    case sensitivity of, 5–6

    changing control's font, 202–203

    character data type, 29

    classes

        applying class interfaces, 130–132

        Class Declaration equivalent chart, 99

        class inheritance in sale price calculations, 145–146, 147–149

        class interfaces in checking account management, 132, 136–138

        creating custom exception, 88

        custom RegEditor, 330, 332–334

        declaring, 101, 127

        destroying with finalizers, 111–113

        extending base class with new methods, 141–142

        generic COM interface, 327, 329–330

        graphic objects drawing, 353–355

        initializing with constructors, 104–105

        instantiating COM, 315

        preventing inheritance of, 145

        StringBuilder, 169–172

System.Convert class, 38–40

writing base class for class inheritance, 139–140

closing, registry keys, 323

collections

adding elements to, 301

declaring, 300–301

examining elements in, 304

logging in user and looping through, 74–76

managing, 304, 307–309

COM objects

including library file for, 314–315

instantiating for late binding, 317

invoking method call for, 318–319

comments in code, 6–7, 8

common financial functions, 294, 296–298

comparing Boolean operators, 58–60

concatenation operators, 44

constructors

inheriting, 144

initializing classes with, 104–105

inputting dates with DateTime, 279

Shared/static, 106

copying, and pasting with Clipboard, 213–215

creating

array of parameters, 318

DataTable object, 257–258

MDI parent form, 207–208

database tables for forward-only access, 254–256

declaring

events with delegate object, 152, 153

properties, 107–110

variables, 9–10, 49–50

directories, 219–223

displaying

application information, 339, 340–341

date and time, 280–282

number of days between dates with TimeSpan class, 283

print preview, 351–352

do loops, 69–70

drawing methods, 355–358

drawing on forms, 347–349

equivalency chart of program fundamentals, 3

event handling in managing checking account, 157–158, 161–163

executing commands, 252

explicit variable casting, 40

files, 223–226

closing, 230

copying, 88–89, 94–97

managing directories and, 230, 234–236

opening, 226–228

reading from, 228–229, 237, 239–241

writing to, 119, 122–124, 229–230, 237, 239–241

finding out what button user clicked in dialog box, 205–206

for each loops, 70–71

forcing inheritance, 145

for loops, 66–68

gaining access to data in another form, 206–207

generating random numbers, 290–291

getting

application-specific details, 336–337

current date and time, 278–279

reference to Type library, 316–317

grouping constants with enumerators, 34–38

handling events, 154–155

if statements, 62–63

instantiating objects, 115–117

interfaces

    defining, 126–127

    implementing, 127–130

Length property, 171–172

linking events to event handler, 155–157

ListBox and ComboBox controls, 196, 209–212

logging errors using Event Log, 342, 343–344

logical operators, 44–45

managing forms, 203–204

message boxes, 201

minimum and maximum numbers, 292, 293–294

modifying

    records, 261–263

    registry keys, 322–323

    scope of variable, 11–12

opening, connection in ADO.NET, 250–251

optional parameters unavailable in, 15

overloading class methods, 113–114

overriding existing methods in, 142–143

parameter arrays, 15–16

Parse() method, 41–42

passing arguments to procedures, 13–14, 253–254

performing date and time calculations, 282–283

PictureBox control, 196, 212–213

procedure declaration equivalent chart, 3–4

processing event messages with DoEvents() method, 200

program flow, 61–62

Project Templates in, 4–5

raising events, 153–154

reading records, 258–261

resizing and repositioning controls, 201–202

retrieving program version number

    with early binding, 324–325

    with late binding, 325, 326–327

switch statement, 63–66

sending documents to printer, 349–351

shadowing variables, 110–111

static members, 102–104

strings, 29–30

    analyzing, 182–185

    converting to and from string arrays, 180–182

    converting to DateTime method, 280

    filling with a character, 175–176

    formatting output with, 185–186

    manipulating input, 186, 189–190

    modifying contents of, 178–180

    trimming, 177–178

    working with characters in, 173–175

structs, 117–118

system registry, 319–323

throwing exceptions, 85–87

translating Visual Basic .NET into, 1–2

traversing the registry tree, 321–322

try...catch...finally error handling, 80–82, 83–85

using enumerators to print employee information, 52–54

variants and objects, 27–28

viewing

    data with DataGrid control, 265–267

    and updating Northwind database, 267, 271–274

while loops, 68

writing

code across multiple lines in, 6

to Event Log, 338–339

See also comparative code listings

calculating

date and time, 282–283

days to birthday example, 284–286

test score functions, 19–23

calling procedures, 17–23

calculating test score functions, 19–23

overview, 17–18

stored procedures, 251–254

camelCasing, 5

Capacity property, 171–172

case sensitivity, 5–6

Catch statements for error handling, 80–85

Ceiling() function, 289

character data type, 29

charts

ADO.NET class descriptions, 247–248

App object equivalent properties in FileVersionInfo class, 335

arithmetic operand conversion, 25–26

Boolean operand conversion, 26

class declaration equivalent, 99

class inheritance equivalent, 139

class interface equivalent, 125

collection class equivalents, 299

collections in .NET System.Collections.Namespace, 304

common members of Clipboard class, 197

custom DateTime format examples for strings, 168

custom numeric format examples for strings, 167–168

data type equivalent, 25

date and time equivalent functions, 277–278

Exception class syntax conversion, 79

file management equivalent functions, 217

of function results for truncating decimals, 289

intrinsic math function equivalents, 287–288

of math functions in .NET, 288–289

members of EventLog class for logging events, 335

possible Try-Catch-Finally scenarios, 82

of procedure declaration equivalents, 3–4

program flow equivalent, 61–62

of program fundamentals, 3

properties/methods to display date and time, 281

relational operand conversion, 26

return value of Compare() method, 182

return values for CheckBox members, 209

standard DateTime format examples for strings, 168

standard numeric format examples for strings, 167

String Manipulation equivalent functions, 165–166

of System.Char members, 166

text file I/O equivalent functions, 217–218

CheckBox control

about, 109

members of, 196

return values for members, 209

Class Declaration equivalent chart, 99

class inheritance, 139–149

in calculating sale price example, 145–149

class inheritance equivalent chart, 139

extending base class with new methods, 141–142

forcing, 145

inheriting constructors, 144

overriding existing methods in base class, 142–143

overview, 139

preventing, 145

writing base class for, 139–140

class inheritance equivalent chart, 139

class interface equivalent chart, 125

class interfaces, 125–138

applying, 130–132

class inheritance and, 139

defining, 126–127

equivalent chart for, 125

implementing, 127–128

implementing multiple, 128–130

managing checking account example, 132–138

overview, 125

classes, 99–124

for ADO.NET, 247–249

applying class interfaces, 130–132

class declaration equivalent chart, 99

class inheritance equivalent chart, 139

common members of Clipboard, 197

declaring, 101, 127

methods for, 106–107

properties, 107–110

defined, 100

destroying with finalizers, 111–113

DirectoryInfo, 219

for drawing graphic objects, 353–355

FileInfo, 223

generic COM interface class example, 327–330

initializing with constructors, 104–105

instantiating

COM, 315

objects, 115–117

knowing when to use String and StringBuilder, 169–172

objects and, 100–101

overloading class methods, 113–114

overview, 99–100

relationship between VB events and, 155

shadowing variables, 110–111

Shared/static constructors, 106

Shared/static members, 102–104

structs, 117–118

TimeSpan, 283–284

With statements, 117

writing to log file example, 119–124

See also base classes; class inheritance; class interfaces; *and specific classes*

Clipboard

common members of class, 197

copying and pasting with, 213–215

closing

registry keys, 323

text files, 230

CLS (Common Language Specification), 2

Collection class

about, 299

declaring, 300

collections, 299–311

accessing and modifying elements, 302–304

adding elements to, 301

chart of class equivalents, 299

collections in .NET System.Collections.Namespace, 304

declaring, 300–301

examining elements, 304

example of managing, 304–311

looping through, 71–77

overview, 299–280

colon (:) designating C# class interface, 128, 130

COM objects

adding references to, 313–314

creating array of parameters, 318

early binding, 313–316

adding reference to COM object, 313–314

getting program's version number with, 324–325

including library file, 314–315

instantiating COM classes, 315

late binding vs., 316

steps for, 316

generic COM interface class example, 327–330

instantiating COM classes, 315

invoking method call, 318–319

late binding, 316–319

creating array of parameters, 318

early binding vs., 316

getting program's version number using, 325–327

getting reference to Type library, 316–317

instantiating for, 317

invoking method call, 318–319

steps for, 319

working with, 313

ComboBox control

about, 209–212

determining user entry in, 211, 212

members of, 196

Command object

function of, 249, 251

instantiating, 252

comments in code, 6–9

Common Language Specification (CLS), 2

comparative code listings

calculating

days to birthday, 284–286

sale price, 145–149

test score functions, 19–23

common financial functions, 294–298

comparing Boolean operators, 54–60

declaring and using variables, 46–51

displaying application information, 339–341

exception handling in copying files, 88–97

of generic COM interface class, 327–330

getting program version number

early binding, 324–325

late binding, 325–327

for handling events in managing checking account, 157–163

logging errors using Event Log, 342–344

managing

checking account, 132–138

collections, 304–311

files and directories, 230–236

for manipulating input strings, 186–191

minimum and maximum numbers, 292–294

RegEditor class, 330–334

using enumerators to print employee information, 51–54

viewing and updating Northwind database, 267–276

writing to log file, 119–124

Compare() method return value, 182

comparing two numbers, 290

concatenation operators, 42, 43, 44

Connection object

    creating, 249

    instantiating in ADO.NET, 250–251

connections

    advantages of ADO.NET, 256–257

    modifying connection string for
        Northwind database, 248–249

    opening ADO.NET, 250–251

constants

    grouping with enumerators, 34–38

    new .NET, 289

constructors

    defined, 104

    inheriting, 144

    initializing classes with, 104–105

    inputting dates with DateTime, 279

    Shared/static, 106

controls, 200–215

    buttons, 208–209

    changing font of, 202–203

    CheckBoxes and RadioButtons, 196, 209

    common members, 193–194

    dialog boxes, 205–207

    DoEvents() method, 200

    forms and, 203–204

    labels, 195, 208

    ListBox and ComboBox, 196, 209–212

    locking, 201

    MDI forms, 207–208

    message boxes, 201

    PictureBox, 196, 212–213

    renaming in Visual Studio IDE, 198–199

    resizing and repositioning, 201–202

    TextBox, 195, 208

    Timer, 213

converting

    between data types, 38–42

        data type equivalent chart, 25

        explicit variable casting with, 40

        overview, 38

        Parse() method for, 41–42

        with System.Convert class, 38–40

    strings to and from string arrays, 180–182

CopyFile() procedure, 88–97

copying and pasting with Clipboard, 213–215

custom exception classes, 88

custom formats

    for DateTime, 168

    for numbers, 167–168

D

data

    access to in other form, 206–207

    ADO.NET passing as XML, 246

    examining in collection, 304

    viewing with DataGrid control, 265–267

data types and operators, 25–60

    arithmetic operators, 42–44

    arrays, 31–34

    Boolean variables, 28

    characters, 29

    comparing Boolean operators, 54–60

    conversion charts

        for arithmetic operands, 25–26

        for Boolean operands, 26

        for relational operands, 26

    converting between data types, 38–42

    data type equivalent chart, 25

    declaring and using variables, 46–51

grouping constants with enumerators, 34–38

logical operators, 44–45

Option Strict option (VB .NET), 45–46

overview, 27

relational operators, 44

strings, 29–30

using enumerators to print employee information, 51–54

variants and objects, 27–28

databases

advantages of ADO.NET connections for, 256–257

modifying connection string for Northwind, 248–249

opening connection in ADO.NET, 250–251

records, 256–265

ADO.NET treatment as object in collection, 259

creating DataTable object, 257–258

filtering and sorting, 264–265

modifying, 261–263

reading, 258–261

viewing and updating Northwind database, 267–276

working with in ADO.NET, 249–250

tables for forward-only access for, 254–256

talking to from ADO.NET, 249–250

viewing

data with DataGrid control, 265–267

and updating Northwind, 267–276

DataGrid control, 265–267

DataReader object, 254–256

DataTable object, 257–258

date and time, 277–286

calculating days to birthday example, 284–286

charts

of equivalent functions, 277–278

of properties/methods to display, 281

displaying, 280–282

getting current, 278–279

inputting dates, 279–283

converting string to DateTime, 280

DateTime constructor method for, 279

displaying date and time, 280–282

overview, 278

performing calculations of, 282–283

storing values for, 278

TimeSpan class, 283–284

DateTime data type

about, 278

DateTime constructor method for inputting dates, 279

formats for, 168

decimals, truncating, 289

declaring

arrays, 31–33

classes, 101, 127

collection, 300–301

constructors in derived class, 144

events, 152–153

methods for classes, 106–107

procedures, 3–4, 12–13

properties for classes, 107–110

and using variables, 46–51

variables, 9–10

default Windows Form source code, 197–198

delegate objects, 152, 153

deleting records, 261, 262, 263

destroying classes with finalizers, 111–113

dialog boxes, 205–207

Dim modifier (VB), 11

directories
  example of managing files and, 230–236
  folders and, 219
  working with, 219–223
DirectoryInfo class, 219
displaying
  application information, 339–341
  date and time, 280–282
  print preview, 351–352
Dispose() method, 112, 113
Do loops, 69–70
documents
  displaying print preview for, 351–352
  sending to printer, 349–351
DoEvents() method, 200
drawing with forms and printers, 345–358
  drawing on forms, 347–349
  graphics, 352–358
    drawing classes for, 353–355
    drawing methods, 355–358
    memory management for graphics
      objects, 346–347
    overview, 352
    working with Graphics object, 346
  overview, 345–346
  printing documents, 349–352
dynamic arrays, 32

E

early binding to COM objects
  adding reference to COM object, 313–314
  getting program's version number with,
    324–325
  including library file, 314–315
  instantiating COM classes, 315
  late binding vs., 316
  steps for, 316

editing records, 261, 262, 263
elements
  accessing and modifying, 302–304
  adding to collections, 301
  examining, 304
enumerated data type
  enumerators of NumberStyles class, 42
  grouping constants with, 34–38
  printing employee information with,
    51–54
errors
  handling, 80–85
  logging using Event Log, 342–344
  raising, 86
  Try...Catch...Finally error handling, 80–82,
    83–85
event handlers
  adding in Visual Studio IDE, 199–200
  linking events to, 155–157
Event keyword, 152
Event Log
  logging errors using, 342–344
  writing to, 338–339
Event Syntax equivalent chart, 151
EventLog class
  logging errors using Event Log, 342–344
  members of for logging events, 335
  steps for using, 338
events, 151–163
  declaring, 152–153
  Event Syntax equivalent chart, 151
  handling, 154–155
    in managing checking account
      example, 157–163
  linking to event handler, 155–157
  overview, 151–152
  processing event messages with
    DoEvents() method, 200

raising, 153–154

renaming controls before adding to, 198–199

using delegate object, 153

examples. *See* comparative code listings

Exception class

creating custom exception classes, 88

syntax conversion chart for, 79

using, 80

exception handling, 79–97

in copying file example, 88–97

creating custom exception classes, 88

Exception class syntax conversion chart, 79

handling errors, 80–85

overview, 79

possible Try-Catch-Finally scenarios, 82

throwing exceptions, 85–87

using Exception class, 80

explicit variable casting, 40

extending base class with new methods, 141–142

Extensible Markup Language. *See* XML

F

file management equivalent functions, 217

FileInfo class, 223

files, 217–241

file management equivalent functions, 217

including library files for COM objects, 314–315

managing files and directories example, 230–236

overview of, 218

text

closing, 230

I/O equivalent functions for, 217–218

opening, 226–228

overview, 226

reading from, 228–229, 237–241

working with, 223–226

writing to, 229–230, 237–241

working with directories, 219–223

See also directories

FileVersionInfo class, 335

filling string with a character, 175–176

filtering and sorting records, 264–265

finalizers, 111–113

Finally statements for error handling, 80–85

financial functions

chart of, 291

example code listing of, 294–298

Floor() function, 289

folders. *See* directories

Font class, 353

fonts for controls, 202–203

For Each loops, 70–71

forcing inheritance, 145

For loops, 66–68

formats

DateTime, 168

formatting string output, 185–186

numeric, 167–168

for string placeholders, 185

forms

access to data in another, 206–207

drawing on, 347–349

finding out what button user clicked, 205–206

managing, 203–204

MDI, 207–208

members of Form control, 194–195

See also Windows Form applications

forward slash (/)

    adding // before C# single-line comments, 7

    adding /// before XML comments, 8

Friend modifier

    about, 11, 12, 16

    determining when methods can be called, 107

    extending base class functionality with, 141

Function keyword, 12, 13

functions

    calling VB, 18

    equivalent charts

        date and time, 277–278

        file management, 217

        intrinsic math, 287–288

        for String class, 165–166

    financial, 294, 296–298

    .NET math, 288–289

    string, 175–185

    in Visual Basic, 12

    See also date and time; math and financial functions; string functions

G

GDI+ (Graphical Device Interface), 345

generating random numbers, 290–291

Get property (VB), 107

graphics, 352–358

    drawing classes for, 353–355

    drawing methods, 355–358

    memory management for graphics objects, 346–347

    overview, 352

    working with Graphics object, 346

Graphics object

    memory management for, 346–347

    working with, 346

H

hash code for objects, 300

I

I/O (input/output), 218

IDE

    creation of source code template by, 197–198

    Visual Studio and VB, 198–200

If statement, 62–63

Image members, 196

implementing

    interfaces

        about, 127–128

        managing checking account example of, 132–138

        multiple, 128–130

    MDI forms, 207–208

inheritance, 139–149

    in calculating sale price example, 145–149

    Class Inheritance equivalent chart, 139

    of constructors, 144

    extending base class with new methods, 141–142

    forcing, 145

    interfaces and, 125

    overriding existing methods in base class, 142–143

    overview, 139

    preventing, 145

    writing base class for, 139–140

initializing array elements, 33–34

input strings, 186–191

input/output (I/O), 218

inputting dates, 279–283

    converting string to DateTime, 280

    DateTime constructor method for, 279

    displaying date and time, 280–282

    performing date and time calculations, 282–283

instance variables, about, 102

instantiating

    COM classes, 315

    COM objects for late binding, 317

    Command object, 252

    Connection object, 250–251

    objects, 115–117

interacting with applications, 313–333

    early binding to COM objects, 313–316

        adding reference to COM object, 313–314

        getting program version number with, 324–325

        getting program's version number with, 324–325

        including library file, 314–315

        instantiating COM classes, 315

        late binding vs., 316

    generic COM interface class example, 327–330

    late binding to COM objects, 316–319

        creating array of parameters, 318

        early binding vs., 316

        getting program's version number, 325–327

        getting reference to Type library, 316–317

        instantiating COM object, 317

        invoking method call, 318–319

        steps for, 319

    overview, 313

    system registry, 319–323

        closing registry keys, 323

        modifying registry key, 322–323

        RegEditor class example, 330–334

        registry class member mapping to registry base key chart, 320

        selecting root key for system registry, 320–321

        traversing the registry tree, 321–322

    working with COM objects, 313

interfaces

    applying, 130–132

    Class Interface Equivalent Chart, 125

    defined, 125, 139

    defining, 126–127

    implementing, 127–128

        multiple, 128–130

    managing checking account example, 132–138

    overview, 125

internal modifier, 16–17, 141

intrinsic math function equivalents, 287–288

L

labels

    about, 208

    common members of Label control, 195

late binding to COM objects, 316–319

    creating array of parameters, 318

    early binding vs., 316

    getting program's version number using, 325–327

    getting reference to Type library, 316–317

    instantiating COM object, 317

    invoking method call, 318–319

    steps for, 319

Length property, 171–172

Let property (VB), 107

libraries

　　adding to projects, 313–314

　　getting reference to Type library, 316–317

　　System.Diagnostics, 336–337

　　System.Math, 288–289

　　System.Reflection, 336–337

library files, 314–315

line continuation characters, 6

ListBox control, 196, 209–212

lists

　　adding items to, 210

　　finding first item selected, 211–212

　　removing items from, 210–211

　　using indexer of Items collection to get specific item, 211

locking controls, 201

logging events, 335

logging in, 206–207

logical operators, 44–45

loops

　　Do, 69–70

　　For, 66–68

　　For Each, 70–71

　　looping through collection, 71–77

　　While, 68

M

managing

　　collections, 304–311

　　files and directories, 218–226

　　　　example code listings for, 230–236

　　　　working with directories, 219–223

　　　　working with files, 223–226

　　forms, 203–204

manipulating input strings, 186–191

math and financial functions, 287–298

　　arithmetic operators, 25–26, 42–44

　　chart of math functions in .NET, 288–289

　　common financial functions example, 294–298

　　comparing two numbers, 290

　　financial functions, 291

　　generating random numbers, 290–291

　　intrinsic math function equivalents, 287–288

　　minimum and maximum numbers, 292–294

　　new constants, 289

　　overview, 288

　　System.Math library, 288–289

　　truncating decimals, 289

MDI (Multiple Document Interface) forms, 207–208

Me keyword, 110

memory

　　allocating for StringBuilder class, 171

　　managing for graphics objects, 346–347

　　set aside for objects, 101

message boxes, 201

method overloading, 113–114

methods

　　declaring for classes, 106–107

　　to display date and time, 281

　　for drawing shapes and objects, 355–358

　　extending base class with new, 141–142

　　for handing events, 154–155

　　invoking call for COM objects, 318–319

　　Move methods unavailable in ADO.NET, 259

　　overloading class, 113–114

　　overriding existing base class, 142–143

　　of System.Convert class, 40

　　See also specific methods

Microsoft .NET Framework. *See* .NET Framework

Microsoft Visual Basic 6.0. *See* Visual Basic 6.0

Microsoft Visual Basic .NET. *See* Visual Basic .NET

Microsoft Visual Studio .NET, 4–5

minimum and maximum numbers, 292–294

Move methods in ADO, 259

Multiple Document Interface (MDI) forms, 207–208

N

.NET Framework

ADO and ADO.NET in, 245

chart of math functions in, 288–289

controls for Windows Form, 197

knowledge of syntax required for, 2

support of inheritance in, 99

New keyword, 115–117

Northwind database

modifying connection string for, 248–249

viewing and updating, 267–276

NumberStyles class, 42

numeric formats

custom, 167–168

standard, 167

O

objects

App, 335–344

displaying application information, 339–341

equivalent properties in FileVersion-Info class, 335

getting application-specific details, 336–337

logging errors using Event Log, 342–344

members of EventLog class for logging events, 335

overview, 336

writing to Event Log, 338–339

classes and, 100–101

declaring

from class that uses interfaces, 130, 131–132

events with delegate object, 152, 153

defined, 100

hash code for, 300

instantiating, 115–117

memory management for graphics, 346–347

raising events from sending, 153–154

variants and, 27–28

See also COM objects; *and specific objects*

On Error Go To statements, 81, 82–83

OOP concepts, 99–100

opening

connection in ADO.NET, 250–251

project template in Visual Studio .NET, 4–5

text files, 226–228

operators

comparing Boolean, 54–60

conversion charts

for arithmetic operands, 25–26

for Boolean operands, 26

for relational operands, 26

logical, 44–45

relational, 44

See also data types and operators

Option Strict option (VB .NET), 45–46

Optional keyword (VB/VB .NET), 15

out keyword (C#), 14

output

    for calculating days to birthday, 284–285

    for common financial functions, 298

    for date and time displays, 281

    for displaying application information, 341

    displaying number of days between dates, 283

    formatting with strings, 185–186

    for generic COM interface class, 330

    of managing collections, 310–311

    for managing files and directories, 236–237

    for manipulating strings, 190–191

    for minimum and maximum numbers, 294

    for reading and writing text files, 241

    for RegEditor class example, 334

    for retrieving program version number

        with early binding, 325

        with late binding, 327

    for viewing and updating Northwind database, 274–276

overloading class methods, 113–114

P

ParamArray keyword (VB/VB .NET), 16

Parameter object, 253–254

parameters

    optional parameters in, 15

    parameter arrays, 15–16

    in SQL statements, 253–254

params keyword (C#), 16

parentheses ()

    declaring VB/VB .NET static sized arrays in, 31

    designating VB/VB .NET dynamic arrays with empty, 32

    in subroutines, 17–18

Parse() method, 41–42

PascalCasing, 5–6

pasting with Clipboard, 213–215

Pen class, 353

PictureBox control, 196, 212–213

placeholders in strings, 185

Point class, 353

print previewing, 351–352

printing

    documents, 349–352

        displaying print preview, 351–352

        overview, 349

        sending documents to printer, 349–351

    enumerated entries, 51–54

Private modifier

    about, 11, 12, 16, 17

    determining when methods can be called, 107

    extending base class functionality with, 141

procedures

    calling, 17–23

    declaration equivalent chart for, 3–4

    declaring, 3–4, 12–13

    modifying accessibility of, 16–17

    passing arguments to, 13–14, 253–254

programmers

    migrating skills from VB 6.0 to VB.NET, 1

    translating languages into VB .NET, 1–2

programs, 3–23

    calling procedures, 17–23

    case sensitivity, 5–6

    comments in code, 6–7

    declaring

        procedures, 12–13

        variables, 9–10

equivalency chart of VB, VB .NET, and C#, 3

modifying

   procedure's accessibility, 16–17

   scope of variable, 11–12

optional parameters, 15

overview of, 4

parameter arrays, 15–16

passing arguments to procedures, 13–14, 253–254

procedure declaration equivalent chart, 3–4

program flow, 61–77

   Do loops, 69–70

   equivalent chart for, 61–62

   For Each loops, 70–71

   For loops, 66–68

   overview, 62

   Select Case/switch statement, 63–66

   testing conditions with If statement, 62–63

   user login and looping through collection, 71–77

   While loops, 68

selecting Project Templates, 4–5

writing

   base class for class inheritance, 139–140

   code across multiple lines, 6

   constructors, 104

   to Event Log, 338–339

   to log file example, 119–124

projects

   adding libraries to, 313–314

   opening and selecting template for, 4–5

properties

   chart of equivalent App object, 335

   declaring, 107–110

   to display date and time, 281

   See also specific properties

protected internal modifier, 141

Protected modifier, 141

Public modifier, 11, 16, 17, 107

R

RadioButton control, 196, 209

raising

   errors, 86

   events, 153–154

random number generation, 290–291

reading and writing text files, 226–230

   closing file, 230

   example of, 237–241

   opening files, 226–228

   overview, 226

   reading from file, 228–229

   writing to file, 229–230

records, 256–265

   ADO.NET treatment as object in collection, 259

   creating DataTable object, 257–258

   filtering and sorting, 264–265

   modifying, 261–263

   reading, 258–261

   viewing and updating Northwind database, 267–276

   working with in ADO.NET, 249–250

ref keyword (C#), 14

registry keys

   closing, 323

   modifying, 322–323

   registry class member mapping to, 320

   selecting root key, 320–321

   See also system registry

relational operators, 26, 44

renaming controls, 198–199

resizing and repositioning controls, 201–202

Return keyword, 12, 13

return value of Compare() method, 182

Round() function, 289

S

Select Case/switch statement, 63–66

SEH, *See* exception handling

Set property (VB), 107

shadowing variables, 110–111

Shared/static constructors, 106

Shared/static members, 102–104

short-circuited logic, 62

signature, 152

simple data types, 27–38

    arrays, 31–34

    Boolean variables, 28

    characters, 29

    grouping constants with enumerators, 34–38

    strings, 29–30

    variants and objects, 27–28

Sort collection, 302

sorting records, 264–265

SQL statements

    executing commands, 252

    parameters in, 253–254

    performing database actions with, 251

square brackets ([]), 31

standard formats

    DateTime, 168

    for numbers, 167

Static modifier (VB), 11

static sized arrays, 31–32

stored procedures, 253–254

storing date and time values, 278

Stream class, 225

StreamReader class, 227–228

StreamWriter class, 227–228

string arrays, 180–182

String class

    equivalent functions of, 165–166

    StringBuilder class and, 169

    using string functions, 175–185

string functions

    analyzing strings, 182–185

    converting strings to and from string array, 180–182

    filling string with character, 175–176

    modifying contents of strings, 178–180

    trimming strings, 177–178

StringBuilder class, 169–172

    adding string to end of variable, 171–172

    equivalent functions of, 165–166

    memory allocation and, 171

    String class and, 169

    using, 169–171

strings, 165–191

    analyzing, 182–185

    converting

        to and from string arrays, 180–182

        to DateTime method, 280

    custom formats

        DateTime, 168

        numeric, 167–168

    filling with a character, 175–176

    formatting output with, 185–186

    manipulating input example, 186–191

    modifying contents of, 178–180

    overview, 169

    return value of Compare() method, 182

as simple data type, 29–30

standard formats

   DateTime, 168

   numeric, 167

string manipulation equivalent functions, 165–166

System.Char members, 166

trimming, 177–178

using StringBuilder class, 169–172

working with characters, 173–175

structs, 117–118

Structured Exception Handling (SEH), *See* exception handling

Sub keyword (VB/VB .NET), 12, 13

subroutines, Visual Basic, 12, 18

switch statement, 65–66

syntax

   declaring procedures, 3–4, 12–13

   declaring variables, 9–10

   for enumerated data types, 34–35

   Event Syntax equivalent chart, 151

   Exception class syntax conversion chart, 79

   format for string placeholders, 185

   knowledge of .NET platform languages required, 2

System.Char members, 166

System.Collections.Namespace, 299, 304

System.Convert class, 38–40

System.DateTime class, 278

System.Diagnostics library, 336–337

System.Drawing class, 345

System.Math library, 287–289

System.Reflection library, 336–337

system registry, 319–323

   closing registry key, 323

   editing, 313

   modifying registry key, 322–323

   overview, 319–320

   selecting root key, 320–321

   traversing the registry tree, 321–322

System.String class, 165–166, 169

   equivalent functions of, 165–166

   StringBuilder class and, 169

   using string functions, 175–185

System.StringBuilder class, 165–166, 169–172

   String class and, 169

System.Text namespace, 170, 171

T

tables

   adding, editing, and deleting records, 261–263

   designing for forward-only access, 254–256

   viewing data in with DataGrid control, 265–267

templates

   creation of source code template by IDE, 197–198

   default Windows Form source code, 107–108

   opening and selecting for project, 4–5

Terminate method (VB), 112

testing conditions with If statement, 62–63

text files. *See* files

TextBox control, 195, 208

throwing exceptions, 85–87

time. *See* date and time

Timer control, 213

TimeSpan class, 283–284

traversing the registry tree, 321–322

trimming strings, 177–178

truncating decimals, 289

Try...Catch...Finally error handling, 80–85

Type library, 316–317

U

underscore (_), 6

upper bound element of arrays, 32–33

V

variables

adding string to end of, 171–172

assigning values to enumerated, 37–38

converting with explicit variable casting, 40

declaring, 9–10, 46–51

modifying scope of, 11–12

shadowing, 110–111

variants and objects, 27–28

VB. *See* Visual Basic 6.0

VB .NET. *See* Visual Basic .NET

viewing

data with DataGrid control, 265–267

Northwind database example, 267–276

Visual Basic 6.0

access modifiers in, 16–17

accessing and modifying elements, 302–304

ADO.NET and, 245

App object in, 336–337

applying class interfaces, 130–132

arithmetic operators, 42–44

arrays, 31–34

Boolean variables, 28

calling procedures, 17–23

case sensitivity of, 5–6

character data type, 29

Class Declaration equivalent chart, 99

collections

adding elements to, 301

declaring, 300–301

examining elements in, 304

managing, 304–306

user login and looping through, 71–73

comments in code, 6–7

comparing Boolean operators, 54–55

concatenation operators, 42, 43, 44

copying file example in, 88–91

creating

custom exception classes, 88

DataTable object, 257–258

declaring

classes, 101, 127

properties, 107–110

variables, 9–10, 46–47

defining interfaces, 126–127

designing database tables for forward-only access, 254–256

destroying classes with finalizers, 111–113

directories, 219–223

Do loops, 69–70

equivalency chart of program fundamentals, 3

Err object and .NET Exception class, 80

events

declaring with Event keyword, 152

handling, 154–155, 157–159

linking to event handler, 155–157

raising, 153–154

executing commands, 252

explicit variable casting, 40

files, 223–226

closing, 230

managing directories and, 230–232

opening, 226–228

reading from, 228–229, 237–238

writing, 237–238

financial functions, 291

For Each loops, 70–71

For loops, 66–68

generating random numbers, 290

graphics of, 345–346

grouping constants with enumerators, 34–38

IDE, 198–200

If statements, 62–63

implementing

interfaces, 127–128

MDI forms, 207–208

multiple interfaces, 128–130

initializing classes with constructors, 104–105

instantiating objects, 115–117

logical operators, 44–45

message boxes, 201

migrating programming skills to VB.NET from, 1

modifying

records, 261–263

scope of variable, 11–12

On Error Go To statements for error handling, 81, 82–83

opening connection in ADO.NET, 250–251

optional parameters, 15

parameter arrays, 15–16

Parse() method, 41–42

passing arguments to procedures, 13–14, 253–254

procedure declaration equivalent chart, 3–4

program flow, 61–62

raising errors, 85–87

reading records, 258–261

Select Case/switch statement, 63–66

storing date and time values, 278

strings, 29–30

analyzing, 182–185

converting to and from string arrays, 180–182

filling with a character, 175–176

manipulating input, 186–187

modifying contents of, 178–180

overview of in, 169

trimming, 177–178

working with characters in, 173–175

subroutines and functions in, 12

System.Convert class, 38–40

system registry, 319–320

using class interfaces in managing checking account example, 132–134

variants and objects, 27–28

viewing data with DataGrid control, 265–267

While loops, 68

With statements, 117

writing

code across multiple lines in, 6

to file, 229–230

to log file, 119–120

See also comparative code listings

Visual Basic .NET

access modifiers in, 16–17

accessing and modifying elements, 302–304

applying class interfaces, 130–132

arithmetic operators, 42–44

arrays, 31–34

Boolean variables, 28

Visual Basic .NET (cont.)

calculating days to birthday, 284–285

calling procedures, 17–23

Capacity property, 171–172

case sensitivity of, 5–6

changing control's font, 202–203

character data type, 29

Class Declaration equivalent chart, 99

class inheritance, 145–147

class interfaces, 132, 134–136

closing registry keys, 323

collections

    adding elements to, 301

    declaring, 300–301

    examining elements in, 304

    managing, 304, 306–307

    user login and looping through, 73–74

COM objects

    including library file for, 314–315

    instantiating for late binding, 317

    invoking method call for, 318–319

comparing

    Boolean operators, 56–58

    two numbers, 290

concatenation operators, 42, 43

constructors

    DateTime constructor method for inputting dates, 279

    inheriting, 144

    initializing classes with, 104–105

    Shared/static, 106

copying, and pasting with Clipboard, 213–215

creating

    array of parameters, 318

    custom exception classes, 88

    DataTable object, 257–258

MDI parent form, 207–208

custom RegEditor class in, 330–332

database tables for forward-only access, 254–256

declaring

    classes, 101, 127

    events with delegate object, 152, 153

    events with Event keyword, 152

    properties, 107–110

    variables, 9–10, 48–49

defining interfaces, 126–127

destroying classes with finalizers, 111–113

directories, 219–223

displaying

    application information, 339–340

    date and time, 280–282

    number of days between dates with TimeSpan class, 283

    print preview, 351–352

Do loops, 69–70

drawing classes for graphic objects, 353–355

drawing methods, 355–358

drawing on forms, 347–349

enumerators for printing employee information, 51–52

equivalency chart of program fundamentals, 3

event handling, 157–158, 159–161

executing commands, 252

explicit variable casting, 40

extending base class with new methods, 141–142

files, 223–226

    closing, 230

    copying, 88–89, 91–94

    managing directories and, 230, 232–233

    opening, 226–228

reading from, 228–229, 237, 238–239

writing to, 119, 120–122, 229–230, 237, 238–239

financial functions, 291, 294–296

finding out what button user clicked in dialog box, 205–206

For Each loops, 70–71

forcing inheritance, 145

For loops, 66–68

gaining access to data in another form, 206–207

generating random numbers, 290–291

generic COM interface class example, 327–328

getting

application-specific details, 336–337

current date and time, 278–279

program version number with early binding, 324

program version number with late binding, 325–326

reference to Type library, 316–317

grouping constants with enumerators, 34–38

handling

errors with Try...Catch...Finally, 80–82, 83–84

events, 154–155

IDE, 198–200

If statements, 62–63

implementing

interfaces, 127–128

multiple interfaces, 128–130

instantiating

COM classes, 315

objects, 115–117

Length property, 171–172

linking events to event handler, 155–157

ListBox and ComboBox controls, 196, 209–212

logging errors using Event Log example, 342–343

logical operators, 44–45

managing forms, 203–204

message boxes, 201

migrating programming skills from VB 6.0 to, 1

minimum and maximum numbers, 292–293

modifying

records, 261–263

registry keys, 322–323

scope of variable, 11–12

new constants in, 289

opening connection in ADO.NET, 250–251

Option Strict option, 45–46

optional parameters, 15

overloading class methods, 113–114

overriding existing methods in, 142–143

parameter arrays, 15–16

Parse() method, 41–42

passing arguments to procedures, 13–14, 253–254

performing date and time calculations, 282–283

PictureBox control, 196, 212–213

preventing class inheritance, 145

procedure declaration equivalent chart, 3–4

processing event messages with DoEvents() method, 200

program flow equivalent chart, 61–62

Project Templates in, 4–5

raising events, 153–154

reading records, 258–261

Visual Basic .NET (cont.)

resizing and repositioning controls, 201–202

Select Case/switch statement, 63–66

selecting root key for system registry, 320–321

sending documents to printer, 349–351

shadowing variables, 110–111

Shared/static members, 102–103

storing date and time values, 278

strings, 29–30

    analyzing, 182–185

    converting to and from string arrays, 180–182

    converting to DateTime method, 280

    filling with a character, 175–176

    formatting output with, 185–186

    manipulating input, 186, 187–188

    modifying contents of, 178–180

    StringBuilder class, 169–172

    trimming, 177–178

    working with characters in, 173–175

structs, 117–118

System.Convert class, 38–40

system registry, 319–323

throwing exceptions, 85–87

translating programming languages into, 1–2

traversing the registry tree, 321–322

truncating decimals, 289

variants and objects, 27–28

VB Err object and .NET Exception class, 80

viewing

    data with DataGrid control, 265–267

    and updating Northwind database, 267–270

While loops, 68

With statements, 117

writing

    base class for class inheritance, 139–140

    to Event Log, 338–339

    See also comparative code listings

Visual Studio IDE, 198–200

Visual Studio .NET, 4–5

void data type (C#), 12, 13

W

While loops, 68

white space characters, 177

Windows Form applications, 193–215

    Clipboard members, 197

    controls, 200–215

        buttons, 196, 208–209

        changing font of, 202–203

        CheckBoxes and RadioButtons, 196, 209

        common members, 193–194

        dialog boxes, 205–207

        DoEvents() method, 200

        forms and, 194–195, 203–204

        labels, 195, 208

        ListBox and ComboBox, 196, 209–212

        locking, 201

        MDI forms, 207–208

        message boxes, 201

        PictureBox, 196, 212–213

        renaming in Visual Studio IDE, 198–199

        resizing and repositioning, 201–202

        TextBox, 195, 208

        Timer, 213

    copying and pasting with Clipboard, 213–215

    default Windows Form source code, 197–198

    DoEvents() method, 200

overview, 197

System.Drawing namespace included in, 345

Visual Studio IDE, 198–200

With statements, 117

writing

base class for class inheritance, 139–140

code across multiple lines, 6

constructors, 104

to Event Log, 338–339

to log file example, 119–124

X

XML (Extensible Markup Language)

ADO.NET passing data as, 246

comments in, 8–9

Apress Titles

ISBN	PRICE	AUTHOR	TITLE
1-893115-73-9	$34.95	Abbott	Voice Enabling Web Applications: VoiceXML and Beyond
1-893115-01-1	$39.95	Appleman	Appleman's Win32 API Puzzle Book and Tutorial for Visual Basic Programmers
1-893115-23-2	$29.95	Appleman	How Computer Programming Works
1-893115-97-6	$39.95	Appleman	Moving to VB. NET: Strategies, Concepts, and Code
1-893115-09-7	$29.95	Baum	Dave Baum's Definitive Guide to LEGO MINDSTORMS
1-893115-84-4	$29.95	Baum, Gasperi, Hempel, and Villa	Extreme MINDSTORMS
1-893115-82-8	$59.95	Ben-Gan/Moreau	Advanced Transact-SQL for SQL Server 2000
1-893115-48-8	$29.95	Bischof	The .NET Languages: A Quick Translation Guide
1-893115-67-4	$49.95	Borge	Managing Enterprise Systems with the Windows Script Host
1-893115-99-2	$39.95	Cornell/Morrison	Programming VB .NET: A Guide for Experienced Programmers
1-893115-72-0	$39.95	Curtin	Developing Trust: Online Privacy and Security
1-893115-71-2	$39.95	Ferguson	Mobile .NET
1-893115-90-9	$44.95	Finsel	The Handbook for Reluctant Database Administrators
1-893115-85-2	$34.95	Gilmore	A Programmer's Introduction to PHP 4.0
1-893115-36-4	$34.95	Goodwill	Apache Jakarta-Tomcat
1-893115-17-8	$59.95	Gross	A Programmer's Introduction to Windows DNA
1-893115-62-3	$39.95	Gunnerson	A Programmer's Introduction to C#, Second Edition
1-893115-10-0	$34.95	Holub	Taming Java Threads
1-893115-04-6	$34.95	Hyman/Vaddadi	Mike and Phani's Essential C++ Techniques
1-893115-96-8	$59.95	Jorelid	J2EE FrontEnd Technologies: A Programmer's Guide to Servlets, JavaServer Pages, and Enterprise JavaBeans
1-893115-50-X	$34.95	Knudsen	Wireless Java: Developing with Java 2, Micro Edition
1-893115-79-8	$49.95	Kofler	Definitive Guide to Excel VBA
1-893115-57-7	$39.95	Kofler	MySQL

ISBN	PRICE	AUTHOR	TITLE
1-893115-87-9	$39.95	Kurata	Doing Web Development: Client-Side Techniques
1-893115-75-5	$44.95	Kurniawan	Internet Programming with VB
1-893115-19-4	$49.95	Macdonald	Serious ADO: Universal Data Access with Visual Basic
1-893115-06-2	$39.95	Marquis/Smith	A Visual Basic 6.0 Programmer's Toolkit
1-893115-22-4	$27.95	McCarter	David McCarter's VB Tips and Techniques
1-893115-76-3	$49.95	Morrison	C++ For VB Programmers
1-893115-80-1	$39.95	Newmarch	A Programmer's Guide to Jini Technology
1-893115-58-5	$49.95	Oellermann	Architecting Web Services
1-893115-81-X	$39.95	Pike	SQL Server: Common Problems, Tested Solutions
1-893115-20-8	$34.95	Rischpater	Wireless Web Development
1-893115-93-3	$34.95	Rischpater	Wireless Web Development with PHP and WAP
1-893115-89-5	$59.95	Shemitz	Kylix: The Professional Developer's Guide and Reference
1-893115-40-2	$39.95	Sill	An Introduction to qmail
1-893115-24-0	$49.95	Sinclair	From Access to SQL Server
1-893115-94-1	$29.95	Spolsky	User Interface Design for Programmers
1-893115-53-4	$39.95	Sweeney	Visual Basic for Testers
1-893115-29-1	$44.95	Thomsen	Database Programming with Visual Basic .NET
1-893115-65-8	$39.95	Tiffany	Pocket PC Database Development with eMbedded Visual Basic
1-893115-59-3	$59.95	Troelsen	C# and the .NET Platform
1-893115-26-7	$59.95	Troelsen	Visual Basic .NET and the .NET Platform
1-893115-54-2	$49.95	Trueblood/Lovett	Data Mining and Statistical Analysis Using SQL
1-893115-16-X	$49.95	Vaughn	ADO Examples and Best Practices
1-893115-83-6	$44.95	Wells	Code Centric: T-SQL Programming with Stored Procedures and Triggers
1-893115-95-X	$49.95	Welschenbach	Cryptography in C and C++
1-893115-05-4	$39.95	Williamson	Writing Cross-Browser Dynamic HTML
1-893115-78-X	$49.95	Zukowski	Definitive Guide to Swing for Java 2, Second Edition
1-893115-92-5	$49.95	Zukowski	Java Collections

Apress Titles Publishing SOON!

ISBN	AUTHOR	TITLE
1-893115-39-9	Chand	A Programmer's Guide to ADO.NET in C#
1-893115-44-5	Cook	Robot Building for Beginners
1-893115-42-9	Foo/Lee	XML Programming Using the Microsoft XML Parser
1-893115-55-0	Frenz	Visual Basic for Scientists
1-893115-30-5	Harkins/Reid	Access SQL to SQL Server Desktop Edition and Beyond
1-893115-49-6	Kilburn	Palm Programming in Basic
1-893115-38-0	Lafler	Power AOL: A Survival Guide
1-893115-28-3	Laksberg/Challa	Managed Extensions in C++ for .NET
1-893115-46-1	Lathrop	Linux in Small Business: A Practical Users' Guide
1-893115-43-7	Stephenson	Standard VB: An Enterprise Developer's Reference for VB 6 and VB .NET
1-59059-002-3	Symmonds	Internationalization and Localization Using Microsoft .NET
1-893115-68-2	Vaughn	ADO Examples and Best Practices, Second Edition
1-893115-98-4	Zukowski	Learn Java with JBuilder 6

Available at bookstores nationwide or from Springer Verlag New York, Inc. at 1-800-777-4643; fax 1-212-533-3503. Contact us for more information at sales@apress.com.

books for professionals by professionals™

apress™

About Apress

Apress, located in Berkeley, CA, is an innovative publishing company devoted to meeting the needs of existing and potential programming professionals. Simply put, the "A" in Apress stands for the "Author's Press™." Apress' unique author-centric approach to publishing grew from conversations between Dan Appleman and Gary Cornell, authors of best-selling, highly regarded computer books. In 1998, they set out to create a publishing company that emphasized quality above all else, a company with books that would be considered the best in their market. Dan and Gary's vision has resulted in over 30 widely acclaimed titles by some of the industry's leading software professionals.

Do You Have What It Takes to Write for Apress?

Apress is rapidly expanding its publishing program. If you can write and refuse to compromise on the quality of your work, if you believe in doing more than rehashing existing documentation, and if you're looking for opportunities and rewards that go far beyond those offered by traditional publishing houses, we want to hear from you!

Consider these innovations that we offer all of our authors:

- **Top royalties with *no* hidden switch statements**
  Authors typically only receive half of their normal royalty rate on foreign sales. In contrast, Apress' royalty rate remains the same for both foreign and domestic sales.

- **A mechanism for authors to obtain equity in Apress**
  Unlike the software industry, where stock options are essential to motivate and retain software professionals, the publishing industry has adhered to an outdated compensation model based on royalties alone. In the spirit of most software companies, Apress reserves a significant portion of its equity for authors.

- **Serious treatment of the technical review process**
  Each Apress book has a technical reviewing team whose remuneration depends in part on the success of the book since they too receive royalties.

Moreover, through a partnership with Springer-Verlag, one of the world's major publishing houses, Apress has significant venture capital behind it. Thus, we have the resources to produce the highest quality books *and* market them aggressively.

If you fit the model of the Apress author who can write a book that gives the "professional what he or she needs to know™," then please contact one of our Editorial Directors, Gary Cornell (gary_cornell@apress.com), Dan Appleman (dan_appleman@apress.com), Karen Watterson (karen_watterson@apress.com) or Jason Gilmore (jason_gilmore@apress.com) for more information.